D1289571

2015

DATE DUE

This item is Due on
or before Date shown.

MIND OVER MONEY

MIND OVER MONEY

Overcoming the Money Disorders

That Threaten Our Financial Health

BRAD KLONTZ, Psy.D.

AND

TED KLONTZ, Ph.D.

BROADWAY BOOKS

New York

Copyright © 2009 by Brad Klontz and Ted Klontz

Published in the United States by Broadway Books, an imprint of the
Crown Publishing Group, a division of
Random House, Inc., New York.
www.crownpublishing.com

BROADWAY BOOKS and the Broadway Books colophon are
trademarks of Random House, Inc.

Library of Congress Cataloging-in-Publication Data
Klontz, Brad.
Mind over money / Brad Klontz and Ted Klontz. — 1st ed.
p.   cm.
1. Finance, Personal—Psychological aspects.   2. Money—Psychological aspects.
3. Self-destructive behavior.   4. Self-actualization (Psychology)
I. Klontz, Ted.   II. Title.
HG179.K573 2010
332.024001'9—dc22   2009023332

ISBN 978-0-385-53101-6

Printed in the United States of America

Design by Debbie Glasserman

10 9 8 7 6 5 4 3 2 1

First Edition

Dedicated to Joe and Sharon Cruse,
who helped us make peace with our own pasts

CONTENTS

Introduction   I

PART ONE: THE BIG LIE

1. Information Is Not Enough   19
2. The Zoo in You   33
3. Belonging at All Costs: Running with the Herd   63
4. The Ghosts of Financial Trauma   90

PART TWO: MONEY DISORDERS

5. What Exactly Is a Money Disorder, Anyway?   129
6. Money-Avoidance Disorders   134
   Financial Denial   136
   Financial Rejection   140
   Underspending   149
   Excessive Risk Aversion   151
7. Money-Worshiping Disorders   154
   Hoarding   158
   Unreasonable Risk Taking/Pathological Gambling   161
   Workaholism   166
   Overspending/Compulsive Buying Disorder   169

8. Relational Money Disorders   175
    Financial Infidelity   180
    Financial Incest   185
    Financial Enabling   187
    Financial Dependency   193

PART THREE: BEATING YOUR MONEY DISORDERS

9. Resolving That Unfinished Business   205

10. Financial Therapy   228

11. Transforming Your Financial Life   262

    Afterword   279

    Do You Have a Money Disorder?   285

    Bibliography   287

    Acknowledgments   297

    Index   301

MIND OVER MONEY

INTRODUCTION

What prompted you to pick up this book? Are you stressed about money? Are you worried about your overspending or your inability to save? Maybe your finances are sound but you still can't overcome your anxieties about money. Perhaps disagreements about spending are driving a wedge between you and your partner, or maybe you're having trouble talking to your children or other family members about money. Whether you're having difficulties managing your stock portfolio or struggling just to make ends meet, know this: You are not alone. Just about everyone has a complicated relationship with money, and more people than you realize have money relationships that are downright dysfunctional. And just about everyone believes the "Big Lie" about personal finance.

What is the Big Lie? It's the accusation that your financial difficulties are your fault, that they stem from your being lazy, crazy, greedy, or stupid. Well, they aren't, and they don't. Trust us on this. We've spent years consulting with, coaching, and counseling couples and individuals struggling with money problems. If we've learned anything from that experience, it's that chronic self-defeating and self-destructive financial behaviors aren't driven by our rational, thinking minds. The truth is, they stem from psychological forces that lie well outside our conscious awareness, and their roots run deep, deep into our past.

Consider the following stories, shared by some of the people we've worked with.

BRIDGET: *I was given up for adoption at the age of two, because my mother couldn't afford me. My birth parents had divorced and my mother couldn't support all five of us children so she gave three of us up for adoption. I was in foster care for about two years and I stopped unpacking my suitcase because I would change foster homes with what seemed like no notice. A family adopted one of my older sisters, and when they found out she had a sister in the orphanage they tracked me down. I remember the day my adoptive parents came to my foster home. They were driving a red car. I remember going up in front of the judge and telling him I wanted to go live with them. I remember feeling like such a big girl, twirling around and around in the big wooden chair next to the judge's desk. I was four and a half.*

My adoptive family was very loving but very dysfunctional. My father was a happy drinker. He wasn't ever abusive but he could certainly tie a drunk on. My mother was, I think, an undiagnosed manic-depressive. She'd be fine one minute and then the next she was horribly depressed, telling us we were about to lose our house and she didn't know where the money was going to come from. I remember, even as a young child, feeling very fearful that if the family ran out of money, they'd send us away again, me or my sister or both of us. Even if we managed to stay together, we might lose our house and everything we had because we didn't have enough money.

What lessons about money do you think that little girl learned? What attitudes about finances did she bring with her into adulthood, and how did they affect her and her relationships? You might expect that she'd come to associate not having enough money with emotional abandonment or that she'd grow up unable to trust or rely on anyone.

And you'd be right. From the time she was a young girl, Bridget constantly worked and saved, but she refused to spend any of her hard-earned money—she believed that money and money alone meant security. But no matter how much she saved, she never really felt secure. She was always waiting for the other shoe to drop.

But you'd also be wrong, because Bridget's sister reacted very differently. While Bridget became compulsively self-reliant, her sister became passive, dependent, unable to believe she could take care of herself at all. She sank into decades of addiction and homelessness before righting herself.

This story illustrates that similar circumstances may have very different effects on different people. That's why each of us has to explore and discover our own money history, without worrying about how we "should have" reacted to the situations we faced.

PAUL: *My third brother died shortly after he was born. During the delivery my mom kept telling the nurse, "There's something wrong! There's something wrong!" By that time she'd been through eight deliveries, so she had some idea when things weren't right. The nurse called the doctor, but he was at the country club playing golf. He didn't make it to the hospital until it was too late and so my brother died.*

A month later, the doctor came out to our house in his brand-new Thunderbird. My father and I were out in the yard. The doctor got out of the car and he told my father to pay his bill or he was going to make sure that my father went to jail. My parents' sense was, this man's need to play golf had killed my brother. So my father grabbed the doctor and threw him up against the Thunderbird and said, "You do whatever you want, but if you continue to pursue me about this bill, I will kill you." He opened the car door and threw this skinny little doctor into the seat and slammed the door. He turned to me and said, "I want you to mark that well, Paul. All he cares about is his money, not the life he destroyed."

That message followed me all the way through my life. I grew up with the idea that the rich are greedy and they really don't care about people. I grew up believing that money had become their god. I decided that money didn't matter and what I needed to do was just work hard, do a good job, and be known for that.

As an adult, Paul didn't want to become known as the kind of person who cared only about money, so he shied away from dealing with money or even thinking about it. He had trouble negotiating for salary increases, saving for the future, or investing, and he had even more trouble when he tried to relax and enjoy time with his family because "working hard" was his only measure of self-worth. And as a helping professional himself, he never wanted to be caught "playing" in case someone needed him in a crisis.

It's easy to see how traumatic experiences like Bridget's and Paul's can make such profound and lasting impressions. But it doesn't take tragedy on this scale to shape our ideas about money, its uses and its meaning. In fact, most of us form our attitudes about money through much more ordinary experiences, doing what all children and adolescents do: observing the influential adults in our lives and puzzling out the reasons for their behavior.

STEPHANIE: *When I was twelve years old my parents moved us to the Upper East Side of Manhattan. We'd come from a middle-*

class community and suddenly we were living in one of the most affluent places in the world. I saw how very privileged people lived their lives, and in some ways my family lived like this, too. We had a big apartment in an exclusive building. We took vacations abroad. There was always money for education, and for art and culture and books. However, my mother often complained about money. We "didn't have enough," my dad "didn't make enough," and she "had to be so frugal." These comments and complaints, always directed at me, were what I now know to be a manifestation of financial incest. Financial incest in the sense that she was talking to me about her and my dad's financial problems, which had nothing to do with me. What was I supposed to do with all of that? She complained that we couldn't afford the fancy clothes or the summer homes that people around us had. On top of that, my mother was really not well mentally and some days she never even got dressed. The apartment was always a mess and I couldn't bring friends home, so even though we lived in this place that was supposed to be so great, so expensive, I was always ashamed.

I trace much of the problem I've had with money as an adult to those conflicting messages about money. Being totally baffled by all things financial. How do you know there's enough? What is important to spend money on, and what isn't? What's the reality, the beautiful building or the horrible apartment inside? I just wanted to ignore the whole issue of money growing up and then later as an adult. After I got married, I just turned all thoughts and decisions about money over to my husband. I never questioned anything. I didn't want to know anything. Even when he asked for my thoughts, I avoided the conversations.

Stephanie's childhood confusion and shame led to her passivity as an adult. She married a man who took control of their finances and their lives, expecting her to stay home and focus all her efforts on raising their children and supporting his climb up the corporate ladder. Grateful for the certainty and the structure, she was happy to go along—until he decided to divorce her, leaving her destitute and alone.

> *Everything went fine until the day he came home and told me he wanted a divorce. He took advantage of my financial ignorance. He told me that we needed to save money and that his lawyer could handle the details for both of us. I found out years later that he had transferred most of our assets to his new flame in the months before he told me he wanted a divorce. Though we had been living a solid middle-class lifestyle, when the divorce was finalized there was nothing left to share. I ended up penniless, homeless, living out of my car, feeling totally defeated with no resources. I lost everything. I didn't have a job or any training for one. It took me seventeen years to rebuild my life, from scratch.*

> LEWIS: *I had a habit of never carrying much money, maybe a dollar in my billfold, because my father was rich and we lived in a small town. I was able to go where I wanted to and get what I wanted and my mother would settle up later with the stores. I really never had any dealings with money. Once in college I got a notice that I had overdrawn my account. When I called home to see what it meant, my mom told me not to worry about it. My father was part owner of the bank, so whenever I overdrew my account, money was just automatically put back in. Sort of like magic. But the other side of that was, I didn't make any of my own decisions. My father picked the car I drove, the college I went to, all that.*
>
> *To sum up, I was raised in a relatively privileged place in the middle of a poor farming community. I found that embarrassing and it made me feel set apart and guilty. Then, being as I was kept away from any information about money or how it worked, and prevented from making my own decisions, even when I went to college . . . what I learned from that was, money has power,*

and it wasn't necessarily the kind of power I wanted. Although, later in my life, without realizing it, I did try to exercise that power with my own children.

Lewis's story shows how, despite our best intentions, money scripts and behaviors are often passed down through the generations. Despite his resentment of the way his own father controlled him through money, Lewis replicated that relationship with his own children. He used money to try to dissuade his daughter from marrying a man that he didn't think was worthy of her, telling her that he wouldn't pay a dime toward their wedding. By withholding financial support, he tried to keep his other daughter from moving away when she wanted to try to make it on her own in New York City. He told his son that he would not support him financially for his college education unless he agreed to attend the one Lewis wanted him to go to. When his children became adults, Lewis would offer them money but always with strings attached. In addition to using money to control his children, he also financially enabled them. They became dependent on handouts from Dad and constricted by all the conditions that went along with them.

ALLISON: *From the time my mother and stepfather got married, when I was almost seven, they've always been what they call "behind the eight ball." They never discussed money problems with us directly but there were always comments like "Money doesn't grow on trees, you know" and "We're one big expense away from real trouble."*

I didn't see it then, but my mother had serious issues with spending. She'd always say we didn't have any money, but then she'd go on these shopping sprees, buying clothes for herself and us and antiques for our house. I'd always pay real close attention, waiting for those sprees, because I knew if I could go along with her, I'd get something, too. My father always took a "head in the sand" approach, very disconnected from our financial situation, agreeing to things even if they didn't make sense, just to avoid a fight. Not good messaging, either way.

When your parents aren't on the same page, when one of them continually warns you, a child, about your family's impending financial devastation, yet spends like crazy, and the other parent acts like everything's fine no matter what, it's very confusing. As a result, I grew up having no real concept of money. I've walked around my entire life thinking, "Oh, money's no big deal, unless you're running out, and then you panic." The concept of making money work for you or knowing how to properly handle it . . . that was beyond me.

Allison's confusion over money persisted for years and years. As an adult, she pushed herself to work hard to earn the money she needed to be independent of her parents but she spent it as fast as she earned it. Unconsciously, she had come to associate having money with anxiety and impending crisis. So, anytime she managed to put something away, her anxiety would increase until she found a way to get rid of her savings: a resort vacation, new furniture she didn't need, dinner for twenty at the most expensive restaurant in town. Though she made a decent salary, she was living paycheck to paycheck.

You've just read five descriptions of what we call *financial flashpoints*—an early life event (or series of events) associated with money that are so emotionally powerful, they leave an imprint that lasts into adulthood. Maybe you recognized a bit of yourself in one or more of these stories. Maybe not. But *all* of us have experiences like these: dramatic, painful, or traumatic early experiences that become the foundation of our financial struggles in adulthood. As you've seen in these examples, financial flashpoints can be heartbreaking and deeply distressing, like Paul's or Bridget's experiences. But as the stories from Stephanie, Lewis, and Allison show, they can also be the result of everyday events that are less dramatic but equally powerful, the slow accumulation of the lessons we learn from the adults around us. Those lessons are often very different from the ones our elders *think* they're teaching us.

Working with our clients, we've found that the lasting power of financial flashpoints has little to do with the events themselves or how we'd interpret them in hindsight, as adults. Rather, they stem from the naive, childhood interpretations that we construct in our efforts to uncover an underlying logic to the baffling, contradictory, often frightening, adult world. And it is from these childhood interpretations of financial flashpoint events that we develop a set of beliefs about money, called *money scripts,* that shape the way we think about and interact with money as adults. Whether or not these interpretations are accurate or rational is not the point; the source of money scripts' power is the fact that *the beliefs made sense* in their original context, in our childhood minds. And the more profound the original event or series of events, the more strongly our emotions lock the subsequent money scripts in place, and the less flexible we are in adapting to changing financial circumstances later in life.

And that's where the problems arise. Even if our money scripts were very useful when they were formed, they can become destructive if we cling to them and act on them unthinkingly throughout our lives. Because money scripts often operate outside of our awareness, lying unexamined in the deep recesses of our unconscious minds, we are at their insidious mercy. To free ourselves, we must first recognize them and their origins, deal with any unfinished business left behind from the circumstances that triggered them, and learn new ways to think about, react to, and deal with money. In times of stress, these old feelings and beliefs about money may creep in, but once we learn to spot these scripts, separate ourselves from them, and ultimately rewrite them, we can learn to adapt to whatever challenges we face.

What to Do When You Know What to Do—But You Can't Do It

So how can this book help? And how is it different from other financial books? First of all, we won't be offering you any advice or tips on managing your money. Many people think that problems with money stem from ignorance about the complicated field of personal finance, and they wrongly believe that the solution lies in gathering more information, collecting more tips and strategies for budgeting and investing. This might help for some people; however, for the majority of us, a lack of information is not the problem. The basics of good financial health are actually quite simple, and more advice telling us to save more or spend less is not going to help.

If you, like the majority of Americans, already know what you *should* be doing but you can't put that awareness into action, your problems with money have little to do with a lack of knowledge. In fact, more information and advice can actually entrench our negative behaviors by making us feel "pushed" in a particular direction, and making us feel bad about ourselves. When we wonder, "I know better, why can't I do better?" the answer we come up with is quite often "There must be something wrong with me." This is not only unhealthy, it's counterproductive because the feelings of shame triggered by these thoughts only increase our ambivalence and entrench our resistance. Nobody likes to be told what to do, especially when we already know it. Case in point: Despite hundreds of books, thousands of newspaper and magazine articles, endless TV programs, films, infomercials, radio talk shows discussing the ins and outs of personal finance, there are still millions who are unable to make major changes in their financial lives.

We believe that scolding you about the risks of not having an emergency fund, or the benefits of budgeting, or how much you should be saving is like trying to treat a brain tumor with aspirin: It addresses a symptom while ignoring the disease. *Financial advice is not enough to change destructive financial behaviors*. So instead of lecturing you on what you already know, we'll help you find the underlying reasons for your self-defeating and self-damaging financial behaviors—and then show you how to get honest about your relationship with money, and take control of and transform your financial life.

First, we'll explore the origins of financial flashpoints, those critical "aha" experiences or influences related to money. The most obvious is the family. As children, we gain insights and make assumptions about the world based on the messages, intended and unintended, passed on to us by those closest to us. When we see the people around us reacting to money in certain ways, we internalize that information, which leaves a lasting imprint on us, especially in our most impressionable years. Moving outside the family circle, we're also influenced by economic events (such as the collapse of local industry, or larger market bubbles and crashes) and cultural influences (such as the media, education, religion, race, gender, and class).

Next, we'll explore money scripts, the assumptions or beliefs about money—what it means and how it works—that each of us takes away from our financial flashpoint experiences. Then we'll talk about the unhealthy behaviors—the *money disorders*—that result. You'll then learn to recognize your own money scripts (and the unfinished business related to them), their origins, and the negative impact they have on your financial life.

We must start by recognizing our self-defeating behaviors and their root causes, because only once we truly get honest about our relationship with money can we overcome and reverse our limiting or self-destructive financial beliefs and behaviors and develop healthier, more productive ones.

Overcoming the Paralysis of Shame

At this point, you might be thinking that the term *money disorders* sounds pretty extreme, maybe a little scary. To be sure, money disorders are extreme reactions, and by their nature they create exaggerated behaviors. But that doesn't change the fact that they are incredibly common, completely normal responses to the difficult life events that we all go through, in some form or another. In our experience, financial pathology typically manifests itself in one of three ways. We might repeat destructive financial patterns learned from our early socialization, either observed within our family or in the broader culture. We might also flee to the polar opposites of those patterns in an attempt to avoid repeating the experiences and consequences of our past. Or we might alternate between those two extremes of behavior, shooting past the middle option in an unhealthy "pendulum swing." Whatever our particular pattern might be, the end result is an equally unbalanced and damaging relationship with money.

Compounding this problem is the fact that people often feel deeply ashamed of their inability to sustain a healthy relationship with money. When we talk to our clients, many of them describe their past financial behaviors as shameful: "I was awash in shame" or "I was so ashamed of myself." When we feel shame, we feel worthless, incompetent, and paralyzed. We don't feel that we're someone who's made some bad decisions; we believe we *are* bad. Shame takes the wind out of our sails. It robs us of power, tells us to just give up. After all, if we're bad and worthless, not simply a person who has made mistakes, then we're unworthy of happiness and grace.

And if we believe we're unworthy, we're less likely to try to change our problematic behavior and we may even unconsciously sabotage our attempts to change. You've probably seen glue traps for rodents; well, shame is an emotional glue trap, keeping people mired in a vicious loop of action, backsliding, and inaction.

But we don't have to remain helpless victims to this cruel, pointless cycle. The first step to breaking free is to recognize that our automatic beliefs about money and the resulting behaviors are not signs that we're bad or worthless or somehow "broken." They're the predictable and normal consequences of experiencing what we've experienced. Our beliefs and behaviors are logical outcomes, given who we are, what we've been taught, and what we've learned to do to survive. Once we embrace our humanity, with all our gifts and flaws, we can begin to take an honest look at our money disorders, and the thinking that underlies them, and make real, ongoing progress toward growth and change. That's our goal: progress, not perfection.

Changing Your Mind

Before we can start to change our behavior, we have to take a look at the place where it all begins: the mind and its fascinating, sometimes contradictory systems for interpreting and responding to the world. Neurological and behavioral research continues to uncover surprising information about how emotions, thoughts, and actions interact, and how they impact our financial decisions. We'll pay special attention to how the brain processes traumatic events and their physical, emotional and behavioral consequences. Although financial flashpoints aren't always traumatic in the traditional sense, they are intense and highly emotional. So understanding the biological and neurological effects of trauma is helpful for understanding the effects of financial flashpoints on our thinking patterns and our behavior.

Throughout the book, we'll be drawing on stories shared by people who've already done the work to resolve their own unfinished business around money, allowing them to heal, transform their lives, and feel at peace in their relationship with money regardless of ever-changing external realities. (We've changed only their names and other identifying details.) We'll also share our own stories, since we come to this process through our own struggles with negative, self-defeating financial behavior. As we like to say, "Our message comes from our own mess."

And here's the most important part of our message: Change *is* possible. In fact, when we remove the mental and emotional blocks, peel off the outer layers, and take a long hard look at the true forces driving our behavior, change is inescapable. Whatever your particular issue is with money, as you read the stories of financial struggle in these pages, you will undoubtedly see something of yourself, and your own story. As you read the real-life transformations from financial pain to peace and prosperity, we hope you will find your own sense of hope and possibility. So if you're frustrated by your inability to make a change in your financial habits, if you're tired of feeling anxious about money, if you long for a sense of financial peace and freedom, don't look for the next aspirin to dull your financial headache. Instead, consider addressing the hidden causes of your pain and using your stress and anxiety as an impetus to radically change your financial life. Now is the time. The benefits can be tremendous.

ALLISON: *Once the fear was removed and I could experience a positive relationship with money, I was able to relax and enjoy the ride. It's made all the difference in my life.*

LEWIS: *We made a list of twenty-five things we needed either to get information about or get done. Within six months we dealt with all but three of those things on our list. All this has made our relationships—between me and my wife, between us and our kids—stronger. We're much better now. There's much more openness.*

STEPHANIE: *The most surprising thing is how much energy has been freed up as I deal with each money issue and become healthier in my relationship with money.*

PAUL: *I was able to see that I can find a middle ground between those original beliefs that money and the people who had it were bad. I have been able to develop more reasonable beliefs and behaviors that make more sense for me, give me greater clarity around the whole issue of money. The most freeing part is being able to have these conversations with my wife and to do all of this consciously.*

BRIDGET: *The whole idea that the amount of money in my bank account equals my image and my self-image—that has shifted. I've realized that I already have enough money to support the simple lifestyle that I've chosen. I've realized that I don't have to sacrifice everything to have a good life. I've accepted that it's okay for me to take a day off, do nothing, and not make any money. It's okay for me to enjoy myself.*

Part One

THE BIG LIE

1

Information Is Not Enough

The basics of financial health aren't complicated, and they're pretty much the same, no matter who you are or your level of wealth. They are even the same whether you're talking about a person, a family, a company, or a country: Save now and invest for the future. Spend reasonable amounts of money to enjoy life and accomplish your goals, but spend less than you earn. Beware of an investment that looks too good to be true, because it probably is.

Pretty simple, right? So why is it that so many of us can't seem to make those rules work for ourselves? Especially now—at no time in recent history has our collective financial health been more compromised. No matter what measure of disaster you pick—foreclosures, bankruptcies, consumer debt, unemployment—the past two years have set records. (How many times in the last eighteen months have you heard or read the phrase "Not since the Great Depression . . .".?) Even if your own finances are in order, the uncertainty wears on you; if you were worried about money before, the constant drumbeat of bad news has likely been enough to send your stress levels through the roof.

On October 9, 2008, the U.S. budget deficit hit the $10.2 trillion mark. The National Debt Clock, which has been keeping track of what we owe since 1989, could no longer display all the numbers so the dollar sign was removed to make room. The Durst Organization, the real estate company that owns and operates the clock, plans to install an updated model sometime in 2009. The new clock will display numbers in *quadrillions*—sixteen digits long. The clock has had several locations over the years and is currently installed near the IRS office. A Durst representative said, "We thought it was a fitting location."

Today, many researchers agree, the biggest source of stress in our lives is money. According to an Associated Press / AOL poll released in June 2008, as many as sixteen million Americans suffered from high levels of debt stress and accompanying health complaints. This was a 14 percent increase over a similar 2004 poll. In October 2008, when the American Psychological Association released their annual survey on stress, what do you think was the primary source of stress for Americans? A whopping 80 percent said it was money and the economy. That makes sense given the current financial crisis yet it's nothing new. Year after year, through boom and bust, the APA poll has shown that for the large majority of Americans—over 70 percent—money is the number one stressor, ranked higher than work, health, or children. But why?

Why Is Money So Significant?

In 1992, psychologists Dr. Joe Griffin and Dr. Ivan Tyrrell developed a new psychological framework about basic human needs. Their *human givens* approach combines current neurological research with earlier work by theorists such as Abraham

Maslow. According to Maslow, all humans have a hierarchy of needs, beginning with the most basic physiological requirements for food and shelter and ascending through social, emotional, and intellectual needs. Our needs must be met at one level before we can begin to address our needs at the next.

Griffin and Tyrell build on Maslow's work by identifying not only universal human needs but also a range of innate resources available to all people to meet those needs. Together, these are the human givens. In this model, each person, regardless of cultural boundaries, has basic needs that are both physical (such as food, sleep, exercise) and emotional (such as security, attention, connectedness). Our psychological health depends on our ability to meet these needs through the exercise of our inherent resources (such as empathy, imagination, and rationality) in effective, productive ways.

In a modern, industrialized society, money is one of the only things that touches on and impacts each and every one of our needs. The effect of money on physical needs is obvious; you can't have shelter, for instance, without enough money to pay rent or a mortgage. But take a look at the list of emotional needs on page 22. Money affects our ability to meet these, too, though some more than others. For example, while it's always possible to feel a sense of competence and achievement without money, this is certainly more difficult in our culture. The same with status or autonomy.

Plus, since money is concrete and measurable in a way that our needs (love, security, attention) are not, it can easily become so closely linked to our emotional needs that we can't separate the two. We come to believe that money *is* love, or security, or attention. Nothing illustrates this better than the story of the Christmas "fancy box."

DENISE: *My father started and developed a very successful business and he uses the fruits of his labor to "reward" us kids. Every*

The Human Givens Institute identifies the following as among our essential, innate needs and capabilities.

EMOTIONAL NEEDS
- Security: a safe environment that allows us to develop fully
- Attention, both given and received: a form of nutrition
- Sense of autonomy and control: having volition to make responsible choices
- Emotional connections to others
- Feeling part of a wider community
- Friendship, intimacy: knowing that at least one other person accepts us for who we are
- Privacy: opportunity to reflect and consolidate experience
- Sense of status within social groupings
- Sense of competence and achievement
- Meaning and purpose: the result of being stretched in what we do and think

RESOURCES FOR MEETING OUR NEEDS
- The ability to develop complex long-term memory, which enables us to learn and add to our innate knowledge
- The ability to build rapport, empathize, and connect with others
- Imagination, which enables us to focus our attention away from our emotions and problem-solve more creatively and objectively
- Emotions and instincts
- A conscious, rational mind that can check out our emotions, question, analyze, and plan
- The ability to "know," to understand the world unconsciously through metaphorical pattern matching
- An observing self: that part of us that can step back, be more objective and be aware of itself as a unique center of awareness
- A dreaming brain that preserves the integrity of our genetic inheritance every night by metaphorically defusing expectations held in the autonomic arousal system because they were not acted out the previous day

Christmas, after all the gifts have been opened, he brings out his "fancy box." That's the real centerpiece of the family gift giving, and it's been that way since I was a child. Inside the box are envelopes with checks inside, addressed to each one of us kids. Or not. Because I'm a girl and because I'm not directly involved in the family business, sometimes there's no envelope for me. Or there might be an envelope with my name on it, but my brothers each get several envelopes. As the envelopes are opened, the amount of the check is announced to all assembled. My check is always the smallest. Last Christmas, my brothers got three-hundred-thousand-dollar checks, but there was no envelope with my name on it.

Of course I've taken a few lessons from this: Money equals love and whoever gets the most money is loved the most. I also learned that money can be used to control and humiliate others. Those lessons have affected my life, all my life.

Given that money is both essential and so emotionally loaded, it's no wonder it takes up so much of our attention, nor is it a surprise that so many people have such tumultuous and self-destructive relationships with it. As financial planning pioneer Dick Wagner says, "Money is the most powerful and pervasive secular influence in the world."

More Money: Not Necessarily the Answer

But even though money is essential, the cruel irony is that more of it doesn't automatically solve our problems or relieve our stress. In fact, many studies have shown that at or above the average American's income, there's no predictable correlation between money and happiness. In his book *Stumbling into Happiness,* psychologist Dr. Daniel Gilbert says, "Americans who earn $50,000 per year are much happier than those who earn $10,000 per year *but* Americans who earn $5 million per year are not much happier than those who earn $100,000 per year." And that's in keeping with what psychologists Dr. Ed Diener and Dr. Martin Seligman found in their research. They analyzed more than 150 studies on wealth and happiness and concluded that money is less important to one's level of happiness than factors such as maintaining strong personal relationships and feeling a sense of accomplishment in one's job.

So if money is the biggest stressor in our lives, yet (beyond the level of poverty) having more of it doesn't solve the problem, what *is* the solution? If we want to improve our psychological and financial health, the solution is not to focus on making more money but instead on developing a better, healthier relationship with it. By facing and resolving the complicated emotions and unfinished business that underlie our financial stress, we can radically improve our current psychological and financial health *and* learn to better manage and cope with future stressful or traumatic experiences. Remember the human givens? Here's where those innate resources come in. By consciously and deliberately drawing on our empathy, imagination, emotions, and rationality—all our inborn strengths—we can not only change our relationship with money but also defeat the power money holds over us.

One financial planner we work with has discovered that for himself:

STUART: *I realized what had controlled my life the most was fear, and now I'm freeing myself of that. I have a sense of serenity about all this. My portfolio may have shrunk by 50 percent, but I'm not 50 percent less than who I was a year ago. I actually feel like I'm* bigger—*more expanded, more peaceful, more grateful than I've ever been. I really feel, for the first time ever, that my net worth as a person has only a little bit to do with my financial net*

worth. I am more at ease with my dis-ease. I know there's still
work for me to do but I'm headed in the right direction.

Stuart didn't come to that place easily, or without struggle. None of the people we've worked with have. Most of them spent years fighting their own inability to change. Even after they faced the unpleasant realities of the past and began taking productive steps to right themselves, they experienced episodes of the old, unhealthy ways of thinking and behaving. Yet they had developed the skills to stop themselves, readjust, and move on.

Why Is Change So Difficult?

When we understand the changes we need to make and yet find ourselves unable to follow through on them, we often add self-abuse to the emotional baggage we're already carrying, and that often just adds to our stress. "Why can't I stick to my budget? I'm such a weakling!" "I know I need to add more to my IRA, but I never do it. How can I be so stupid?" And even if you don't say those things to yourself, you'll hear talk-show hosts shouting them, and worse, at people just like you. Whether it comes from ourselves or others, a big dose of criticism just ends up making us feel worse, and erodes our motivation to change: "If I'm such a loser, why bother?"

The fact is, you are not stupid, crazy, or lazy. You are a highly evolved human being behaving exactly like a person who has come from where you've come from, witnessed what you have witnessed, and experienced what you have experienced would likely behave! So we invite you to let go of the shame. And don't beat yourself up for having a hard time not beating yourself up, either. You'll just put yourself into another shame spiral, and that won't help at all.

What *will* help is getting to the real source of the problem. When you truly understand what has gotten you where you are, it all makes sense. There are deep-seated, complicated, and even adaptive reasons why changing your money behaviors is so difficult. Once you understand and accept those reasons, you can learn to overcome the roadblocks standing in your way.

Often we're not fully aware of our resistance to change, let alone its source. Our inability to do what we know we should do is frustrating. Remember Stephanie, from the introduction, who had a hard time facing and dealing with her adult financial issues because she grew up receiving confusing and mixed messages about the role of money in her life? When she came to us for help, we worked on dealing with her unfinished business and rewriting her money scripts, using exercises we'll share with you later in the book. First, she dug down and articulated the unhealthy beliefs about money that she'd retained all these years. Then she modified those beliefs to better fit her true goals and values, and came up with a money mantra to help her reinforce the new beliefs when the old ones resurfaced.

Here Stephanie talks about how she was able to put these new perspectives and capabilities to work, removing her hidden resistance, and enabling her to talk calmly and directly about money issues.

STEPHANIE: *I would write out my checks for my IRA and not send them in, out of fear that my business cash flow would not be able to cover it. It never occurred to me that I could tell my accountant how I felt and adjust the amount of the payment. That was my old "ignore it" approach to money reappearing and I didn't even realize it. So I continued with this behavior until I got a call from my accountant about the checks I had written but not sent in. I felt so ashamed that I hadn't followed through on this commitment to myself! But once I was able to move past that, I felt free to ask for what I needed, and I got it. I finally had the courage to tell her what was going on in my mind, and as a result we now have established a different IRA amount which I am more comfortable with. And I'm sending the checks in, every month.*

The Tilted Table

Imagine sitting at a table that has one leg shorter than the others. If the imbalance is slight, it's just mildly annoying. But if the legs are really uneven and the table tilts too far, it becomes unstable and unusable. The short leg needs to be propped up or repaired in order for the table to be functional.

The human brain under stress is a lot like that tilted table. Anxiety, fear, and shame make us feel off-balance, and the brain seeks out substances or behaviors that seem to repair or rebalance it, at least temporarily.

That rebalancing stimulus may be a substance that's consumed, such as food, nicotine, or alcohol, or it could be the neurochemical effect of a wide range of human behaviors. Some of the most common behaviors in this category are shopping, working, hoarding, sex, and cleaning, but virtually anything can become a means of alleviating negative feelings. Because our brains are different, each of us has a particular substance or behavior that we find balancing and soothing, which is very much based on our own unique DNA as well as the specific choices, opportunities, and challenges we've faced. It's impossible to predict which behavior or substance will have the strongest balancing effect for a specific person. Our brain seeks this stimulus in times of stress, especially when we're already feeling down on ourselves. And as stress increases—as the table tilts more and more—it takes more and more of that behavior or substance to restore balance.

Even though we each have specific substances or behaviors we're more likely to turn to in times of stress or anxiety, certain ones have wide, almost universal, appeal. Consider the following study, by researchers at Arizona State University and Erasmus University in the Netherlands. After testing students' self-esteem, they ask the students to write on one of two essay topics: a visit to the dentist or their own death. Later, each subject was offered plates of cookies as well as the opportunity to select items from a shopping list. Students with low self-esteem who'd written about their deaths ate more cookies and picked more goods than students with similar self-esteem levels who'd written about a dentist visit. As the researchers explain, thoughts of death (our own or someone else's) make us uncomfortable, increasing our level of anxiety, and both the cookies and the material items provided an "escape from awareness." In other words, eating and spending provide distraction from unsettling feelings, from the tilt of that table.

But all too soon, these effects wear off and the table will once again start to tilt. In fact, it will probably be a little more unstable than before because of the guilt, shame, and negative consequences that the person experiences afterward. Despite the aftereffects, the simple fact that the calming stimulus works, even temporarily, creates in some people an overwhelming compulsion to return to it again and again. This lies at the heart of addictive and self-destructive behaviors. The alcoholic, the overeater, the compulsive shopper—they're all seeking escape from similar feelings, each in the way that works for them. Unfortunately, the desire for that short-term pleasure or anxiety relief can quickly rage out of control, causing serious problems in the long run.

Our client Phyllis and her husband learned this the hard way. A few years ago, they were faced with aging and illness and responded by overspending, digging themselves deeper and deeper into debt.

PHYLLIS: *Before the Christmas holidays, I told Carl, my husband, I couldn't work at the current pace much longer. Since Carl did the bill paying and I did most of the spending, I rarely went over the bills. When I sat down to see where we might cut back, it was obvious that we were spending too much. At the time we were receiving at least two or three applications a day for zero-interest credit cards. So, feeling like I was doing something really good and huge, I transferred everything to the new cards and tucked away the paid-off ones in the safe deposit box, just in case we needed that credit for an emergency.*

That spring, Carl was diagnosed with a tumor in his lung. I knew it was time for me to really slow down. He had been fighting cancer for years, and whatever time he had left, I wanted us to enjoy our marriage. I cut back my hours and got ready to retire, but we never changed our spending habits even though the income was declining. Soon enough, we'd spent up to the limit on the new credit cards. In early summer, Carl had his surgery and—can you believe it?—the tumor was benign. It was time to celebrate our good fortune! I planned a wonderful retirement party with old friends, family, and colleagues. I really enjoyed it. Afterwards Carl said, "Let's go visit your daughter and her family." Well, he didn't have to ask me twice.

We pulled out the paid-off credit cards in our safe deposit box, since the ones we'd been using were maxed out, and we went east for two and a half weeks. We had a blast. We decided to treat ourselves and our family to a stay at a resort. Carl and I treated everyone. One day I had to take the youngest grandchild to the bathroom at the concession stand. He was four years old then. He wanted some ice cream and I said, "Honey, Grandma didn't bring her money with her. It's down on the beach with Mommy." He pointed at the ATM and said, "That's okay, here's the money machine. Just go there and it will give you money." I tried to explain that it didn't quite work that way, but he was just too young to get it. Funny thing is, I was behaving not much better than my

*grandson. If someone had looked at my behavior, they'd see that I
didn't get it, either.*

*We had a wonderful trip, one I will never forget, but then it
was time to go home and our finances were a disaster. It was like
we'd been on a money drunk. I know now that on that entire trip
I was in denial, pretending I could afford anything I wanted like
I used to be able to do. It made me feel better, but just for a while.*

Phyllis and her husband were spending too much even
when she was working; after she retired, they began spending
even more. She overspent because she was subconsciously
trying to distract herself from the uncomfortable reality of illness and impending old age. She also wanted to be a generous, loving mother and grandmother and to celebrate her
husband's clean bill of health. Because of her personal history
as a pampered and indulged only child, that meant spending
money on everyone. If she'd been asked, "Is going further into
debt the best way to distract yourself?" or "Would your family
love you any less if you didn't pay for everything?" she would
have, of course, answered no to both questions. But her rational, conscious mind lost out to the powerful emotional
brain—as it often does.

In the next chapter, we'll talk more about the emotional and
rational parts of your brain and how they work together and
sometimes against each other. Right now, the important thing
to understand is that your financial struggle isn't a measure of
weakness or failure. It is a predictable response, often triggered by stress and anxiety, to your early money experiences.
The good news is, you *can* change.

Now What?

Today it seems that the entire world is suffering from the aftereffects of financial trauma. This is not the first time local,

national, and world events have affected our financial well-being, and it certainly won't be the last. The silver lining is that the recent economic crisis offers a unique opportunity for us to really look hard at self-limiting and self-destructive beliefs about money, and in turn change our behaviors. But we can't do that until we take several steps.

As with any problem, the first step is acknowledging that there is, in fact, a problem. This is quite often the biggest hurdle, because in the short run denial is so effective and so tempting. Until we learn to accept that we have a problem not even the current financial crisis, as massive as it is, will be enough to change our money behaviors on a long-term basis. The fact is that we are highly resistant to change, and without rewriting the scripts that underlie our self-destructive behaviors, we run the risk of repeating them over and over again.

Case in point: In early 2009 the *New York Times* interviewed several people who'd survived terrifying plane crashes within the previous several months. It wanted to find out how many survivors had vowed to make changes in wake of their near-death experience and how many had actually followed through. Almost all had vowed to make changes, and a few had been somewhat successful in making modest ones, such as complaining less about everyday irritations. But most passengers shared the frustration of the man who said, "The old saying 'Time heals all wounds,' it's true. It kind of lasts a real brief amount of time, at least for me. Then the realities of life set in. I think it's really easy to fall back into those old habits."

Or look at what happens with cardiac patients. Bypass surgery is expensive, risky, traumatic, and invasive, with a long recovery period. It's no one's idea of fun, and making lifestyle changes—better diet, more exercise—can significantly reduce the chances of having to go through it again. So you'd think those who have had this painful surgery would have no problem making these behavioral changes. But according to Dr. Edward Miller, dean of Johns Hopkins Medical School, that isn't the case. "If you look at people after coronary-artery bypass grafting two years later, 90 percent of them have not changed their lifestyle. And that's been studied over and over and over again. And so we're missing some link in there. Even though they know they have a very bad disease and they know they should change their lifestyle, for whatever reason, they can't."

It seems that narrowly escaping death isn't enough to motivate us to make permanent changes. Neither is the trauma of having our sternum cut with a saw, cracked open, and wired back together. So what would make us think this financial crisis will automatically change our relationship with money?

It won't. There's nothing automatic about it. We *can* make changes, but only if we're willing to use this opportunity to take a closer look at our relationship with money. Without this basic healing, our brain will drive us along the path of least resistance. We'll revert back to behavioral patterns that have helped our ancient ancestors survive in the past. Our prehistoric brain doesn't know the circumstances have changed, that old beliefs and ways of behaving may not be useful anymore. It can't understand that the same mechanisms that kept our ancestors alive in the jungles and savannas are the same ones that can trip us up today. In the same way, it can't know that the conclusions we drew about money from our early life experiences, the beliefs that helped our young minds make sense of the world, can sabotage our financial health as adults. But *we* can know and understand. That's why we have to retrain our prehistoric brain to adapt to our current financial realities so we can avoid repeating our mistakes.

Before we go on, take a moment now to list three things you need to do or have been told you should do financially but can't seem to act on. What would have to happen before you truly committed to making the changes?

2

The Zoo in You

Imagine a very small cagelike enclosure containing three living creatures: a crocodile, a monkey, and a scientist. Is it possible for them to peacefully coexist? To cooperate or communicate in any meaningful way? Can all of them even survive in such close proximity?

Believe it or not, this is exactly what is going on in your head, day in and day out. Your brain is made up of three interconnected systems that react to the world in very different ways. For you to function optimally, all three systems have to coordinate their responses. The scientist, the monkey, and the crocodile all have to work together. Amazingly enough, that's exactly what happens most of the time. The crocodile—the most primitive part of the brain—focuses its attention on potential threats. The monkey—the emotional center of the brain—keeps busy exploring and investigating, and the scientist—the rationalizer—observes and analyzes the information coming in. When all three combine their efforts, they accomplish amazing things none of them could manage alone. But if something frightening occurs, there's no doubt who's really in charge of the situation. Here's a hint: It's *not* the person in the lab coat holding the clipboard. In times of great stress, all bets are off.

This model for how the brain functions has profound implications for our mental and financial health. It explains why we persist in our self-destructive and self-limiting financial behaviors even when we know they're causing us harm. Because when it comes to money, more often than not, our impulses and emotions—our inner crocodile and monkey, not our scientist—are running the show.

The Triune Brain

In the 1950s the neurologist Paul MacLean developed a theory of brain structure that identified three separate areas, each of which controlled different functions and, he suggested, marked a different stage of our evolutionary development. Of course no simple metaphor for something as incredibly complex as the human brain will ever be entirely accurate, and later research indicates that evolution wasn't quite as linear as MacLean thought. Even so, his model is still a useful way to understand how our brains are organized and how that organization affects our thinking and our behavior—especially when it comes to money.

The *reptilian brain*—represented by the crocodile—is made up of the brainstem and the cerebellum, connecting to the spinal cord. The reptilian brain controls reflexes, balance, breathing, and heartbeat. It also acts as a collector of sensory information but the processing of that information into thoughts and feelings takes place elsewhere. The reptilian brain's singular focus is on survival. As you can imagine, reptiles aren't good at forethought and planning. They *are* good at biting things, running away, or freezing in place, whichever action is deemed in its best interest for survival.

BRAD: *This was illustrated for me one night soon after I moved to Hawaii. While I was watching television I noticed some movement on the wall and saw two geckos, a baby and a larger one. The big gecko approached the smaller one and they paused in what looked like a kiss.* How cute, *I thought.* Then the larger gecko attacked the smaller one. I watched, shocked, as the smaller gecko's wriggling tail disappeared into the larger one's mouth. Having won that contest for survival, the larger gecko went on about its reptilian business. No remorse. No concern regarding cannibalism. No loyalty. Just reflex. Just survival. That's our inner reptile.*

The *limbic brain*—represented by the monkey—sits on top of the reptilian brain. MacLean called it "the old mammalian brain." It's here that emotions and thoughts begin to kick in and for this reason, researchers sometimes refer to it as the *emotional brain.* It's composed of several different structures, the most important of which are the amygdala, the hypothalamus, and the hippocampus. The hippocampus helps us remember and navigate three-dimensional space; it also plays a role in transferring experiences to and recalling them from long-term memory. The hypothalamus connects the nervous system to the endocrine system, and so it controls the release of hormones, such as adrenaline, critical to the fight-or-flight response. The amygdala is crucial in creating and storing memories related to emotional experiences. (We'll talk more about the amygdala later, when we discuss the effects of trauma.) As a whole, this part of the brain plays an essential role in memory, and in learning from experiences—especially intensely emotional ones. Taken together, the limbic system is the part of the brain involved in behaviors like taking care of one's offspring or developing relationships with other members of a herd, pack, family, or culture.

The term *monkey mind* will be familiar to almost anyone who's ever taken a class in yoga or meditation. The phrase comes to us through Buddhism and refers to the way our thoughts jump around, like a monkey swinging from branch to branch. Calming or distracting the monkey mind is one of the most difficult and most essential aspects of meditation. In *Healing and the Mind,* journalist Bill Moyers and cancer researcher Michael Lerner talked about monkey mind.

LERNER: Meditation quiets your mind. It is a way of simply sitting quietly and allowing your mind to empty of all content, either by focusing on something, such as a sound, or your breathing, or an idea, or else by just emptying the mind and allowing things to come in and go back out again. There are a variety of meditation techniques.

MOYERS: It's hard to do this, though, because the mind is constantly full of chatter. It's like monkeys up in trees, chattering back and forth. If you quiet the monkeys in this tree, the monkeys in that tree begin to sound off.

LERNER: The mind is well recognized as being a monkey. We all have a monkey mind. In meditation you give that monkey something to do. For example, one traditional image is to tell the monkey to stand a hair on end. An equivalent of that is giving the monkey a sound to repeat, or telling the monkey to focus on his breathing so that you can get beyond the conscious mind to a place where there's some quiet.

The *neocortex*—the scientist—is where everything that makes you "you" is generated: your thoughts, your hopes, your dreams, your goals. It's the analytical part of the brain, the part at work when you weigh the pros and cons of various possible actions. The neocortex also controls self-consciousness and speech, and it's the part of the brain responsible for organizing, planning, and—not least—controlling the more primal impulses that come from other parts of the brain. However, the neocortex is also the smallest and most recently developed region of the brain and, in times of stress, it's easily hijacked by the other two.

We're not getting you ready to perform brain surgery so we'll simplify all this. The reptilian brain (the crocodile) and the emotional brain (the monkey) often work together to generate our more primal impulses and emotional responses, so we'll call the two of them the *animal brain*. We'll refer to the neo-cortex (the scientist) as the *rational brain*.

Most of the time, the different parts of your brain divide up the work of observing and reacting to the world. The animal brain processes memories and feelings, creating, storing, and retrieving associations from past experience. It also takes in and responds to current sensory information from the outside world (as when it increases our breathing rate when oxygen levels are low). Then, the rational brain develops narratives to explain what's going on and makes decisions about what to do next.

Most of the time, the animal brain and the rational brain work together seamlessly and almost effortlessly. In fact, it is this unique ability our brains have to analyze and express physical states, feelings, and emotions that has allowed our species to dominate the animal kingdom. But while the animal brain has been tested and refined over hundreds of millions of years, the rational brain apparently began developing in our ancestors relatively recently—less than two million years ago. The animal brain is the faster, more powerful of the two. It also has its own circuitry and thus can operate independently of the thinking brain. There are about five times more nerves traveling from the animal brain to the rational brain than there are going in the opposite direction. This means the conscious, reasoning part of our brain has lots of material to work with, but it also has less influence over what happens elsewhere and is slower to respond than other regions of the brain.

This is why, when our anxiety level becomes too high—when we experience something startling and unexpected, something the animal brain interprets as a threat to its existence—the partnership between the animal brain and the rational brain falls apart. The rational brain instantly gets shut out as if it were behind a door that's suddenly slammed and locked. The scientist is removed from the decision-making process, leaving the crocodile and monkey in charge. You've probably looked back on a tense, fast-moving situation and said to yourself, "Why didn't I say this?" or worse yet, "Why did I say *that*?" That's the result of the animal brain taking over, pushing us into one or more of three reactions.

Fight, Flight, or Freeze

When our animal brain perceives a threat, whether that threat is a saber-toothed tiger in a prehistoric jungle or a looming economic disaster, the hypothalamus signals the body to load up the bloodstream with hormones such as adrenaline, cortisol, and norepinephrine. This sets off a chain of physical responses that prepares us to fight to defend ourselves, run away, or freeze in place until the threat goes away. Our heart beats faster and our breath quickens, circulating more oxygen. Digestion slows down and blood vessels in some parts of the body constrict, while the circulatory system for our large muscles begins to dilate. Our mouths get dry. We develop tunnel vision. Our hearing becomes strangely attuned. We're *ready*.

And then what do we do? Well, that's determined by the specific circumstances we face and whether or not we have memories of similar experiences to draw on. Making connections between current cues and previous experiences is one of the major roles of the animal brain, and we'll be talking more about that soon. The fact is, our initial responses under stress aren't determined by our rational brain. Once we're in fight, flight, or freeze mode, the animal brain takes over and our rational mind has little or nothing to do with the resulting behaviors.

We once saw a perfect illustration of this on *America's Funniest Home Videos*. One Halloween night, a homeowner dressed up as a scarecrow and sat, still and silent, in a chair on his porch. As trick-or-treaters collected their goodies at the front door, he'd suddenly reach out and grab the unsuspecting visitor. Most people screamed and ran away (the flight response), except for one young man. In a flash, he punched the scarecrow in the head and *then* ran. After a few moments, he came back to apologize.

This is how the animal brain operates to keep us alive. The young man sensed a threat, immediately acted to fight it off, then fled—fight, *then* flight. All those actions were completely unconscious and automatic, and only after he was out of harm's way did his rational brain come back online. That's when he analyzed the situation, realized he was wrong to have punched his mischievous but harmless neighbor, and apologized.

What does all this have to do with money? A lot, actually. Because when we get scared enough about the economy or stressed enough about our finances, our animal brains take over. Once we're operating in this mode, we make decisions based on our emotions, such as excitement and fear, rather than logic. And this can be dangerous because these emotions, left unchecked, can lead to irrational and self-defeating behaviors—the kind of behaviors that underlies all economic bubbles and crashes. (We'll go into this in more detail when we talk about the sources of financial flashpoints.) Right now, let's take a look at some of the common ways we respond to financial stress:

Fight: Some people react with anger and blame. In a subconscious effort to avoid taking personal responsibility for their financial problems, they blame others: their uncle for giving them a bad stock tip, their bank for predatory lending practices, a particular political party, short-sellers, and on and on. Someone in fight mode might call his financial planner and complain or threaten to sue, or lash out at his or her spouse or kids for overspending. These responses not only fail to solve the problem but they can also injure relationships and lead to even more strife and stress. Sometimes this angry reaction is directed internally, where the person beats themselves up for behaving in ways that through hindsight they believe they shouldn't have. This, just like being angry at someone else, is an attempt for the person to relieve their overwhelming anxiety.

Flight: Others respond by trying to get as far, far away from that source of stress as possible. If the problem is a loss from a bad investment, for example, a person might rashly pull all their money out of the market and run in a different direction.

> BRAD: *I talked to someone recently who's cashed out of the market completely. He's buying as many gold and silver coins as he can get his hands on, he's bought a floor safe, an assault rifle, and he's stockpiling his home with a year's worth of food. That's an extreme flight reaction!*

It's also not unprecedented. During the Great Depression many of the wealthy fled the cities in fear, holing up in country homes stockpiled with canned goods. Some families went as far as mounting machine guns on the eaves of their houses to protect themselves and their hoards against a threat that never came.

Freeze: Another common reaction is to feel so overwhelmed that one takes no action whatsoever. These people go into denial (one of the disorders we'll talk about in the next section) about the problem and freeze up. To use another animal metaphor, they "play possum." They avoid thinking about their financial situations and may even stop looking at their investment reports or bank statements altogether. They stop following the news and they repeatedly ignore recommendations from financial advisers. Many times they will remain frozen until they're jolted into action by some catastrophic event, such as major losses in the market or a foreclosure on their home, only to get frozen into inaction again as soon as the crisis is stemmed.

TED: *When I decided to start investing in my own retirement, I talked to our CPA who helped me determine how much I could afford to send him every month, so he could have it invested for me. The first month, I felt really proud of myself. At the age of fifty-three, I was starting to do my part to take care of myself in terms of saving for my future. The second month came and I wrote the check but didn't send it. The third month, the same. The fourth, fifth, sixth, all the same. I would write the check, but I couldn't send it in. My CPA would call and ask me where the checks were. The answer was always the same: "They're right here, I just haven't sent them to you yet." I had lots of excuses, but I knew there had to be some unfinished business there. It was literally impossible for me to send the checks in, until I dealt with what was really stopping me.*

What should you do if you find yourself in a financial fight/flight/freeze reaction? Here are four simple steps that will help calm you down and enable you to make better, more rational decisions.

Step 1: Recognize that when you are emotionally keyed up—either afraid or excited—you'll be inclined to act irrationally. Remind yourself that financial decisions made in these emotionally charged states are almost always ill advised; that can help get your rational brain back on-line. Give yourself permission to delay making a big decision until it does.

Step 2: Take a few deep breaths. This might sound silly, but there are actual physiological reasons why it works. When we're stressed and angry, we automatically take shorter, shallower breaths. Taking several deep belly breaths can help initiate a relaxation response. With each breath, repeat in your mind a comforting word or phrase: "Relax" or "Take it easy." This helps bring the rational mind back online and prevents it from being shut out of the decision-making process.

Step 3: Evaluate the accuracy of your thinking. Just because a thought pops into your head doesn't mean it's true. What is the evidence that supports your assumption? What's the evidence against it? Is there a better explanation? What's the worst thing that could happen? Could you live with that? What's the most realistic thing that might happen? If a friend or loved one was in this situation and planned to do what you're thinking of, what would you tell him or her?

Step 4: Don't make any rash decisions. Put some time between your emotional reaction and whatever action you take in response. When we're distressed, it takes about twenty minutes of calming thoughts to quiet the animal brain enough to allow the rational brain to take control again. Even then, we can still be swayed by our emotions, so consider seeking professional financial advice before making big financial decisions.

The fight, flight, or freeze responses serve an adaptive purpose. They developed over the ages to ensure the survival of our prehistoric ancestors, and they're still essential when we're faced with life-threatening danger. But for most of us, this response is not really helpful in handling the stressors of daily life. In fact, it can be counterproductive. Our animal brains don't know this, so when we experience what should be a minor annoyance—a car cutting us off in traffic, an argument with our partner or spouse, an unexpected ATM fee—it may register as a major threat, especially if stress levels are already high. That means we'll have a tendency to overreact, even when our conscious selves know better. The good news is that the emotional brain can be trained to suppress its hardwired survival responses in certain situations. In fact, sustained financial health is dependent on our ability to do just that.

Training Takes Over

Spc. T. J. Vallejos, a field medic attached to Charlie Company, Third Platoon, 2-27, describing his experiences while stationed in Kirkuk: "I prepare myself for the worst and hope for the best. The first time I assisted soldiers after an incident, the adrenaline was pumping, my training took over, and I knew what to do."

Volunteer firefighter Stephen Price, who broke out a window in a burning SUV to rescue trapped passengers: "Training took over. I mean, I didn't think anything about it. All I knew was someone was in trouble and needed help."

Pamela Isaza, stay-at-home mother and former EMT who rescued a boy from drowning: "He was blue, not breathing, no pulse. My training took over."

Police officer Chip Reynolds, who risked his life to rescue a hostage from an armed robber: "He could have shot me but this wasn't in my mind. My training took over. I was waiting for the right moment to control the situation."

These are all examples of the rational brain learning to control the animal brain—obviously not through conscious decision making in real time but by relying on repetitive, focused preparation or training. The word *training* appears over and over again in the examples above because any job that requires performing specific actions in highly stressful situations also requires intensive training of the emotional brain. Elite law enforcement personnel spend hours practicing the precise muscle movements needed to draw a gun and move into a firing position. Airline pilots spend hundreds of hours in flight simulators, training to handle every imaginable situation they might encounter in the air. Soldiers are subjected to live fire drills and taught to continue advancing despite explosions all around and bullets whizzing overhead.

Training also helps us master our responses in situations that aren't life and death, like sports. As collegiate athletes ourselves, and later as scholastic coaches of baseball, football, basketball, tennis, and soccer, we have devoted a great deal of time to high-pressure situational drills. In practice, we'd replicate game situations over and over until the players could perform in a particular way in the game itself, without even having to think about it. Whether it's bunting situations in baseball, out of bounds plays for basketball, defending against reverse plays in football, lobbing over an opponent coming to the net in tennis, or corner kicks in soccer, all kinds of complex physical reactions can, and must be, made second nature through repetition and mental training if an athlete or team is to be successful. For example:

BRAD: *For our tennis players, we set up high-pressure game scenarios that are meant to increase the player's anxiety while they execute certain skills, such as hitting second-serves or lobbing over a player at the net. During these exercises, players are taught to use skills aimed at reducing the amygdala's impact on the body by taking deep breaths, visualizing success, and using positive self-talk. An intense focus on what you're doing and intending to do in the here-and-now of the game allows you to play your best. Worrying about the outcome of the shot or the game is a recipe for defeat.*

TED: *Volunteering to stand directly in the path of a rock-hard object flying toward you at seventy to a hundred twenty miles an hour—in other words, stepping in front of a batted baseball—is an unnatural act. When I coached baseball, I'd teach my players to overcome this natural tendency to shy away from baseballs by having them catch ground balls with wooden gloves. To successfully catch a baseball with such a contraption they would have to have perfect fundamentals. Their feet, hands, their arms, their entire body had to be in the right position; aligned perfectly to execute the catch. Using the wooden gloves forced their emotional brains to figure out how to successfully accomplish the task. That meant that during a game, when stress levels were high, their emotional brain would "know" what to do.*

So how can you apply this principle of training to help you deal with financial stress? Just as we can train ourselves to respond a certain way to a line drive coming at our head, we can train ourselves to exert the same kind of control over our emotional reactions to financial events, both personal and global. If we train ourselves to recognize potentially stressful financial situations before they happen, the rational brain can act ahead of time to exert control over the emotional brain. In other words, if we can train ourselves to recognize when our animal brain is trying to hijack a financial decision, we can learn to tame it.

First, we encourage our clients to take a few minutes every day for meditation and for focusing on the body and what it has to say. The ability to read our physical cues, especially those signaling approaching stress, is essential in resisting the takeover of our rational brains.

STAN: *The idea that my emotions, my body, and my financial behaviors were connected—that was novel to me. Now I'll notice that my stomach is tight, and I'll realize that I'm feeling fear, which is my biggest emotion. That's oftentimes my first sign that there's some old stuff going on, and then I can explore what's driving that sensation. I have learned that though I have the impulse to act, to relieve my anxiety, it is absolutely the wrong time to do so.*

Stan's example shows how the body registers uneasiness or anxiety long before we become consciously aware of it. He's learned to use that emotional guidance system to help him identify old self-defeating thinking patterns so that he can take rational, conscious steps to reverse them.

It also shows that training ourselves to keep our thinking from being hijacked starts after the fact, by observing and learning from situations when our thinking *was* hijacked. Think of a financial situation that ended badly. Let's say it's a shopping trip during which you spent far more than you intended. As much as you'd like to forget the whole thing, sit down and really *think* about it, in detail. How were you feeling when you went to the mall? Did you have certain purchases in mind, or was this an impulse visit? If you were shopping for something specific, how did you find yourself even looking at the other items you bought? Concentrate on remembering your thoughts and emotions at each point. Pretend that you're a detective investigating a crime and trace your actions back to whatever prompted them. When did you lose control of the spending? What were you feeling at that moment?

Intense emotions overwhelm the rational brain. We liken it to a flood: When the emotions come rushing in, the rational brain retreats and waits for the flood to subside. By paying attention to and gently analyzing your mistakes and missteps, without shame or criticism, you'll gradually build an awareness of what it feels like when an emotional flood is about to arrive. When you sense that wave coming, take a few deep breaths—really deep, deep enough to move the belly. Then, before you do anything, count to a hundred by fives, recite the alphabet, sing a verse or two of that awful pop song you secretly love—to yourself, of course. That gap between impulse and action is often enough to let the flood subside and the rational brain take over.

When it's possible, seek the advice of others before you take action. This is a very important skill in relationships, which we discuss in more detail later. You might be surprised to learn that many of the top financial planners in the country have financial planners of their own. This is because no matter how much expertise we might have, when we're emotionally charged, we're rationally challenged. *All* of us are susceptible to emotions flooding our rational brain.

You can also plan ahead by giving your rational brain a comeback to the emotional brain's urging. We've all been in a situation where we came up with the perfect response to an argument—five minutes after it would do any good. (The French phrase for this is *esprit de l'escalier,* literally, "staircase wit"—the zinger you think of while you're walking downstairs to go home.) It may be annoying when it happens, but here, your after-the-fact realizations and observations are actually useful. Think of that about-to-flood moment. Think about what your rational brain would have to say if it weren't busy retreating. Then practice saying it over and over, and your rational brain will have it ready the next time a flood threatens.

For instance: You realize that a bad day at work (anxiety and anger) means that you're more likely to "treat yourself" to an impulse purchase you really can't afford. Your comeback might be, "I know I only feel like buying this because I'm mad at my boss and I'll regret spending the money once I cool down. I won't buy it now; if I still want it tomorrow, I can buy it then."

Or: "I'm upset and I don't trust my decision making when I'm upset. I'm sticking to my shopping list and I won't even look at anything that's not on the list." The key is to anticipate the situations—the settings, the emotions, the people—that tend to prompt flooding and prepare yourself to resist them.

There are a number of ways we can train our thinking. We know one financial planner who makes it a point to "drill" his clients on the normal range, or standard deviation, they might expect on their investment returns, based on how aggressive or how conservative their portfolios are. After reviewing the portfolio, he says, "You might expect it to go up x percent, or down y percent over the coming year. Either would be perfectly normal." He makes sure they pay attention to the "or down" part instead of focusing only on the optimistic forecast. Though his clients have lost money over the last year, just like everyone else invested in the market, the important point is that none of them have panicked and acted rashly, because their emotional brains have been trained to anticipate losses as well as gains.

The Overactive Explanatory Mechanism

Clearly, one thing getting in the way of our financial health is the tendency of the animal brain to derail rational decision making. But the brain presents another, surprising obstacle: It's not that great at accurately interpreting events and forming explanations. In fact, contrary to our beliefs, we really don't know much about the origins of our own choices and actions. To understand how this phenomenon impacts your financial life, we first need to take another quick look at the structure of the brain itself.

While the elements of the triune brain are nested on top of one another, like measuring cups, the brain is also divided in half, front to back, like a walnut in its shell. Each hemisphere is the mirror image of the other and there's a certain amount of overlap in function. (That's one reason why people, especially children, can sometimes make remarkable recoveries from a brain injury to one side of the head; the other hemisphere picks up the slack.) A thick bundle of nerve tissue called the *corpus callosum* connects these two hemispheres and acts as the bridge between them.

But despite the similarities, there are distinct differences in each hemisphere's functions. One of the biggest ones is that each hemisphere communicates with a different half of the body. In a sense, we're wired backward: You may already know that the right brain hemisphere processes sensory information from and controls motor function on the left side of the body, while the left hemisphere handles input and movement on the right side. Since the mid-1860s, researchers have been exploring the other ways brain function is divided. Some of the most interesting research has come from working with split-brain patients, people who've had the corpus callosum, the connection between hemispheres, severed. (This is one treatment for patients suffering from extreme, debilitating epilepsy, intended to reduce the frequency and violence of seizures.)

Almost forty years ago, neuroscientists Dr. Joseph LeDoux and Dr. Michael Gazzaniga studied split-brain patients and discovered some surprising things about how the brain works. Earlier experiments had shown that speech and language processing was handled in the left hemisphere alone. But that raised an interesting question: How does the left hemisphere respond to something the right hemisphere does, and vice versa? Gazzaniga and LeDoux designed an experiment to find out. A split-brain subject was shown a split image: The left side (seen only by the right brain) depicted a snowy outdoor scene and the right (seen only by the left brain), a bird's foot. In front of the subject were two groups of four smaller pictures: on the left side, several tools, including a snow shovel, and on the right, a variety of animals and objects, including a chicken. The subject was asked to pick the most appropriate small picture to go with the larger one and, correctly, he picked the shovel with his left hand (controlled by the right brain) and the chicken with his right (controlled by the left brain). Makes sense, right? Well, here's the interesting part.

When the subject was asked *why* he'd selected the shovel, he came up with a response that's both logical and nonsensical. The right part of his brain, which made the choice based on the snowdrifts, couldn't communicate its reasoning, and the left part of his brain, which *could* speak, had never seen the snow that had prompted the selection. The resourceful left brain came up with an answer anyway: "I picked the shovel to clean up after the chicken!" In the absence of information needed to explain a decision, the brain sorted through what it knew about chickens and snow shovels, found a way to connect the two, and convinced itself that this connection actually explained the choice.

Gazzaniga calls this tendency to add information and details to memories and create links between unrelated events the *interpreter mechanism*. According to Gazzaniga, new findings over the past two decades "suggest that the interpretive mechanism of the left hemisphere is always hard at work, seeking the meaning of events. It is constantly looking for order and reason, even when there is none—which leads it continually to make mistakes. It tends to overgeneralize, frequently constructing a potential past as opposed to a true one."

This holds true for all of us. We're *all* wired to seek out connections and meanings, even when they don't exist. And it is this tendency of the brain to misinterpret and draw erroneous assumptions from random or unrelated events that helps explain how people end up drawing irrational, unproductive, and self-destructive lessons from financial flashpoint experiences. We might think: "I lost money on my first investment, so there's no point in investing in anything ever again" or "My parents used to fight all the time about money and they got divorced so if I want to stay married I'll never talk to my spouse about finances."

And these kinds of scripts, however flawed they might be, are incredibly resilient. Once the explanatory mechanism settles on a narrative, it takes real effort to change that story, no matter how outlandish it is. These stories are anchored in the animal brain, which is focused on survival, not constructed through careful consideration and reflection. When we hear what we think is a big cat in the jungle, we don't have time to consider all of our possible responses, weigh the pros and cons of each prior to taking action. Our animal brain acts on pure instinct and feeling, and it acts immediately. The response is the same whether that threat turns out to be a hungry tiger or a terrified mouse, because the animal brain doesn't have time to wait and find out which it is. Similarly, our money scripts remain static and rigid even though our situations or circumstances may have changed.

Each of us carries around many different money scripts, and because they're not the result of conscious and rational thought, they're often contradictory. Yet all of them are powerful and deeply held. Money scripts have already worked for us and others we know, at least to some degree, so we have faith in them and cling to them, even when they're causing us distress and disaster in daily life. Our primary obstacle in dealing with money scripts is that we're often unaware of them, which only enhances their ability to exert absolute control over our lives. That's why before we can begin to change a behavior, we have to consciously understand the script or story our interpreter mechanism has created.

TED: *I was working with a couple who had their finances mapped out well but they were balking at buying life insurance—especially the husband. They had several children, all under eight years of age; they owned and ran a multimillion-dollar company; and they flew in their own private jet together, quite often without the children. At several meetings, I'd press them on the real need for life insurance and they'd wave me off.*

Finally I drilled down a bit, asking questions to get at the source of this irrational behavior. I discovered that the client's grandfather, who had founded the company, went without life insurance for decades. Finally, when he was in his sixties, he took out a policy—and within a year he was dead. As a young boy, our client overheard his family talking about the sad coincidence of the insurance purchase and the death. His interpreter mechanism made the connection between the two and now, more than thirty years later, he was still convinced they were connected. When I pointed that out to him—"Does that mean if I never buy life insurance, I'll never die?"—he and his wife both laughed. He said, "I guess that is a ridiculous way to run our lives, isn't it?"

A few days later they called to let me know that they'd purchased life insurance.

As counselors, we have no problem believing that many of our financial decisions—and those of the whole marketplace—are based on something other than logic and rationality. That's how we are trained to see the world. But three renowned economists came to the same conclusion. We'll include one observation here and the other two elsewhere in the chapter.

For indeed, the investor's chief problem—and even his worst enemy—is likely to be himself.

—Benjamin Graham, the father of modern value investing,
   Warren Buffett's mentor, and author of *The Intelligent Investor*

Deciding Under Stress

We've seen that stress interferes with our ability to make accurate assessments. And stress over money is no exception. Whether it results from watching a 401(k) plunge in value or trying to figure out how to make ends meet, financial stress tends to make us feel out of control, which further adds to stress levels and impairs our rational thinking.

This was demonstrated in a set of six experiments, by Dr. Jennifer Whitson at the University of Texas–Austin and Dr. Adam Galinsky at Northwestern University, testing people's ability to accurately perceive patterns when they felt a lack of control. The researchers induced that feeling in their subjects in two ways: by asking them to recall a time when they'd been in a situation where they lacked control, or by giving them feedback on a series of tests that had nothing to do with the subjects' actual performance. Then the researchers asked participants to look at a set of grainy images and pick out which ones, if any, had hidden patterns. Sure enough, the participants with the induced uncertainty had more false positive responses. In other words, the people who felt out of control were more likely to detect patterns that weren't there.

Most interesting for our purposes, Whitson and Galinsky then asked people to analyze financial information. In this case, the control group was given information that described the stock market as stable and predictable, while the other subjects read descriptions of the stock market as volatile and unstable (much like the news reports we take in these days). They were then asked to analyze a series of financial statements about two different companies. The "volatile" group did a much worse job analyzing the information than the control group; they overemphasized insignificant factors and ignored more important ones. Indeed, when primed to think about stressful situations out of their control, their ability to accurately spot patterns in the information was alarmingly impaired.

> *The heart has its reasons that reason knows not of.*
> —Blaise Pascal,
> seventeenth-century scientist and philosopher

In his best-selling books *Fooled by Randomness* and *The Black Swan,* Nassim Taleb highlights the fact that we have a tendency to underestimate the degree to which randomness plays a role in both our successes and failures. In terms of financial decisions, Taleb makes a convincing argument that we exaggerate the validity and predictive power of our beliefs, often to our financial detriment. We're also prone to making false-positive conclusions, convincing ourselves of a causal link between two unrelated events. This thinking is what underlies many superstitions and rituals, such as knocking on wood to keep bad luck away, or believing that an itchy palm means money is on its way to you. It is also what underlies so many cognitive biases, like attributing your success in the stock market to your shrewd and savvy investing, instead of the overall bull market.

So under stress, the rational brain is kicked off line and we do what the nonrational parts of our brain urge us to do. Afterward we create reasons why we reacted the way we did. We convince ourselves we are right and shut out any evidence to the contrary. We even seek out others who share or confirm our conclusions. We are drawn to these people. We call them friends. We go from rational human beings to rationalizing ones.

Chocolate Cake or Fruit Salad?

As if that weren't bad enough, studies have found that our over-loaded schedules and relentless multitasking may further impair our ability to make wise decisions. Stanford researchers Baba Shiv and Alexander Fedorikhin tested the effects of distraction on decision making. The title of the resulting paper—"Heart and Mind in Conflict"—is a good thumbnail summary of their find-ings, and a good shorthand explanation for so many of our self-destructive financial behaviors. In the experiment, students were told they were participating in a memory test and asked to mem-orize a specific number, either two digits or seven digits long. On the way to the room where the supposed memory testing was to take place, they were offered a choice of snacks—chocolate cake or fruit salad—that appealed to two different and powerful men-tal processes: the cognitive (our rational, thinking selves) and the affective (our impulsive, emotional side). Obviously, the healthier, more rational and reasonable choice would be the fruit salad, and indeed, only 27 percent of the people remembering a two-digit number gave in to temptation and chose the cake. On the other hand, more than twice as many—59 percent—of the people try-ing to hold a seven-digit number in their heads picked the cake. Why? Because it turns out that a single part of our brain, the prefrontal cortex, deals with both working memory—tasks like holding on to a number or keeping track of a to-do list—and the rational control over our impulses—decisions like resisting a tempting snack that's bad for us or avoiding a questionable but desirable purchase. If we load up the prefrontal cortex with too many tasks, we significantly reduce our ability to talk our-selves out of the powerful impulses (*"Must have* cake!" *"Need* flat-screen TV!") that come from other parts of the brain.

What's the takeaway from these experiments? Two points: Our rational brains are much less powerful than we like to believe, and stress weakens them further by impairing our ability to make decisions. And when we remember the fact that 80 percent of Americans name money as their biggest source of stress, it no longer seems surprising that so many of us make irrational financial decisions, does it?

Flexibility Is Essential

You've just reached an important milestone in taking charge of your financial life. Recognizing and understanding your inherent tendency to be overconfident in your scripts and beliefs about money, especially when you're feeling stress, is essential if you're going to take charge of your relationship with money. But that insight isn't transformative on its own. As we've seen, people tend to create an external financial reality that fits with their internal reality. To create a new financial life, we must first make the necessary internal shifts in beliefs, knowledge, insight, and emotion. If we do not make this internal shift, we will inevitably drift back to old habits.

> *Even apart from the instability due to speculation, there is the instability due to the characteristic of human nature that a large proportion of our positive activities depend on spontaneous optimism rather than on a mathematical expectation, whether moral or hedonistic or economic. Most, probably, of our decisions to do something positive, the full consequences of which will be drawn out over many days to come, can only be taken as a result of animal spirits—of a spontaneous urge to action rather than inaction, and not as the outcome of a weighted average of quantitative benefits multiplied by quantitative probabilities. . . . Thus if the animal spirits are dimmed and the spontaneous optimism falters, leaving us to depend on nothing but a mathematical expectation, enterprise will fade and die;—though fears of loss may have a basis no more reasonable than hopes of profit had before.*
>
> —John Maynard Keynes, macroeconomist and advocate of government intervention in faltering economies on the topic of animal spirits

An uncertain global economy only makes this more imperative. History shows us countless examples of disaster and downfall brought about by a failure to adjust to changing circumstances. In fact, you could even say we owe our nationhood to it; the Redcoats, trained to fight formalized Napoleonic battles, couldn't adapt quickly enough to the revolutionaries' more free-wheeling methods of combat. The former Soviet Union, too, was the model of rigidity, sticking to policies and systems long after they'd proved unworkable. And Jared Diamond's book *Collapse* analyzes the disappearance of several cultures that failed to adapt to changes in climate, natural resources, or trade alliances.

On an individual scale, similar failure to mentally adjust to changing circumstances can be just as disastrous. Lack of flexibility explains why so many people who come into money suddenly, through an inheritance, an insurance settlement, or a lottery win, end up squandering it. Adaptability in thinking and openness to new information are essential protective factors that help us survive and thrive in this transformative era. To change your financial future, you must be willing to challenge and change what you think you know.

Emotions: Our Internal GPS

We've been talking a lot about how our emotional responses interfere with our ability to make decisions. By now you might be thinking that the problem would be solved if we could somehow get rid of those erratic emotions and stick with pure logic. Not true. It turns out that our emotions are often an essential component to good decision making.

In *Descartes' Error,* neurologist Antonio Damasio describes working with patients who'd suffered damage to a specific part of the brain that caused them to be completely devoid of emotions. Their cognitive skills were intact and they scored normally on tests designed to detect various psychological problems. Their difficulties arose from the fact that they had no real response to or engagement with others. And their behavior was strangely contradictory, both obsessive and impulsive. In some circumstances, such as sorting papers to be filed, they'd become stuck at one step in the process, unable to distinguish between the minor task and the overall objective. Yet they'd also embark on fraudulent investments, disastrous marriages, and all sorts of obviously ill-advised, impulsive choices. Two incidents with a particular patient (we'll call him Bob) explain the paradox.

> It's the psychology that leads to panics and recessions.
>
> Economists cannot avoid being students of human nature, particularly of exuberance and fear. Exuberance is a celebration of life. We have to perceive life as enjoyable to seek to sustain it. Regrettably, a surge of exuberance sometimes also causes people to reach beyond the possible; when reality strikes home, exuberance turns to fear. Fear is an automatic response in all of us to threats to our deepest of all inbred propensities, our will to live.
>
> Inbred human propensities to swing from euphoria to fear and back again seem permanent: generations of experience do not appear to have tempered those propensities.
>
> —Alan Greenspan, former chairman of the Federal Reserve Board and author of *The Age of Turbulence* on factors beyond the numbers that influence the economy

Bob drove to Damasio's clinic on a day when the roads were unusually icy. When he arrived, Damasio asked if he'd had any trouble on the way. Bob said he hadn't, but he'd seen the car ahead of him hit a patch of ice. The driver panicked and hit the brakes and the car spun into a ditch. But when he himself reached the same ice patch and began to slide, he calmly steered himself out and drove on, and here he was. Now, imagine yourself relating this story. Would you be a bit shaken? Bob wasn't. Would you express some concern for the driver ahead of you? Bob didn't.

The following day, when Bob's next visit to the clinic had to be scheduled, Damasio offered two different dates; Bob took out his appointment book and, for the next thirty minutes, drove the clinic staff crazy with his inability to make a simple decision. As Damasio describes it: "Just as calmly as he had driven over the ice, and recounted that episode, he was now walking us through a tiresome cost-benefit analysis, an endless outlining and fruitless comparison of options and possible consequences." Finally, Damasio reached the limit of his patience and suggested the later date. Bob said, "That's fine," and put away his appointment book. The ordeal was over.

In the first incident, Bob's lack of emotion served him well. Unlike the driver ahead of him, who was overcome with panic at the initial skid, he felt no rush of fear and was able to calmly respond as he'd been taught to do. But when he tried to make a simple decision between two dates, that same lack of emotion was crippling. Why?

It seems that emotions are essential to decision making in several ways. First, they help us to project ourselves into the world and understand the responses of others. Without the ability to experience emotion, Bob wasn't able to recognize the nonverbal cues through which the staff surely communicated their growing annoyance and impatience. Second, emotions produce what Damasio calls *somatic markers*: those instantaneous "gut feelings" that we so heavily lean on, for better or for worse, when we make choices. Operating below the level of awareness, somatic markers are mental records of past experiences that act as an internal guidance system. Somatic markers help shape our decisions by shifting us toward or away from specific choices depending on how similar choices worked out in the past. For example, let's say you ate salmon for dinner and became violently ill. The next time you're offered salmon, your animal brain all but shouts at you, "Don't eat that!" But these markers can operate at more subtle levels, too, which escape our conscious awareness. If the tablecloth at that wretched salmon dinner was red and white checkered, you might feel slightly queasy at the sight of that pattern without knowing why. These kinds of somatic markers are the source of our hunches and gut feelings.

In his book *How We Decide,* Jonah Lehrer describes a remarkable example of the power and subtlety of the gut feeling. During the first Gulf War, Michael Riley, a lieutenant commander in the British navy, was part of a mission protecting offshore alliance battleships as they shelled a Kuwaiti military base occupied by Iraqi troops. Riley's job was monitoring radar screens hour after hour, following the blips that represented aircraft and allied missiles, watching for anything out of the ordinary. Early one morning, a blip appeared, traveling from land toward the battleship USS *Missouri.* For no reason he could pinpoint, that blip filled Riley with dread, made his heart pound and his hands go clammy. Was it an Iraqi missile? Or was it an American fighter returning to its nearby aircraft carrier? Because of a range of human and mechanical errors, Riley couldn't try to contact the blip or evaluate its altitude. He had to decide what to do on his own, and the costs of getting it wrong were immensely high. Riley trusted his gut. He issued the order to fire, then waited to find out if he'd brought down a missile or an American pilot.

Riley made the correct call. The mysterious blip was an Iraqi Silkworm missile and his decision saved the *Missouri* and its sailors. Riley still couldn't say why that blip had struck him as fearsome or threatening, only that it had. Cognitive psychologist Dr. Gary Klein was determined to find out why. After exhaustively reviewing the radar tapes, watching those crucial seconds over and over, Klein finally got his answer. Flying at low altitude, the missile didn't show up on the radar screen until several seconds after a jet would have—on the third radar sweep, instead of the first. It broke the pattern Riley's brain had come to recognize and expect. The difference was miniscule, so much so that it escaped Riley's conscious awareness. But his animal brain noticed and reacted.

Finally, our emotions are also helpful because they allow us to "try on" new behaviors, through imagination and visualization, which helps us predict how we will feel about the outcome of a decision before we actually make it. Given that the majority of our wisdom is outside of our conscious awareness at any one time, our emotions also act as a safeguard, letting us know, at a visceral level, that something is wrong, or about to go wrong.

Of course, no one suggests you should make financial decisions based on emotion alone. But emotions shouldn't be ignored completely; they should be recognized, acknowledged, and then examined as objectively as possible. It is critical that we become students of our emotions—a curious observer of our anxieties, our assumptions, and our internal dialogue, the constant internal chatter and self-talk. If we don't, we will forever be subject to their insidious control over our financial decisions. Identifying our financial flashpoints, acknowledging our hurts and the lessons we have learned, enables us to recognize that we are separate from our emotions and automatic thoughts. Only then can we choose our financial actions in a mindful and proactive way.

So what does a mindful and rational decision-making process look like? First of all, don't rush into anything. Do your research. Think about the likely consequences of each choice. Listen to your body; if you're feeling signs of anxiety, try to figure out the source. Are you stressed about having to make a decision at all? Is your anxiety connected to one of the choices? Does your anxiety have more to do with a bad experience in your past than your current reality? Your animal brain—source of those gut feelings—certainly isn't infallible but it is worth listening to.

And once you've made your decision, let it go. Don't agonize over what might have been. Whatever happens, it's probably not life and death. Seventeenth-century philosopher and economist Adam Smith said the same thing, much more eloquently.

> *The great source of both the misery and disorders of human life, seems to arise from overrating the difference between one permanent situation and another. . . . Some of those situations may, no doubt, deserve to be preferred to others: but none of them can deserve to be pursued with that passionate ardor which drives us to violate the rules either of prudence or of justice; or to corrupt the future tranquility of our minds, either by shame from the remembrance of our own folly, or by remorse from the horror of our own injustice.*

3

Belonging at All Costs: Running with the Herd

Have you ever been in the middle of a stampede?

If you're imagining thundering hooves stirring up clouds of dust, the answer will almost certainly be no. (Otherwise you wouldn't be here to answer at all.) But the fact is, everyone who's ever been a member of a group—in other words, each and every one of us—has undoubtedly been caught up in the human equivalent of a stampede. You may even have led one.

We've seen the thundering-hooves kind of stampede at the Black Hills Wild Horse Refuge outside Hot Springs, South Dakota. We've spent considerable time there watching the wild horses and observing their behavior and interactions with each other. There always seems to be a leader or a group of leaders who determine what the group does—not through force, but simply by example. If the leaders suddenly begin galloping away, the entire herd goes with them. It doesn't matter if they're galloping because they've caught a whiff of mountain lion, or because they've stumbled into a hive of ground-nesting hornets, or because they're just feeling in the mood for a good gallop—where the leader goes, so does the herd.

The lead horses might be taking the herd toward safety. They might also be leading it, by mistake, to the crumbling edge of a cliff. None of the other horses knows for sure. But all the horses *are* sure that they do not want to be left behind and they do not want to be the slowest. After all, to escape from a large predator, a horse doesn't have to be the fastest in the herd. It just has to be faster than at least one other horse. To the members of a herd, being left behind means certain death—if not now, then soon.

A common belief is that financial decisions are driven by greed. We disagree. We believe that financial behaviors are driven by fear: Like the horses in a stampede, our decisions about what direction to take, and the speed with which we take them, are driven by the fear of being left behind.

Humans are social animals. Our very survival for thousands of years depended on being a part of the tribe. Being kicked out meant being alone, and being alone meant death. We are wired to connect with others. Though this is an ancient instinct, one that evolved in our prehistoric past, it's still one of the strongest impulses we have. MySpace, Facebook, LinkedIn, and Twitter are just modern-day examples of the ancient herd instinct, and their success is testament to the power of that need to belong. That desire is not only still alive, but still powerful, even though it typically operates below our immediate awareness. When activated, it will take charge and throw rationality out the window.

Think of the lead horse taking the entire herd over a cliff. This wasn't a rational, conscious decision—it was an instinctual one. In humans, the herd mentality—the blind following of some de facto leader—can result in anything from riots, to gang violence, to bullying among children. Herd instinct can go out of control in the most unlikely of settings—as it did on Black Friday, 2008, the day after Thanksgiving, when a temporary worker at a Long Island Wal-Mart was knocked down and trampled to death by a "herd" of shoppers eager to snap up bargains.

The human herd mentality, too, applies to financial behaviors, and as such, can play an important role in shaping our money scripts. Many behaviors that seem to be random and irrational are, in fact, the result of a highly predictable social dynamic—our innate desire to "stay with the herd." It is this desire that keeps us from breaking free of our *financial comfort zone,* or the socioeconomic herd in which we are most comfortable. Until we are willing to venture outside of our financial comfort zone, to leave our own herd and enter the territory of another, we will continue to unconsciously engage in financial behaviors that keep us stuck in, or draw us back to, our own.

Financial Comfort Zone

Picture the neighborhood you lived in the longest. You probably got to know it pretty well. You knew where to get groceries. You knew the quickest way to get to the hospital emergency room. You knew the friendly neighbors and the not-so-friendly ones. You knew where the closest hardware store was. Drugstore. Coffee shop. Playground. Dry cleaners. You *knew* your neighborhood. You felt comfortable there. You felt safe there. You *belonged* there.

A financial comfort zone works the same way. It's the financial neighborhood that makes you feel safest and most at home. We often find ourselves in a particular financial comfort zone as a consequence of our birth and family of origin. We didn't choose it originally, but many of us never realize how much a part of us it becomes. We can leave—but even if we do, the original boundaries we learned are very strong. Those boundaries may be arbitrary and drawn by others, but we soon learn to live within them, anyway. Just as you learned not to throw a ball into the cranky neighbor's yard, these financial boundaries set the parameters for what is acceptable for you to do with your money. They become second nature. They define our reality. Because they are automatic and lie outside our awareness, these financial boundaries, left unexamined, become glass ceilings and floors.

Each financial neighborhood has its own set of values and mores. It has its own answers for questions like: What is the financial role of fathers and mothers? When if ever is it acceptable to take on debt? What is the best way to use my money? What are we supposed to put up with to meet our financial obligations to others (for instance, working at a job you don't really like much)? How acceptable is it to flaunt how much I have and what I spend it on?

Your financial comfort zone also dictates how *poor* and *rich* are defined (as we'll see in a minute, these in fact are highly relative terms) and at what point you move from one position to the other. We know of one young lady from an upscale neighborhood who was planning her wedding. Her parents told her that they would give her a certain amount of money to spend but set a limit to what they would be willing to contribute. Shocked, the young woman said, "A budget? Mother, that's what poor people do!" The point is, the wealthy and the poor think very differently about money, and without a significant shift in thinking, it is difficult to move from one group to the other.

Our goal is to teach you to stretch your own financial comfort zone. We want to help you become more flexible in your thinking, so you can become comfortable at any financial level and develop the mental and emotional framework you need to reach and maintain the financial level you aspire to.

This flexibility is something that has to be consciously learned. Without awareness, new knowledge, and skills, it's hard to overcome the pull of our upbringing. As long as your financial status is compatible with your financial comfort zone, you'll feel as if everything is fine. The problems begin when your income level or standard of living significantly increases or decreases, or when that comfort zone limits your potential success.

When your circumstances bring you beyond the top boundary of your financial comfort zone, you will begin to feel unsettled or anxious. You probably won't even be aware of that anxiety or the reasons for it. After all, more money should be a good thing. It's having less money that should be stressful, right? Wrong. In our work, we have found that feeling stress about having more money is just as common, if not more so, than feeling stress about having less. For example, all other things being equal, people with 401(k)s are much more anxious about stock market declines than those without. In many ways, the more we *have,* the more we *have to worry about.* True, stress sometimes comes from having less money, but also from the feelings that arise when you find yourself in an unfamiliar financial place, away from your herd. Under unfamiliar circumstances, the alarm in the animal brain sounds a danger alert and your unconscious mind will attempt to pull you back to familiar ground. For your animal brain, it is an issue of life or death.

This is why we experience such stress any time we face a change in our financial status. And if we aren't conscious of this financial comfort zone and what we are experiencing, we'll begin to behave in unconscious ways that will move us back into our comfort zone. We will, without awareness, do what we have to do to restore our sense of equilibrium and comfort, even when that is to our financial detriment. We'll make automatic, often totally unconscious money decisions that are designed to reduce our exposure to that uncomfortable top boundary and pull us back into safer, more familiar confines.

After all, moving above that boundary might require a move to a different neighborhood, where we may not know the rules or speak the same language. Where we might feel judged, unsafe, isolated, or out of place. Where we might be misunderstood or "evicted."

TED: *I once owned a twenty-five-year-old truck to haul things around the estate that we owned. I had picked it out, but before I could buy it my daughter got it for me as a gift. It cost eight hundred dollars. In the part of the country I lived in, everyone named their trucks, and the neighbors affectionately named mine "Junior."*

The day after I took possession of Junior, I noticed the engine missed and backfired quite a bit. I could also tell that it needed a new muffler and the steering was a little loose, in that Junior tended to wander from side to side as "he" was driven down the road. I took it into the local garage for a tune-up and left it there.

When I got home, the mechanic from the garage called and said that when he went to remove the old muffler, he saw gasoline running out of the gas tank and that I'd need a new one. He also noticed that the entire exhaust system had rusted and needed to be replaced. I gave him permission to fix all those things.

The next day, I got another call from the mechanic. He informed me that they couldn't fix the "miss" in the engine and they suspected a bent valve. He also said they didn't do that kind of engine work and I should take Junior to the local dealer to have that done.

I took the truck to the dealer and they told me that if they rebuilt the top end of the engine their concern was that the bottom end of the engine would then go out, so they suggested an entirely rebuilt engine. I said fine. A week later, I couldn't get Junior into gear, so back to the dealer he went and got a new clutch as well as new brakes.

Two weeks later, my eight-hundred-dollar truck had a new engine, radiator, clutch, and brakes; a rebuilt transmission and differential; and a custom-fabricated driveshaft. The repair bills totaled sixty-seven hundred dollars, but I wasn't driving a truck worth seventy-five hundred dollars. Junior was still a twenty-five-year-old truck worth about eight hundred dollars, with almost seven thousand dollars of repairs. Obviously, I could have afforded a seventy-five-hundred-dollar truck, so why didn't I buy one in the first place?

Because I lived in a little town where the average guy drove a twenty-five-year-old pickup truck, I didn't want people to think I thought I was better than them. Looking back, it's obvious I didn't fool anyone. By their standards, and· most people's, I was rich. I owned the big house and seventy acres on the hill. I owned and ran a multimillion-dollar business that operated out of that site. We employed about twenty of the local folks in our business.

The need to appear to be just like them cost me thousands of dollars. I was trying to fit into the herd. And truth be told, I was having trouble leaving my own financial comfort zone, the one I grew up in.

(Five years later I sold Junior. For five hundred dollars.)

BRAD: I grew up in a working-class family, in a working-class neighborhood. My parents divorced when I was young, which led to financial hardship for both of them. My father spent the next decade living in rented rooms in other people's houses. My mother remarried early, but times were tough. We turned our backyard into a family farm, growing fruits, berries, and vegetables, which we canned for the winter months. Often, we hunted wild game and fished to supplement our food.

I grew up very aware that others had more money than we did, and that meant they could do things I couldn't do. I was often

*jealous. I wanted to try downhill skiing but knew it was too ex-
pensive for us, so I didn't even ask. And even though my parents
were divorced, they seemed constantly in conflict over money.
Many times one of them reminded me that I couldn't do or have
something because the other wouldn't pay for it or wasn't being
fair. Many things were promised but not delivered. I fantasized
about what it would be like to have money—to be able to do
things I wanted to do and go places I wanted to go. To have nice
clothes. To have reliable transportation. To travel to Europe during the summer instead of working. I was very attracted to the
wealthier herd, but I knew I didn't belong there.*

*It wasn't until I entered graduate school that I realized I was
in the company of a new herd. I began to notice that many of
them thought much differently than I did. I encountered clas-
sism, hearing discussions about how "tacky" certain poorer people
are and anger toward the "white trash" element in our society,
who are racist and stupid. Since I had a doctorate, people assumed I came from a more privileged background and would invite me into the conversation. I heard jokes about people who eat
squirrels and like monster trucks, jokes that were just as dismis-
sive and contemptuous as the ones my herd often made about
greedy, shallow rich people. In this new herd, I often felt
ashamed. I felt like an impostor, a fraud about to be exposed.*

*At the same time, trips home became increasingly uncomfort-
able. I noticed that my own people were seeing me as different—
richer. It felt horrible. I found myself frequently offering up
details about how much debt I had accrued in graduate school,
and minimizing how much money I was making: "I know it
sounds good, but I'm a hundred thousand dollars in debt." I felt a
profound emotional need to pull myself back into the herd.
When I started making six figures a year, my efforts to appear less
successful intensified. My house was almost empty, with just a
Ping-Pong table in the living room, some folding lawn chairs,*

and a third- or fourth-hand bed and dresser. I had two plates, two mismatched forks, one pot and one pan. I had two cars, one that cost four hundred dollars and one that cost five hundred dollars. They took turns breaking down and I'd drive one while fixing the other. I would empty my bank account into retirement funds I couldn't access and continue living paycheck to paycheck. Although I was making more money than anyone in my extended family, I had structured my life so that day to day I was living as if I had less than any of them.

Then, in 1999, I was bitten by the dot-com bug. After watching friends become day traders and make thousands of dollars with a few mouse clicks, I jumped in with both feet. For a while I made money, but then the bottom fell out of the market. I lost everything I'd "made" and half of what I started with. Looking back on it, I can see my recklessness as another attempt to get back to my financial comfort zone.

This experience, as painful as it was, was worth every penny I lost. I took the opportunity to reflect on my feelings, thoughts, and decisions. I researched the history of stock bubbles and crashes and saw that I had fallen victim to emotional finance, like others before me have been doing for centuries.

And as I began to examine my financial flashpoints and money scripts, I was able to make the move out of my financial comfort zone and become more and more comfortable with who I am and what I earn. It is a work in progress. Some of my relationships have been maintained, and some I have lost. Expanding my financial comfort zone has helped me be more comfortable around those who have more and those who have less. However, some people in my life have been unable to expand their financial comfort zones to include me, and we have drifted apart.

As you can see from our personal stories, any event that triggers the animal brain's fear of not belonging to our community, our tribe, causes us to use incredible energies to do whatever it takes to stay in the neighborhood. There's intense internal pressure to stay within the socioeconomic boundaries we're familiar with.

There's also external pressure to stay within the confines of our financial comfort zone—the crab-barrel effect. When live crabs are caught, collected, and put into a barrel, it seems there are always a few enterprising crustaceans bent on escaping. But as they scramble to the top of the pile and make their way up the side of the barrel and get near the top, their barrel mates reach up—sometimes in their own attempts to escape—and pull the leaders back down. Occupants of a particular financial comfort zone or neighborhood will do the same thing, but instead of using legs and claws, people use the one thing the ancient part of our brains are most afraid of: social isolation. We're all terrified of being kicked out of our tribe and having nowhere to belong. Most people instinctively know this, and will play on that fear to try to drag us back into the barrel where they believe we belong.

Consider Tomás's story. He came from a very poor family near the Pacific Ocean in Central America and he was aware that his father could barely make enough money to feed the family. When he was six years old, a visiting couple from Australia asked to adopt him, offering to educate him and even bring him back to see his family every year. His father told Tomás he could go but made it clear he would essentially be abandoning his family and that he'd probably never see them again. Tomás knew the couple was offering him an incredible opportunity for a better life, but after talking to his father Tomás felt intense pressure and guilt and so he made the decision to stay.

After that, Tomás took jobs after school and on weekends. By the time he was twelve, he was going out on tiny fishing boats for up to five days at a time. Sometimes he'd go into town and sell cheese and other things that his mother made. He saved all the money he earned and was very set on improving his and the family's future.

One day his father became very ill and needed some medicine that he couldn't afford. He asked Tomás's mother to borrow the money from a local loan shark. When Tomás heard this, he offered his savings to his father to buy the medicine. Sick as he was, his father beat Tomás severely with his belt. He accused Tomás of thinking he was better than his own father, but he took the money, anyway.

From that day on, Tomás made the conscious decision that he wouldn't save money; there was no point in it. He married young and now, whenever he gets money, he turns over to his wife what she needs for the month's expenses and then spends the rest, usually on getting drunk. Tomás had tried to get out of that barrel—twice. The first time by trying to go live with the Australian couple, the second time by earning and saving so that his family could have a more comfortable life. And both times, his father—whether out of jealousy, petty resentment, or macho pride—used the threat of alienation to pull him right back down. Sadly, this is not uncommon behavior among those insecure about their own financial situation or station in life, and the results can be incredibly damaging.

Or consider the story of our uncle and great-uncle Jim. He was one of seven children who grew up on a small farm in southern Ohio. As a young man, he decided that there wasn't much of a future for him on the family farm. So he signed up for the service and after his enlistment was up, he decided to try his luck in Florida. One thing the farm had taught him was how to work hard. He started as a laborer on a builder's crew, then eventually founded his own construction company and, after decades of hard work, dedication, and attention to detail, he became a very wealthy man. He had definitely left the financial comfort zone that he was raised in.

Each summer Uncle Jim would bring his family to Ohio to visit our grandparents, uncles, aunts, and cousins. The reaction of the people he left back on the farm was quite predictable.

"Guess how Jim is going to get here? (He's going to fly, just to show off how much money he has.)"

"Guess who's too good to have us pick him up from the airport? (He's going to waste money renting a car. A Hertz, even!)"

"Guess who's too good to stay at one of our houses? (He's going to rent a room at a motel. A motel with a swimming pool, of all things.)"

"Guess why he's doing all this? (Just to show us all up.)"

"Guess who thinks he's better than us?"

What do you think the effect was on Uncle Jim's nieces and nephews as they listened to their elders tear down the one relative who'd moved away and made a lot of money? Would they grow up thinking that ambition and initiative are positive attributes or signs of arrogance? Is there a chance they'd feel so much fear of being cast out of the tribe, like Uncle Jim, that they'd fight against any desire they might have to emulate him?

And what might Uncle Jim himself have felt, as he left his financial comfort zone? As we mentioned, the pressures to stay inside our zone are both external and internal, and when people move past the upper limit suddenly or with little preparation—such as after a big windfall—they're likely to feel tremendous subconscious pressure to move back toward the security and familiarity of that lower zone. They might give away chunks of money, go on an extended or extravagant vacation, or otherwise fritter away the newfound wealth. Or perhaps they decide to invest in a business, build an addition to the house, or play the markets. These aren't horrible ideas in and of themselves, but since these people often have no experience in managing that kind of wealth, they may make poor business or investment decisions that end up losing money.

This automatic drive to restore our equilibrium holds true as we approach the lower limit of our comfort level, too. In some cases, this desire can work to our advantage. Think of successful business owners whose businesses fail and who, within a few years, have developed another successful one. Falling below their financial comfort zone drives them to focus all their skills and resources on returning to their original comfort level. Perhaps this explains the fact that, on average, millionaires make 3.1 major business mistakes compared to 1.6 for those who are not millionaires. They may fail more often, but each failure only inspires them to try again.

Sometimes, even when we do manage to move successfully out of our zone, we continue to *act* like we are still in the old zone—like the ex-billionaire who goes bankrupt but continues to drive BMWs, buy expensive clothing, and spend like there's no tomorrow. Or on the flip side, think about the self-made millionaire who buys a split-level home in a neighborhood of mansions, continues to drive his used Hyundai, and wanders among the rich while remaining socially isolated. Both situations are unhealthy for our psyche and can severely compromise our happiness.

The unconscious reluctance to move out of one's comfort zone may also explain why so many young adults get into trouble with excessive debt. Moving out into the adult world, in many cases, requires starting at or near the bottom of the career ladder, with the accompanying lower income that won't support the lifestyle with which they have grown accustomed.

But those who overspend in an attempt to live as though they are in their comfort zone might find the "comfort" very expensive in the long run.

Regardless of whether we move past the top or the bottom of our financial comfort zone, the stress comes from a sense of losing our place. If we move out of this zone, who are we? What will the people we know think of us? What will we think of ourselves? What would it mean to become like one of those people who exist outside our zone? What are the social rules and norms of this new zone? Whenever we find ourselves shifting in either direction, if we don't take the time to consider these questions, we will be at significant risk for poor financial decisions.

Another reason we so stubbornly cling to our comfort zones is that the money scripts that anchor the upper and lower limits of our financial comfort zones help us not only to define who we are, but also to identify ourselves as part of a group, or one of the herd. And one way we try to create a sense of belonging is to rationalize and justify our own positions by making judgments about people who are above or below our zone, like, "Rich people are selfish" or "Poor people are lazy." Like a gated development or a small town, a financial comfort zone is not a place where being described as "different" is a compliment.

Because our comfort zones are so closely tied to who we are, it can be very difficult to develop and sustain friendships with people in different zones—in other words, different socioeconomic classes. For the wealthier couple or individual, the challenge is to be sensitive to the disparity in income and resources; for the less affluent, it can be a struggle to keep embarrassment, jealousy, or resentment at bay. Consider the challenges in managing the following scenarios.

Dining out

Poorer friend/family member: What do you do if you are invited to eat at a restaurant you can't afford? Do you ask for separate checks and eat only an appetizer? Do you ask to go to a cheaper place? Do you accept your friend's offer to pay? If so, how often?

Wealthier friend/family member: Do you take your friend's financial situation into account when you plan for eating out? Do you offer to pay for their meal? Are you worried they may be offended if you offer or don't offer? Do you avoid going to pricier places with this friend and not invite him or her when you plan to go to more upscale restaurants? If so, do you conceal this from them because you don't want to make them feel bad?

Travel

Poorer one: Are you comfortable with your friend flying first class while you fly coach? Do you feel pressure to say yes to staying in a more expensive hotel than you can afford? Do you feel embarrassed having to decline certain activities—like a Broadway show or private hang-gliding lessons—that cost too much money?

Wealthier one: Are you comfortable flying first class while your friend is flying coach? Do you sacrifice your own comfort or desires so as not to make them feel uncomfortable? Do you feel guilty, like you should be paying for part or all of their way?

Emotional intimacy

Poorer one: Can you talk about your worries about paying your bills to your friend without worrying about them feeling guilty? Can you listen to your friend's legitimate frustrations regarding losing thousands or millions of dollars in an investment gone bad without being resentful that they had the money to lose in the first place? Do you feel ashamed of your financial status around your friend? Do you avoid inviting them over to your house because you will feel that they are judging you?

Wealthier one: Can you talk about the reality of your financial situations or worries without feeling guilty? Do you avoid certain topics? Are you reluctant to invite them over to your home because you feel guilty or don't want them to feel jealous or resentful?

As you can see, differences in financial status can pose serious challenges to relationships between friends and family members. For this reason, people may drift away from their old family and friends if their financial situation changes very much. To resist this drift, people who receive large amounts of money rapidly, without time to adjust their skills and knowledge and without finding financially responsible ways to support their friends and family, are prone to getting rid of it, often by giving all of it to friends and family. Predictably, their friends and family are often just as ill prepared to hold on to it or make good use of it, often using it in unproductive or harmful ways. The end result: Nobody has anything to show for it, and the relationship can be ruined.

If you want to achieve and succeed at a higher income level, or become more comfortable with less, you must first come to terms with what it means to step out of your financial comfort zone. For many, this might involve moving into a new financial neighborhood, at least metaphorically, or *learning how to be okay with having more or less money than those closest to you*. If you do not take care to prepare yourself for this transition, you will be at high risk for unconsciously sabotaging your financial success or, on the flip side, living beyond your means to maintain your self-perception, comfort level, and relationships.

If you want to feel *more comfortable with having less,* a situation imposed on many of us recently by the world's economic situation, the same principle applies. Interact with those who have less. Become a student of how they make their financial situation one of meaning, comfort, and ease. This will help you maintain flexibility in your thinking, which is critical to achieving and sustaining financial and mental health.

Relative Deprivation

Four young men are walking through a Las Vegas casino. Their attention is immediately drawn to the craps table where everyone seems to be having a raucously good time. But the young men don't have the money to play such a high-stakes game, so after watching for a few minutes, they move on.

Three days later, these same four guys return to the casino. Turns out, they were in town for an NFL draft. This time, all four are fresh off signing professional contracts, one of them for millions of dollars and the rest for substantially more than they or anyone they know earned before, but still substantially less than their friend. Once again they're drawn to the fast-moving excitement of the high-stakes craps table. Now one of them has enough money to play. Even if he loses twenty thousand or thirty thousand dollars, it won't make much of a dent in his newfound riches. But for the other three, losing ten thousand dollars would still be a significant financial hit.

The new multimillionaire strides up to the table and begins to play. What do the others do? Rather than be left out, they may join in the game even though they cannot really afford to. Once again, the power and pull to belong can overcome good judgment.

Never keep up with the Joneses. Drag them down to your level. It's cheaper.

—Quentin Crisp, writer and raconteur

This story illustrates another effect of the herd instinct: relative deprivation. You've probably heard people—maybe your grandparents or older neighbors—say things like, "We were all poor, but we didn't know it." They didn't know it *because* everyone around them was poor as well. They didn't have anyone else to compare themselves to so they assumed that what they had, however little, was all there was to have. Today, it would be almost impossible to find such a group inside the United States; our consumer culture has been built on the concept of relative deprivation. Today, we compare ourselves not just to our friends and neighbors, but to the people on our television screens, in the gossip columns, on the covers of magazines like *Us Weekly.* Think of all the shows that celebrate spending, portraying it almost as a competitive event. *Lifestyles of the Rich and Famous* was one of the earliest and it's been followed by dozens of others, most recently shows such as *Cribs, My Sweet Sixteen,* and *The Housewives* of wherever. Shows like this skew our idea of what's "normal," what we can reasonably expect to own and spend. They make us feel "poor" by comparison, which makes us feel miserable.

In his recent book, former Fed chairman Alan Greenspan describes a study conducted with Harvard graduate students. The students were asked to make a choice between two options: earning a yearly income of fifty thousand dollars while their peers made twenty-five thousand or making one hundred thousand dollars a year while their cohorts made two hundred thousand. The majority chose fifty thousand dollars. In other words, they'd rather have half as much money than see their peers outearn them. This illustrates both relative deprivation and the old saying "cutting off your nose to spite your face."

Why is there a magic cutoff between money and happiness at fifty thousand dollars per year in the United States? Perhaps it is no coincidence that when that research was conducted, that was the average household income in the United States. This also helps explain why, although we have more money per person, Americans are significantly less satisfied with their financial situation than people in much poorer nations. Perhaps no one has told those people from less affluent countries that they are poor, or no one has been successful in selling them the myth that greater happiness can be achieved by having more money and more things.

Blowing Bubbles

"In reading the history of nations, we find that, like individuals, they have their whims and their peculiarities; their seasons of excitement and recklessness, when they care not what they do. We find that whole communities suddenly fix their minds upon one object, and go mad in its pursuit; that millions of people become simultaneously impressed with one delusion, and run after it, till their attention is caught by some new folly more captivating than the first."

These words are no less true now than they were when Scottish journalist Charles Mackay wrote them, over 150 years ago. In *Extraordinary Popular Delusions and the Madness of Crowds,* Mackay detailed several historical episodes of herds gone amok: wild market bubbles, mob violence against supposed witches, and so on. The most interesting for our purposes are the market bubbles. The classic bubble Mackay describes, and one of the oddest, is the tulipomania that swept Holland in the seventeenth century.

The tulip was introduced to western Europe from Constantinople (now Istanbul) in the mid-1500s and soon became the toast of the Netherlands. The flower became so prized that by 1634, according to Mackay, "it was deemed a proof of bad taste in any man of fortune to be without a collection of them." That year, tulip popularity crossed some sort of tipping point, growing into a tulip craze that swept through all levels of Dutch society, "even to its lowest dregs." The tulip was the flower everyone *had* to have. Merchants, clerks, and bankers; millers, cobblers, and bakers—all began neglecting their usual business in favor of trading in tulip bulbs. Rare bulbs were fiercely sought after, and prices soared. In 1636, two bulbs of an especially rare variety, 'Semper Augustus', went up for sale. One was traded for "twelve acres of building-ground" and the other sold for "4600 florins, a new carriage, two grey horses, and a complete set of harness."

Tulips began to be traded on the stock exchanges of major cities throughout Holland, just like commodities with proven underlying value, such as cattle or wheat. Small towns had tulip notaries, schooled in the laws of the trade and authorized to conduct and supervise exchanges. As tulip prices kept climbing, speculators stepped in and made tremendous amounts of money. This only drew more people and more money into the market. "A golden bait hung temptingly out before the people, and one after the other, they rushed to the tulip-marts, like flies around a honey-pot. Every one imagined that the passion for tulips would last for ever, and that the wealthy from every part of the world would come to Holland, and pay whatever prices were asked for the bulbs."

In November 1636, the honeypot began to sour. Prudent investors, recognizing the delusions for what they were, started withdrawing their funds. "It was seen that somebody must lose fearfully in the end. As this conviction spread, prices fell, and never rose again." The courts were tied up for years as people fought over exactly who would "lose fearfully."

The tulipomania Mackay described matches the trajectory of every market bubble that's been seen before and since, not least the recent dot-com and real estate bubbles and crashes. Market bubbles are a subject of intense interest and study among economists, and there are several different theories to explain the factors behind them. Various aspects of the herd instinct come up repeatedly.

> *For indeed, the investor's chief problem—and even his worst enemy—is likely to be himself.*
>
> —Benjamin Graham, the father of modern value investing, Warren Buffet's mentor, and author of *The Intelligent Investor*

One such aspect is relative deprivation. Recently, researcher and neurologist Dr. Read Montague set up an experiment that allowed him to scan the brains of test subjects while they made investments in a stock market. Using functional magnetic resonance imaging, Montague was able to see exactly what events activated the parts of the brain associated with pleasure and happiness, and he found that when people invested conservatively and then made money, they were happy—until they saw that others who'd invested more had made even *more* money. When these thoughts about how much more others had made were present, the portion of the brain associated with regret showed lots of activity. That sense of missing out then influenced the subjects' behavior in the next rounds. Those who had experienced the regret put more and more money in the market, pushing it higher and higher until it crashed. This replicates what we see in market manias, people watching others making it big and then jumping in.

Other experiments and mathematical models have identified

definite signs of follow-the-leader herd behavior in markets. Writer Virginia Postrel spoke to a number of economists who use elaborate investment games to study market patterns. And what she found was that given certain fundamental truths about human nature (truths that the economists saw manifest themselves in experiment after experiment), bubbles are almost inevitable. One of the researchers said, "If you put people in asset markets, the first thing they do is not try to figure out the fundamental value. They try to buy low and sell high." The speculators jump in first and, as the market goes up, they're followed by "momentum investors," who chase market trends—herd instinct in action—and almost always end up buying high and selling low.

In their experiments, with successive rounds of the game, the bubbles happen faster as each trader tries to get out before the peak. Then, on the fourth round or so, the bubbles stop. The market value of the securities has been established, and so have the trading patterns of all the players. But the researchers got the bubbles going again by changing the trading rules and rearranging the groups of subjects, so people were trading with unfamiliar faces. Once the context changed, the bubbles started again. Why? Because now the investors had a whole new set of people with whom to compare themselves and compete against.

Herding behavior also depends in part on who is leading the herd. In the most recent bubble, it was professional traders, brokers, hedge fund managers: people who do this for a living. The rest of us assumed that they must know what they're doing—plus, they were making tons of money—so we followed their lead. The problem is, as we have so painfully been reminded, today's market is so volatile, so dependent on new, complex financial instruments such as credit default swaps, that even the experts were novices. "Now we have new instruments," said Caltech economist Charles Plott, one of the pioneers of experimental economics. "We have 'leaders,' who one would ordinarily think know something, getting in there very aggressively and everybody cuing on them—as they have done in the past, and as markets should. But in this case, there might be a bubble." (Postrel's article ran in the December 2008 issue of the *Atlantic,* and so the interview with Plott may well have taken place months before. Otherwise, he should get a prize for understatement.)

Joseph Kennedy, father of JFK, is often credited with this observation: "When the shoeshine boy is giving you stock tips, it's time to get out of the market." A less well-known investor during the Roaring Twenties, Bernard Baruch, expanded on the idea in his memoirs: "Taxi drivers told you what to buy. The shoeshine boy could give you a summary of the day's financial news as he worked with rag and polish. An old beggar who regularly patrolled the street in front of my office now gave me tips and, I suppose, spent the money I and others gave him in the market. My cook had a brokerage account and followed the ticker closely. Her paper profits were quickly blown away in the gale of 1929."

When everyone you know on Main Street is talking about selling land to buy tulips, spending their retirement savings on a technology company's initial public offering, or getting their real estate license, you are likely witnessing a bubble. As we've said, bubbles are human nature. Any one of us can fall victim to them if we aren't careful. But we've found in our practice that unaddressed financial issues can make people even more vulnerable to the lure of the herd instinct, of the bubble.

Consider how Ruth, one of our clients who grew up in an unstable home, impoverished both in money and in spirit, gave in to the herd instinct during the dot-com bubble.

RUTH: *Our 401(k) money, mine and my husband's, was invested in a slow-growing, safe fund for maybe ten years. Then during the late '90s I kept hearing stories of how other people—the smart*

*people, who grew up in the normal families I watched and wanted
as a kid—were making the big bucks because they were smart and
they were risk takers. I decided I could be a smart risk taker, too. I
partnered up with a multimillionaire friend and asked him to
mentor me, which he did. Well, that amounted to the blind leading the blind. We were naive. We did not know that companies
could lie. We bought into two companies that went bankrupt, just
as the whole market collapsed. We didn't get back a dime. He lost
thirteen million dollars and I lost fifty thousand. The blow, however, was the same for each of us. Our nest eggs were wiped out.*

Fortunately, the worst experiences can be the best lessons.
If we're willing to look honestly at our mistakes and motiva-
tions, we're much less likely to make the same mistake twice.

BRAD: *During the height of the real estate frenzy I sat next to a
man on a flight who told me he was a recently licensed Realtor.
With great excitement he described how he'd recently sold his
business and invested all of his money on several pieces of land,
planning to flip them in a year when they had doubled in value.
"It's an entirely new market," he said. "Real estate will always go
up. It's the best investment you can make."*

*I recognized the "bubble babble" from my very expensive ad-
venture in online day trading. All the experts, all the investors
had said the same things about technology stocks. Only now, I
recognized it for what it was. This time, while I felt the very familiar emotional pull, I didn't join the herd.*

*He gave me his card and encouraged me to get in on the game.
I wished him well, respectfully declined, gave him my card, and
told him to call me if his plan didn't work out as anticipated
and he needed to sort out his emotions. Six months later, there
were thousands of properties for sale in his area, where property
values had dropped 50–70 percent. I never did get a call from my
seatmate.*

Though he was an immigrant to the United States, Charles Ponzi had a shrewd sense of what would appeal to Americans and help him avoid a life of toil and drudgery: a neat and dapper appearance, with shined shoes, carefully knotted tie, and diamond stickpin. Top it with a jaunty straw hat. "And then, of course, there was the smile. Always, the smile; for a smiling man was not worried—and who would give money to a worried man?" For a few exciting months in 1920, people gave millions to Ponzi and made him richer than he'd ever dreamed. When it all fell apart, the fraud gained so much attention that we now call a whole class of crimes "Ponzi schemes."

Carlo Ponzi arrived in the United States in 1903 at the age of twenty-one. In the years that followed, he'd come up with a number of get-rich-quick schemes, a few of which had landed him in jail. But none had been the pot of gold he was looking for. He found it in international reply coupons, or IRCs. These could be bought in one country, sent to another, and redeemed for return postage. In the wake of the Great War, there was great instability in European monetary systems. By carefully selecting where and when IRCs were bought and redeemed, it would be possible to make money on each trade. Ponzi opened the Security Exchange Company to take advantage of the situation, which would have been perfectly legal—if he'd ever made any IRC trades.

Ponzi offered investors a 50 percent return in forty-five days. Workmen and shop owners invested their savings and when the earliest investors got the promised return, word quickly spread. In February 1920, Ponzi had $5,000 in investments; by May, he had $420,000; by July, he was taking in millions. As the money poured in, Ponzi used it to pay earlier investors. He also bought a mansion with a heated pool and brought his mother over from Italy on a luxury liner.

On July 26, the *Boston Post* began running a series of articles pointing out some uncomfortable facts: Ponzi was not invested in his own company; there was no sign of bulk purchases of IRCs; the amount of money Ponzi took in would have purchased more than ten thousand times the number actually in circulation. Ponzi staved off an initial run on the company by handing out about two million dollars but by August 12, the Securities Exchange Company was defunct and Ponzi was in jail.

He spent three and a half years in jail for mail fraud and, after a few more tangles with the law, he was deported in 1934. Charles Ponzi died fourteen years later, penniless, in a charity hospital in Brazil.

How Madoff Made Off with the Money

The herd instinct also explains why smart people fall prey to frauds, especially Ponzi schemes. The fifty-billion-dollar fraud carried out by Bernie Madoff is the perfect example of this. Madoff was able to operate the world's largest Ponzi scheme for years, possibly decades, largely because of the herd instinct.

Madoff ran two very different companies: a brokerage firm, which apparently thrived on legitimate trades, and a private money management firm that took in billions but may never have invested anything on behalf of his clients. Madoff did his record-breaking damage through the money management firm, and he did it very cleverly. First, he promised, and delivered, steady returns of 10 percent to 12 percent, year after year. But even more shrewdly, he relied on personal relationships and the allure of exclusivity to recruit clients. Satisfied clients recommended him to family and friends. But Madoff didn't take on everyone referred to him, which only made becoming one of Bernie's clients more desirable. "The best thing in New York City was to get to Bernie Madoff," one of his victims said. "Everybody wanted to be there." According to one early investor, "Everybody said, 'You got to go with Bernie.'" One observer described the phenomenon as "country-club investing, where, once one person who everybody thinks is smart gets in on something, everybody wants in on it, too. It's a herd instinct."

We will never rid ourselves of the impulse to run with the herd. But we can learn to become careful students and observers of the triggers that set off that impulse. When we are aware of the triggers, we gain power over them; we are no longer subject to their ever changing whims. Careful observation brings our rational brain back on line. When the reptile, monkey, and scientist are working together, nothing can stop us. However, when the animals take over the zoo, lock the scientist up, and stampede to the exits, all bets are off. When it comes to our financial health, we must make sure the scientist stays in control of the situation.

And don't forget that our strong desire to bond with other human beings and run with the herd doesn't have to lead us on the path to financial ruin. In fact, it doesn't have to be a bad thing at all; it can be an incredible asset to our humanity, and it can even offer a bit of comfort when the going gets tough.

NEIL: *During these unprecedented times, there's a prevalence of fear and anxiety among many people; ironically, at some level, it is comforting. I don't have the belief, "Oh, if I had just done this or that I could have made it out." Everyone is down financially. We're all suffering together, which feels better than, "All those people are getting rich and I'm sitting over here not knowing how to make this work."*

4

The Ghosts of Financial Trauma

Our financial flashpoints, or intense emotional experiences relating to money, shape the money scripts—or patterns of thinking and acting—that we write for ourselves. And while each of us has flashpoints or experiences from childhood that shape our relationship with money, some of these experiences are more painful and traumatic than others. In our work helping people overcome the lasting effects of financial trauma, we've found that the more traumatic the flashpoint, the more serious the lasting effects. But the good news is that our responses to emotional trauma often follow specific, predictable patterns, and with careful thought and introspection, we can learn to identify, detect, and overcome them. Consider the following examples.

> LESLIE: *When I was a girl we would get paid for doing chores around the house, and we were told that half had to go into a savings account at the bank and we could spend the other half on candy or whatever we wanted. I'd save half in my piggy bank and*

then, once a month or so, I'd go to the real bank to make a deposit. I liked looking at the numbers on the passbook, thinking about my little pile of money getting bigger and bigger.

One day, when I was twelve or thirteen, I went to the bank to make a deposit and check my balance. The teller said there was nothing there, that my dad had withdrawn it all. When I confronted him about it, he just laughed and said, "That's my money." I was just so shocked that he would do that.

I stopped putting money into the savings account. After that, whenever I got any money, I spent it all. I'd spend it when I had it, before someone else could take it away.

This was a profound financial flashpoint for Leslie. She felt a deep sense of betrayal, and her entire "reality" about how money was supposed to work was changed in an instant. As a child, her behavioral adaptations were limited. After all, she couldn't open up a bank account without an adult cosigner, and she obviously couldn't trust her parents with her money. So in an effort to never feel betrayed again, Leslie arrived at what seemed to her like a logical conclusion—spend money before it can be taken from you. After a while, long after Leslie's rational brain had put the incident with her father behind her, this habit became so ingrained, it took on a life of its own. As a result, she became an overspender (one of the disorders we'll talk about in the next section). She lived paycheck to paycheck, accumulating more and more debt, never putting aside any savings.

CARLA: *All I remember as a child is chaos, around money and in every area of my life. One of my first memories, at maybe age three or four, was when my mother was in jail for writing bad checks. For the next five years Mom was constantly being arrested, in and out of jail. We were always running from the law, hiding from creditors, moving from house to house, one step ahead of the sheriff.*

When I was nine, Mom finally had a kind of breakdown. She was weeping and crying, just inconsolable. Finally, I said, "Mom, call Dad." Amazingly, she did. The very next day, we moved into a house that was better than anyplace we'd ever lived. We were just six houses down from Dad, and I thought it was great to be so close to him. My parents had divorced when I was sixteen months old so I never knew him that well. But now I saw him a lot and we had a nice place to live and food to eat, and things were going better than they ever had.

Early one Saturday morning, I was still asleep when my mom and my uncle roared into my room. They said, "Grab what you want to take with you. We're leaving and we're not coming back." So I grabbed my goldfish and ran out the back door. They plopped me down in the back seat of a little sports car with a little U-Haul trailer behind it. We took off and drove straight through all day and all night, only stopping for gas. We drove fifteen hundred miles to our new home, and it all started up again.

That did it for me. Something seemed to break inside. I gave up. I learned that I couldn't trust anything or anyone, that nothing will ever work out and I have no power to change anything. From that point on, whenever things got stressful, I just pretended like I didn't notice. I just tried to look good, just get by. That was all I could do.

When I got out on my own, I did pretty well financially. I was taking care of myself, acting responsibly, paying my bills, saving money. All that went away when I married my husband. I married someone who behaved, in many ways, just like my mother. All my old scripts came rushing back, scripts like "I have to help him and I'll do that by putting everything I have into our relationship, and never questioning him."

So for the next twenty years, through lost job after lost job, after many, many moves all over the United States, after promises from him that he'd change his behavior, and lots more chaos, I just gave up. I believed I had no power over my life. I believed *that I didn't deserve to get my needs met. I just shut down, blindly trusted, and just gave up.*

Strange as it may seem, these beliefs kept me sane during that difficult time. As long as I didn't pay attention to what was going on, I didn't feel a lot of anxiety. I didn't feel a lot of anything, and that seemed okay.

Despite the human capacity to survive and adapt, traumatic experiences can alter people's psychological, biological and social equilibrium to such a degree that the memory of one particular event comes to taint all other experiences, spoiling appreciation for the present. This tyranny of the past interferes with the ability to pay attention to both new and familiar situations. When people come to concentrate selectively on reminders of their past, life tends to become colorless and contemporary experience ceases to be a teacher.

—Bessel Van Der Kolk and Alexander McFarlane, researchers in psychological trauma

---

Carla's story demonstrates how unfinished business from childhood can affect our choices as adults. We're drawn to people, places, and things that feel familiar, often in an unconscious effort to replay the past and "fix it" this time. This rarely succeeds. Notice too how her scripts served her well, in the short term, in a specific situation. They allowed her to survive until she gathered the strength to confront her husband and begin putting together a plan for her own future, despite the fact that her husband was not able or willing to join her in that process. Yet these same scripts were what led her into the painful situation she had to escape, and they would have led her into other self-destructive situations if she hadn't taken steps to heal.

When people talk about trauma, they often think that only unusual events qualify: armed combat, a mugging, sexual assault. But the fact is that any event, however mundane it might seem, that causes emotional distress and pain can be traumatic. There are differences in degree, not kind. Financial flashpoints don't have to be shocking or rare events, like finding out that your father has robbed you of your savings, or seeing your mother being hauled off to jail; many common, everyday experiences—a hurtful comment from a parent, an embarrassing moment in front of peers—can leave similar lasting imprints, and have similar and lasting negative effects on our financial and mental health. The effects of these traumas may not be as immediately noticeable or easy to pinpoint, but they are just as real.

This chapter looks at the fundamental role traumatic experiences play in shaping disordered money behaviors. First we'll explain how emotionally charged or traumatic events associated with money can actually change the physical structure of the brain in such a way as to make future financial reactions primal and automatic, bypassing the logical brain that would otherwise allow us to make informed decisions. Then, we'll look at the various types of early trauma and the impact such events have on our adult patterns of thinking and acting.

The Neurobiology of Stress and Trauma

In chapter 2, we talked about various brain structures and how they interact. Here we'll be focusing on a specific portion of the brain that plays a huge role in our response to trauma: the amygdala. This pair of small, almond-shaped bundles of neurons is nestled deep in the animal brain, acting as a kind of early warning system, much like a burglar alarm or smoke detector in your home. Both your amygdala and your home alarm respond as they've been programmed to do—instantly and indiscriminately. When the amygdala senses a threat, it triggers a potentially lifesaving fight, flight, or freeze response.

Besides its function as an alarm, the amygdala also acts as

an archivist: It prompts the animal brain to store as many details of the incident as possible, cross-referencing them with our emotional response to the situation. This makes adaptive sense; by associating dangerous or traumatic events with negative emotions like fear or anxiety or sadness, we are better able to recognize, and avoid, those life-threatening situations in the future. However, because the animal brain isn't always very good at sorting out real cause and effect, many of the emotions we associate with a traumatic event may actually have nothing to do with the event or situation itself.

The amygdala also helps determine whether or not certain events or details of events become stored in our long-term memory. The more disturbing an event, the more likely it is to be seared into our brains, often resulting in *flashbulb memories,* or haunting and vivid recollections of the event triggered by similar situations or sensory details. We were once near the end of a session with a client when a helicopter passed overhead at an unusually low altitude. Our client dove under the table, shouting, "Get down! They're coming for us, get down!"

He'd served three tours of duty in Vietnam, and several times he was rescued from firefights by helicopter. However, when the rescue helicopters would appear, they would do so suddenly and their arrival would draw intense enemy fire. His survival had depended on recognizing that pattern and acting on it: finding cover until the 'copter was close enough to reach. Forty years later, the neural pathways those experiences had created were still intact and powerful enough to create the flashbulb memory he experienced in our office.

The working of the amygdala also explains why our emotional associations are so long lasting, so resistant to facts and logic. The neural pathways from the amygdala to the neocortex— where reasoning and logic take place—are much stronger than those running from the neocortex to the amygdala. In other words, our emotions shape our thoughts far more powerfully than our thoughts shape our emotions. This is why the emotional brain stores "truths" about our history that often lie outside of our conscious awareness.

In the last chapter we learned about our brains' tendency to generate false positives. This can also help explain why we respond so readily to cues that trigger emotions associated with our financial traumas. In terms of human survival, this false positive makes a certain amount of sense. Imagine our prehistoric ancestors hearing a rustle in the bushes. If they didn't pay attention to and try to determine the source of the sound each and every time—no matter how often the cause turned out to be a gust of wind or a falling branch or a small scurrying animal—they'd probably end up as dinner. But in modern-day terms, reacting so instinctively and dramatically to every perceived threat only adds to our stress level.

Recent advances in technology have revealed that we not only make mental connections and associations between emotions and traumatic events; the brain actually undergoes *physical* changes in response to trauma. Historically, human brain function could only be studied indirectly, as in the split-brain experiments. Researchers asked subjects to perform tasks, observed the results, and then, based on those observations, drew conclusions about how the brain worked. Modern medicine has changed that. A century ago, the invention of X-rays allowed us to study the skeleton; today, advanced technology, such as magnetic resonance imaging (MRI), lets us peek inside the skull and get a look at the brain itself. Recently, functional magnetic resonance imaging (fMRI) allows us to watch the brain in action, in real time. The fMRI detects which specific regions of the brain are most active as the subject performs all kinds of tasks—anything from solving mathematical equations to thinking of a loved one to viewing emotionally charged photographs. Using data from thousands of subjects, it's now possible to map out the pathway of the brain, identifying which regions are associated with which activities and emotions. One thing neuroscientists have found is that traumatic experiences create neuropathways in the brain that remain long after the event itself is over. If the experience is repeated often enough, either in reality or in our memory, the reshaped and rewired neuropathways become permanent, like ruts worn in a well-traveled path.

More evidence that trauma changes the physical structure of the brain has also been found in studying changes in *size* of certain parts of the brains of those who have experienced severe trauma. For instance, two crucial portions of the brain—the prefrontal cortex and the hippocampus—are markedly smaller than average among combat veterans diagnosed with posttraumatic stress disorder, and people with chronic severe clinical depression also show significant reduction in the size of the hippocampus over time.

We've been privileged to work with a pioneer in the field of electroencephalography (EEG) research: Lee Gerdes, founder of Brain State Technologies and author of *Limitless You: The Infinite Possibilities of a Balanced Brain*. Gerdes identifies two types of trauma: infringement and abandonment. Infringement involves an act of physical threat, violation, or perceived threat, while abandonment occurs through betrayal or neglect. Using EEG readings (which measure electrical activity produced by the firing of neurons within the brain) to detect emotional states, Gerdes found not only particular patterns associated with early trauma but also distinct patterns resulting from each type of trauma.

We recently worked with Gerdes to measure the brain activity of people who report disordered money behaviors to see if they displayed specific brain patterns, including those typically seen in trauma. We helped design a questionnaire to assess the presence of several disordered money behaviors, which participants were asked to complete at the time of their brain scans. The data from 604 subjects showed some clear patterns. For example, one question we asked was "At any time, does your spending or gambling endanger the financial well-being of you and/or your household?" Gerdes found that people who answered that this statement was "very true" showed distinct brain patterns associated with a lack of connection to self and others.

Coupled with this finding, Gerdes noticed another interesting pattern in the frontal lobes of the brain. People who answered the same question in the affirmative had a brain wave pattern consistent with a tendency to see the world as hopeless or overwhelming. This is the type of pattern that may lead people to register a stack of paperwork or bills as too huge to deal with, prompting procrastination rather than action. (The healthier response would be to break down the daunting task into smaller steps and tackle them one at a time.) In terms of spending, such a brain pattern would be associated with an impulsive approach to financial decisions and situations. They might say, "Why not get the bigger car with higher payments? I work hard and I deserve it," as opposed to "I'll get the smaller car now because I can afford the payments on my current income. The bigger car will have to wait until my salary goes up and I get some bills paid off." Like the procrastination mentioned earlier, this impulsiveness reflects a difficulty in focusing on smaller details and component steps—a difference in brain function we can see in action through the EEG.

The point we want to stress is this: The changes in the brain caused by trauma are real. As such, behavioral manifestations of trauma are not caused by a failure of will, nor are they a sign of weakness. They are expected, predictable, normal, biologically based responses to the painful events we all experience at one time or another. Whether it's of the everyday or the extraordinary variety, trauma is an unavoidable part of life. Financial trauma—divorce, bankruptcy, foreclosure, significant market loss, being the victim of a crime (embezzlement, Ponzi schemes, theft, or mugging), job loss, or living through an economic meltdown—is just as common. The current global financial crisis is an ongoing financial trauma for all of us. For millions, it has not only significantly threatened our ability to provide the most basic needs for ourselves and our families; it has had a major impact on our beliefs about money and our outlook toward the future.

So whether your trauma originated on a personal, familial, or national level, learning to come to terms with it by acknowledging it is the first step to healing. In the pages that follow, we'll teach you some of the tools and strategies for dealing with the lasting negative effects of trauma that have formed the heart of our work, helping thousands of people successfully change their persistently troubling financial behaviors.

Family Financial Trauma

When we can't seem to learn from our mistakes, when we can't seem to do what we need to do around money, when we know better but can't help ourselves, when we try to change and can't, when our emotional response is more intense than the situation warrants—then it's likely the result of unresolved trauma. Often—but not always—that trauma has its roots in the family experience.

It comes as no surprise that dysfunctional family systems often result in financial dysfunction. Given money's powerful influence on every aspect of life, and its symbolic connections to emotions like comfort, security, and affection, it's only natural that we are quite prone to misinterpreting money's role in painful family systems. Money itself may not be the primary issue, but it can very quickly become associated with family pain or problems. For children, the situation is even more complicated. With still-developing brains and coping skills, limited perspectives, and little ability to distinguish between actual threats and imagined ones, a young child can experience almost anything as traumatic: a visit to the dentist, a first haircut, a momentary separation from one's parents, overhearing a heated argument between adults. Children are programmed to pick up the subtlest of clues with regard to threat or danger. As such, they are much more likely than adults to draw false conclusions or interpret benign situations as threatening. And because children are so focused on taking in information and making sense out of their world, small events can take on what seems to be, in retrospect, outsized significance. It doesn't matter whether or not the incident is something our adult selves would consider traumatic. If the emotional component is strong enough, if the message is powerful enough, a child will carry it forward into adulthood.

Additionally, children form their view of the world from observing and modeling adults. They learn what they're supposed to fear and avoid, and what they should want and pursue. The more stressed a parent is about money, the more likely the child will develop money anxiety also. Or a child who grows up in a wealthy but painful family system, where money is used as a means of control, may erroneously equate wealth with distress and heartache and spend the rest of his or her life repelling it. Another possibility is that child could grow up equating the amount of money one spends with how much love is felt. Remember Denise's story from chapter 1, about the Christmas checks kept in her father's "fancy box"? She still struggles with separating love and money. Conversely, a child who grows up in a poor and painful family system may erroneously equate a *lack* of money with distress and heartache, resulting in a life spent pursuing enough wealth to bring happiness (which never materializes). Often that pursuit manifests in one of two extremes: workaholism or crime.

ELLEN: *My mom was one of twelve and they were very poor. She dropped out of high school to help take care of her younger brother and sisters and had her first child at nineteen. There were many things that she couldn't have and she adopted a "by any means necessary" attitude toward getting what she wanted. Getting something for nothing, having a "hustle," was just a way of life. She was determined that we would have "everything she never had" and that meant that she would hustle, steal, borrow, do anything to get what she wanted. My mother never saved any money. She spent every dime she made. She was a maid for a wealthy family and she stole from them. Eventually she was caught, she lost her job and we eventually lost our home.*

Early in life I remember feeling it was okay to take things and there was a thrill to getting away with it. Fortunately, I learned very early that I didn't want to live that legacy. As a mother and grandmother, I don't want to look like I'm a taker so I give excessively. I have difficulty accepting anything, whether it's money or gifts or friendship, offered by people who care for me and simply want to be kind.

Ellen grew up exhibiting a textbook case of one of the disorders we'll talk about in the next section—rejection of money. Because of the behavior her mother modeled, and the trauma that resulted from her mother's behavior, she grew up to associate money with dishonesty and shame, so it's hardly shocking that as an adult she wanted little to do with it. Today, Ellen is a highly trained professional who works primarily with the economically disadvantaged. She volunteers to take on projects and work for free, even when the federally funded projects she heads up offer to pay her. She literally returns the money she does earn, because she wants to preempt any criticism from anyone that she is just "doing it for the money." Of course, the criticism comes from only one place: her own mind. It would be one thing if she didn't need the money, but at age fifty-five, her financial situation is one of living from day to day, one paycheck at a time, with no savings or retirement plan.

One other source of confusion for children about money is the silence around it. In many families, even though issues involving money are ever present, they are rarely talked about or expressed. This silence can be just as traumatic as experiences like Ellen's—if not more so, because the issues are swept under the rug and never dealt with. When money is never talked about in front of the children, common and predictable responses include the child growing up financially dependent, living in financial denial, or developing an avoidance of money (three common disorders we'll discuss shortly). While it's important to protect children from worries they're too young to handle, it's much healthier to include them in financial decisions appropriate to their age.

All families have histories. Traumatic events are often a part of that history. And when families experience stress or trauma, they respond like individuals do: They create unspoken scripts to try to reconcile that trauma with an acceptable, or at least minimally painful, version of reality. These scripts are compiled into family anthologies and these stories—not to mention the unhealthy habits and behaviors that go along with them—get passed down like heirlooms. And they can exert a powerful and profound effect on families for generations.

Exploring and revealing your family's financial history can be tremendously rewarding and enlightening. In doing so, you'll realize that your beliefs are not your own—that they've been passed down to you, taught to you (deliberately or not) by your family members. That discovery can be very freeing, opening the door to learning and growth.

As father and son, we share a multigenerational financial

legacy, one that went unexamined until we faced our own financial difficulties.

TED: *One day in my midthirties, I collapsed into bed at 11:30 p.m. and silently said to myself, "At least they can't call me lazy." I had gotten out of bed that morning, as usual, at 3:30 a.m. to feed and care for the six horses I was in charge of. By 5:00 a.m. I was at the gym I owned, working out myself before opening it for customers at 6:00 a.m. By 7:15 a.m. I had traveled the twenty miles to my day job as a high school teacher and coach (for baseball, and boys' and girls' basketball). I would be done with practice by 6:30 or 7:00 p.m., go close the gym by 10:00 p.m., come home, tend to the horses once again, and get something to eat myself. I'd fall into bed about 11:30 p.m., only to start again in four hours. "At least they can't call me lazy"—where did that voice come from? It made absolutely no sense. No one had ever suggested such a thing. It wasn't until years later that I began to understand the power of my family's unspoken legacy.*

My father's family had been very wealthy landowners in Virginia prior to the Civil War. As the war began, they were forced to abandon their holdings and move away in the middle of the night. They settled in southern Ohio, and records show that at one time they were on the county dole. One of the sons enlisted in the Union army and the family used the bonus money for a down payment on some land. He was killed in the war and the death benefits were used to pay off the purchase, much to the everlasting shame of his mom and dad and the succeeding generations. They felt they'd profited from their son's death.

My paternal grandfather didn't work much. It could have been because of his bad vision; it could have been because he had injured his foot as a young man; it could have been because he didn't choose to. The story is a bit unclear. The point is he didn't do much, and everyone knew it.

My paternal grandmother lost her own mother, who died

delivering her. Her father died just months later and she was raised in an orphanage. As an adult, she supported the family by working for other families: taking in laundry, doing mending, caring for their children, whatever domestic duties she could barter for what her family needed. The family was exceedingly poor.

My father grew up hearing his mother complain about his father and how little he did to support the family. He started helping neighboring farmers when he was six years old, and he was held up and honored by his mother. She tried to shame her husband into working harder by unfavorably comparing him to his own son. It didn't work for that purpose, but as a result, working became the centerpiece of her son's, my father's, life.

When I was a child, my father always had several jobs at the same time. He went to work at his regular job, then came home and worked for one of the neighboring farmers. When he finished that, late at night, he'd repair a piece of equipment for yet another neighbor or friend. As with his mother, he was held up by everyone around him for being such a hard worker and doing his best to provide for his family. Every event in our lives was organized around his work. Every hobby turned into some kind of business venture. In our family, being called lazy was one of the worst things that could be said about someone.

I grew up watching this and for as long as I can remember, I wanted to be known as a hard worker, too. I wanted people to admire me the same way they did my father and so I became a hard worker. I worked until the job was done, whether that meant I ate meals or not. Work came before anything else, always. Long after my days on the farm were over, long after my grandparents were dead and gone, I was still trying to live up to the standard that would guarantee that no one can ever call me lazy.

I was so focused on working hard that I left myself at the mercy of others in terms of what happened with my financial life. I never took control of my finances, because I believed that work was about proving my worth, not about making money. I trace *that script back to one afternoon at my grandfather's farm. This was my maternal grandfather and he did work hard. I often worked for him and one day, when I was about ten, I finally mustered up the courage to ask him if he'd be willing to pay me a dollar a day to help bale, pick up, and store the hay we were putting up. He'd hired other boys my age, many of them friends of mine, and he was paying them a dollar an hour to do the same work I was doing. I knew he'd never pay me a dollar an hour, but I thought maybe a dollar a day would work. I'll never forget his answer. His words became the guiding principle of my life for the next thirty years. He said, "I will decide whether or not I think you're worth anything, and if I do, I'll pay you. Furthermore, you should feel lucky that you have something to eat, a place to sleep, and clothes to wear."*

End of conversation. I never got a cent. Every job I worked at for the next thirty-five years was one where other people decided what I was worth and what I'd be paid.

BRAD: *This was a powerful story for me. Until recently, I had never heard it. As a child, I saw my father work. A lot. On weekends he'd take me into the office with him, where I would mill around while he worked. At home, I'd see his back for much of the day, as he worked on whatever he was doing. As we grew older, my sister and I would joke that he had "ADS Disease"— Always Doing Something. He and I never had a discussion about work, but I knew it was all-important. Whenever my sister and I argued, her knockout punch was to call me a "slug," implying I was lazy. Even as a child, this comment sent me over the edge. The biggest sources of shame in my life involve the times that I have left a job unfinished or didn't follow through on a promise. Hard work and integrity meant everything.*

After high school, I spent the next ten years in school full time. Part of me wanted to take some time off to travel but I couldn't allow myself to do that. I finished my doctorate in four years. I paid off ninety thousand dollars in school loans in three years, while driving a four-hundred-dollar car and living in a home with no furniture. I was working seventy hours a week, but I felt like I wasn't doing enough, that I was being lazy.

At the same time, I saw how my father consistently worked for much less than he was worth, did not save and did not take even moderate risks with what little money he accidentally accumulated. After all, we were poor people, from generations of poor people. As I was growing up, I decided, I'm not going to be poor; I'm not going to play it safe.

Without any training or real knowledge about finances or the stock market, I began buying and selling stocks. For me, the real risk was not taking any risks. In the end, I lost over half the money I initially invested. This was a life-changing experience for me. I felt a great deal of pain and shame. I had no conscious understanding about my hidden generational beliefs and my personal relationship with money. In trying to "do it differently" from my parents, I made a big mistake and ended up just like them, with little money.

My family legacy and its impact on me became clear when I heard my father was working a hundred hours a week and felt lazy compared to his father. This awareness was freeing for me because I saw how ridiculous it was for him to feel that way. After all, I had seen him be a workaholic my whole life. To hear that he felt that he was lazy compared to his father helped me put my own automatic thoughts and guilt into perspective. It helped me come to terms with how inaccurate my thinking is in this area, and gave me permission to have a healthier work–life balance, stop taking excessive risks, and not succumb to guilt or shame.

Societal Financial Traumas

Large-scale societal traumas like a war or a depression can have a tremendous influence not only on those who lived through it but on their children and often their grandchildren as well. We recently heard a powerful interview with a man re-calling the effects of his Great Depression–era childhood on his family. James Bost's father had managed to keep his job as a salesman but worked himself into a heart attack just trying to keep his family afloat. Once he recovered, the elder Bost was determined not to lose the meager savings he'd almost died trying to accumulate. He withdrew all his money from the bank, put it in a suitcase, and buried it in the backyard. "He didn't trust the banks for a long time," Bost said. "And this made an impression on me." Bost himself recently withdrew several thousand dollars and hid the cash. "I think it's kind of silly in some ways and kind of stupid," he said. "But at the same time, the Great Depression made a big impact on me. And I can't forget it."

This mistrust of banks and impulse to hide money is not uncommon during such times. In her book about the Great Depression, *The Invisible Scar*, Caroline Bird describes the lengths people took to protect their savings: hiding bills be-tween the pages of books, sliding them behind the lining paper of framed pictures, rolling them up and hiding them in bicycle handlebars, gluing gold coins inside walnut shells. "In January 1932, a schoolteacher asked a 12-year-old boy why he was scratching himself and discovered a thousand dollars in big bills taped to his chest. He explained that his parents were afraid of banks."

It's very likely that this boy's parents retained their extreme anxiety around money long after the Depression ended, and chances are the boy himself also developed a money disorder of some kind. Many survivors of the Depression, in fact, de-veloped hoarding behaviors that persisted even in times of prosperity. Having lived through a period of such utter scarcity, deprivation, and uncertainty, they developed an in-tense and irrational fear of being once again wiped out and left with nothing. So they prepared by stuffing money under mattresses, building up stores of food, saving everything from scrap metals to fuel oil. And, like so many other disordered behaviors, these hoarding tendencies often got passed down to family members. We know many children of Depression-era hoarders who became hoarders or underspenders by modeling their parents' habits. Paul, for example, didn't live through the Great Depression himself but its legacy was strong in his family.

> PAUL: *I grew up hearing stories constantly about the Depression, about how that impacted people. One of my first jobs as a kid was to sit out on the garage floor with a big iron brick, a bunch of old bent rusty nails, and a hammer. My job was to straighten the nails so we could reuse them. I can do that again if I have to. I think that the lessons that my parents learned and taught me from the Depression, and the fact that we actually lived in a financially depressed house or family—all that taught me that you can survive anything. I guess that just really grounds me.*

Unfortunately, these days we're all too well aware of how traumatic an economic meltdown can be for countries, communities, and families. But social trauma doesn't always stem from a singular major event like a depression. The ongoing effects of race, class, and gender on a society or segment of society can be equally traumatic. Let's look at how socioeconomic, cultural, and gender roles can shape our attitudes toward money.

Socioeconomic Issues

While it's often uncomfortable to talk about class in this country, it's true that your family's economic status has a tremendous influence—good and bad—on your financial attitudes.

People who grow up in a low socioeconomic class (or what they perceive as a low class relative to those around them) develop very different scripts than people who grow up wealthy. Some common ones include "If one of us makes it, they owe the rest of us a hand up," "If we get it, we need to spend it before it is taken away from us," "There will never be enough," "It's okay to spend money we don't have by going into debt," or "Wealthy people got that way by taking advantage of people like us."

These types of scripts encourage a fatalistic scarcity mentality, the belief that life is relatively hopeless, that one is helpless and powerless over one's own life events. People with these scripts believe that the bigger decisions in life are controlled by forces much greater than themselves: the government, the boss, the universe. This leaves them to manage the cash that comes in their pockets the best they can, most often by spending it before it can be taken away. Of course, not everyone who had an impoverished childhood reacts this way. Like all human responses, reactions to growing up poor range widely and often unpredictably, from rejecting money altogether to obsessing about it and hoarding it or other possessions. It's no surprise that poverty has negative effects. But it can also instill qualities and attitudes that serve us well in later life. You just read some of the positive influences Paul received from his upbringing, such as a sense of resilience and a strong work ethic; here, he goes into more detail on how his family's financial situation influenced him in adulthood.

PAUL: *We grew up very, very poor, and we were taught that money is totally unimportant, that it didn't matter. Looking back, that was a brilliant way for my parents to rationalize and deal with the fact that we didn't have any. As long as money was unimportant, not having any was nothing to worry about. What we focused on was figuring out how could we have fun, how could we produce. How could we make things and make do with things without having money?*

There's both a positive and negative side to that. The positive side is I didn't, and still don't, worry about it. I'll survive. I don't care what happens, I will survive, and that comes out of that very impoverished place. The negative is, it's hard to deal with money. I keep hearing my father's voice: "The rich get rich off the backs of poor people. Rich people are greedy and they really don't care about other people. Money has become their god."

I only had one pair of shoes and one pair of jeans that I wore to work on the farm and then go to school, and I'd be laughed at because they were dirty, or my shoes had manure on them. I got frowned on in church because I wasn't wearing what they considered Sunday best. This is the church that my great-great-grandfather founded.

There's story after story after story of my feeling caught in the middle. Being poor was a shameful thing, but being rich was evil. I don't think it's any accident that I went on to work summers in college, doing public aid as a caseworker. I grew up with the message that my responsibility was to help those less fortunate than myself.

It may not come as a surprise to find out that Paul ended up pursuing a career in public service. He later went into private practice as a counselor and he subconsciously rejected wealth by undercharging for his services compared to what his education and experience warranted. He focused his practice on people with limited financial resources who were often uninsured; this resulted in his working long hours and living from paycheck to paycheck.

Similarly, growing up at the other end of the financial spectrum often has both positive and negative effects. Obviously, having a high net worth eliminates certain worries. But contrary to the popular belief that having more money makes people happier, anxiety about money often increases proportionately with net worth; the more a person has, the more they are afraid of losing. If they have any underlying issues about money—"I don't deserve this" or "I'm going to screw this up"—their wealth only magnifies that anxiety.

Kristen's story shows how large amounts of money can lead to alienation; compare her experience with her family to Paul's relationship with his.

KRISTEN: *We children seldom had direct contact with our parents and we didn't really create a bond with them. It was more like we were grandchildren and our parents were grandparents. They'd dote on us from time to time but for the most part they weren't around. The people who took care of us day to day were all hired to do it, and they told us that if we were bad, they'd lose their jobs, and if they lost their jobs, our parents already had plans to send us to an orphanage.*

I heard all the time, "You are so lucky to have money. You should be grateful. Don't complain. Look at what you have." I'd look around, and I'm surrounded by eight staff people in a huge house and yet there was no one there that I really had any bond with. That's what I really wanted. I'd glom onto other people's families, families where their entire house would fit into my parents' bedroom. I really loved the part where the father came home for dinner. The kids would talk about their day, Mom and Dad would talk about theirs, and I was invited to talk about mine. I wished they could adopt me.

It was embarrassing to be driven to school by chauffeurs. I'd say, "Drop me off at the corner." My parents never came to school for anything but the governess used to come instead, dressed in her uniform. It was just really embarrassing. When I would mention how uncomfortable all this was, everyone would once again tell me how lucky I was, that I just would have to face up to the fact that I was different than the other kids.

I didn't want to be different. I already felt this huge gulf in my home, an inability to connect. I wanted to be the same as everyone else. I grew up believing that because I didn't feel as lucky or as grateful as I was supposed to, I was a terrible person. I believed you have to pay for people to take care of you. You are not entitled to any money; you're lucky that you were born into it but you're not entitled to it. You can do a lot of things because of money, and you were different because of money, and different wasn't always good.

Growing up, Kristen learned to associate money with shame, guilt, detachment, and alienation from others. She was repeatedly given the message that she had no right to feel lonely or isolated. Her father said to her as an adult, "The only reason that people ask you to do things is because you have money. If you were poor, they wouldn't give you the time of day." In itself, money can't provide love, connection, or nurturing. It could not provide Kristen with what she needed most. Later in life, this script resulted in a number of negative behaviors. For example, she allowed herself to stay in abusive relationships. When we met her she was serving on over two dozen nonprofit boards all across the country and as a result she was never home. She overworked, yet she felt like she was never really contributing anything of value other than her money. At one point in her life she drank excessively. She lost her marriage and her children were estranged from her. She never knew for sure whether someone who had befriended her had done so because of who she was or the money she had. Secretly she herself wasn't sure she had anything of value to offer people other than her money. She and her siblings fought over the family money, bringing out the worst in each other. She never felt like she belonged, anywhere.

Another interesting thing about the socioeconomic class we grow up in is that we can tend to get stuck in it. This is the financial comfort zone we talked about in the last chapter. Our class can become so tied to our sense of self and identity that we cling to it, even when our circumstances change. In other words, if we grow up poor but later come into wealth, we continue to think and act like a poor person would, even when it's unnecessary or detrimental to do so. If we grow up in a rich family, then lose our nest egg, we tend to still live and spend like a wealthy person, even if it is no longer within our means. Rigidly adhering to an outdated set of money scripts in this way can be detrimental to our egos, our relationships, and our financial well-being.

Culture

It can be hard to separate the economic effects of culture from those of class but our not-so-distant history offers very clear cases of the impact racial discrimination can have on a cultural group's economic situation. African Americans, for example, are still dealing with the economic effects of centuries of slavery and ongoing racial hostility—effects that can have a negative impact on their money scripts and beliefs about what is possible to achieve financially.

Over the past decade, several studies have shed some light on the financial difficulties and challenges faced by African Americans. Compared to white college students, black students tend to carry more credit card debt—and report higher levels of stress because of it. African American women who seek help at battered women's shelters are more likely than women of other ethnicities to report income below the poverty line; because of their limited economic resources, these women have drastically reduced options for escaping their situation. Another study that followed African American girls through adolescence found that the girls who reported the most financial stress at home were most likely to do poorly in

school and to become pregnant at a young age. Lack of education and teen pregnancy are strongly correlated with poverty,
so these girls, and their babies, face a future that's likely to be
bleak.

In *The Hidden Cost of Being African American,* Thomas
Shapiro points out that low income is not the only financial
difficulty African Americans face. He writes that they're also
more likely to be "asset poor"—renting instead of owning their
homes, with smaller or nonexistent investments—and less
likely to leave a financial inheritance for the next generation.
Thus, we can see how the effects of slavery and Jim Crow still
touch the current generation: Because African American families are often unable to leave an inheritance, their children
have to start from scratch. Contrast this with many middle-
class white families who, in addition to whatever they earn,
have access to inherited financial assets that they can draw on
to pay for college tuition, professional training, a first home—
large expenditures likely to not only anchor them in the middle class but help them, or their children, rise beyond it. In
the absence of such a cushion, black families of the same income level often must depend solely on wages and salary to
provide not only the essentials of daily life but also pay for
those "capital investments." This has obvious implications for
long-term class stability and mobility. As Shapiro says, "I
talked to a single mother who called income 'life support' and
referred to assets as 'moving-ahead money.' "

What's more, a cultural history marred by racial discrimination can have a powerful influence on a group's beliefs and
assumptions. For example, the internment of Japanese immi-
grants and Japanese American citizens during World War II
demonstrates how blatant racism can trigger all kinds of self-
defeating money scripts and behaviors. Consider the following
story.

In January 1942, one month after Pearl Harbor was attacked, Kiyoshi Kagawa enlisted as a twenty-one-year-old army private. He considered himself American first and Japanese second, and wanted to fight for his country. On February 19, 1942, FDR's Executive Order 9066 paved the way for the internment of more than one hundred thousand ethnic Japanese living primarily on the West Coast. Kiyoshi's mother, father, and brother were among the thousands forced to abandon their homes, businesses, and belongings and move to the barren, desolate concentration camps. Kiyoshi's younger brother was released from the internment camp and he enlisted in the 442nd Regimental Combat Team, the Japanese American unit that fought in Europe (and later became the most highly decorated military unit in the history of the United States). Kiyoshi himself served as an Intelligence Officer under General Douglas MacArthur during his return to the Philippines and the occupation of Japan.

That same year, a young woman named Fumiko Momonoi turned eighteen in a desolate internment camp thousands of miles from her home in Seattle. Before the war, Fumiko's family had lived the immigrant success story. Her father, Yoshio Momonoi, had been in the Japanese merchant marines prior to coming to America. In December 1910, he was on a ship making its way along the Columbia River; he and two friends jumped overboard into the freezing water. Miraculously he made it to the shore. In the thirty-two years that followed, Yoshio, through hard work and dedication, went from being a cook to owning his own successful restaurant, which he even managed to nurture through the Great Depression. But in 1942, the Momonois were sent to an internment camp in Rowher, Arkansas. Like most other resident Japanese and Japanese Americans, they lost everything. Savings accounts, farms, stores, restaurants, homes—in total as much as three billion dollars in assets (worth trillions today) was seized, stolen, or destroyed.

But the internees' losses went far beyond their financial ones. According to historians David O'Brien and Stephen Fugita, "the stress from long periods of uncertainty, separation from family members, economic loss, and stigmatization have left their marks." Many understandably came away from the experience traumatized, harboring a deep distrust of the government and a profound reluctance to talk about that time. As a group, they refer to internment as the watershed event of their life histories; there is life "before camp" and life "after camp." For those who, like the Momonois, sustained devastating economic losses, those memories of pain and suffering became tangled up with their feelings about money.

Flash forward to 2009. Fifty-six-year-old financial planner Rick Kagawa, son of Kiyoshi Kagawa and Fumiko Momonoi, is president of Capital Resources and Insurance, based in Huntington Beach, California. Eighty percent of Rick's clients are Japanese Americans, over half of whom, like his own mother, lived through the internment, usually as children. Rick still sees the lasting symptoms and witnesses the ongoing effects of that financial trauma in the financial lives of his clients. And in his own family, he sees the sharp contrast between the financial beliefs and behaviors of his mother, who was interned, and those of his father, who was not.

RICK: *My mother graduated from high school while in the camp. Like many at the time, she didn't have the chance to go to college, which was how it was supposed to be in the Japanese American culture at the time. She ended up being very reluctant to spend money and doesn't really know how to enjoy it. She's had a very high savings rate her whole life, but she never wants to take any risks around money, and her creativity and imagination were stifled. My dad was different. He was in the army during the internment years, and afterward he was a risk taker, an entrepreneur. He ended up being very successful in business after the war.*

I've asked my mom if she would talk about her experiences, but to this day she won't discuss it. Most of my clients don't want to talk about it, either. They just want to put it behind them. You can see the effects, though: They are all very high savers. Since they didn't want to take risks and many missed their chance to go to college, the majority of them ended up working for other people. My average client started out making $5,000 per year and ended earning a yearly income in the high $30,000. They saved 10–15 percent of what they earned, year after year. They put the money in CDs because that was safe, but they weren't able to make their money really work for them. Many of them now have $250,000 to $500,000 in the bank, and they own their houses. Financially they're comfortable, but the hardest part is getting them to enjoy their money now that they're retired. They can't seem to make the transition from saving to spending. They might take a vacation every now and then, but mostly they live at a bare subsistence level, spending as little as possible on themselves. The majority can't enjoy their own money.

During the internment we lost a whole generation of earnings. Our community was hit with two Great Depressions within twelve years, and the second one took everything. We had to start all over. My clients who lived through it are still being affected by it all. Paranoia and fears that are so powerful become intergenerational. This is something you actually get from your parents. I have some of my parents' money issues but mine aren't nearly as severe. But I see the signs.

Clearly, Rick's parents grew up with very different ideas about money. Because of her experience, Rick's mother, like other internees, never believed that her money was truly hers. Unconsciously, she expected everything to be taken away at any moment and she lived as frugally as possible, so she wouldn't miss it when it was gone. On the other hand, Rick's father, who experienced the war as a soldier, was able to take ownership of his money, seeing it as a tool to be used instead of a source of heartbreak and loss.

Gender

The idea that women shouldn't worry about money, or that it's not ladylike to be good with money, is thankfully going the way of the eight-track tape and the 56K modem. Still, many women who are adults today grew up with some version of that lesson.

> DENISE: *Dad did not, and still doesn't, believe that girls have what it takes to be in business. He would tell you that he doesn't believe that they have the emotional strength to succeed: "Women are too emotionally fragile." As the only girl, it was clear that he thought of me and treated me differently than my brothers.*

For Denise, this consistent message from her father that she could never succeed in her own business led her to stifle her dreams of entrepreneurial pursuits, and remain financially dependent on her parents for decades.

> MADELYN: *The biggest lesson for me growing up in a household with a dominating sexist father and being the youngest of four girls is that to get what you want, sex is the currency. I have watched my mother totally manipulate my father with that. I saw my sisters do the same, as one by one, they attached themselves to financially successful young men. They are still playing that role today in their marriages and grooming another generation of young women, my nieces, to do exactly the same.*
>   *When I began working as a young adult, I quickly realized that for most of the jobs I had, sex was part of the services expected to receive a paycheck. Part of the employment contract. Even though I never directly received money for sex, I did receive*

a paycheck and in exchange it was understood that using my sexuality as a commodity was required. For example, though I worked in a professional office and was college educated, I knew that it was important—at least as important as the work I did— to look good, to dress to please, and get (and keep) the attention of my male boss. I knew that I was supposed to respond to his flirting by being flirtatious myself. I knew that I was supposed to laugh at his jokes about sex and all that goes along with that. I knew that I was competing with all the other women in the office for his attention. I learned that if I played that game well, I got the promotions. All of this even led to my having an affair with the boss. No one ever was confused about what was going on. It was obvious that all of this was just an exchange. They got what they wanted, and I got what I thought I needed. More money.

Like my sisters before me, I married someone because of his financial success. Once again, sex was essentially exchanged for money and what I thought was security. While I was in the middle of all this, I deluded myself, never owning up to the fact that I had connected money so tightly to intimacy and sex.

Finally, as a result of a lot of work and self-examination, I realized the beliefs my life had been based on and where the lessons came from. Slowly, over time, I came to believe that not all relationships are built on that kind of exchange. My current marriage is one built on equality and a sharing of who we are—something very new for me, and sometimes hard to trust.

Obviously, this is an extreme case of something many women grow up with—the notion that it is a man's job to provide financial security, or what we call the "Prince Charming" money scripts. These include "Money is the man's territory," "Someone else will always take care of me financially," and "Money equals love." Scripts like these encourage the woman to wait for someone to come and sweep her off her feet and into a glorious new life. They place her in a position of financial dependence, both before she marries and after. Financially dependent women may lack even the most basic financial know-how, such as balancing a checkbook or reading a bank statement, leaving all that to her husband. (We'll talk about financial dependence and its ramifications in more detail later.) This passivity is very unwise. About half of all marriages end in divorce and even in long-lasting marriages, women outlive their husbands by an average of seven years; chances are a woman will be on her own at some point in her adult life. Financial dependence won't serve her well during those periods.

But even women who don't grow up believing in the "Prince Charming" script can end up developing equally negative and self-destructive scripts about gender and money. Consider Vanessa's story.

VANESSA: *Before I was born, my maternal great-grandfather lost most of his fortune in the Great Depression. As a result my grandmother became very interested in money and made many of the money decisions in her family. She invested in the stock market and eventually parlayed my grandfather's salary into a sizable sum. Her husband would periodically take interest in managing finances, stock picking, and otherwise, with results sometimes detrimental to the family's wealth. I eventually inherited a portion of the money from my grandparents.*

When I was growing up, my father started a business that eventually failed. The story I made up was that men are dreamers and dilettantes without much sense when it comes to money. Women, on the other hand, are steeped in common sense and will make the right decisions to preserve the money. So I was always very practical about money.

"A fool and his money are soon parted" was a common expression in our family. The women in my family portrayed the men as fools—but secretly and behind closed doors. After all, the men

were the ones who were supposed to be in charge. We all agreed on several things: Money is very, very important, very serious busi-ness. Money is a scarce resource that must be properly managed and respected. To mismanage money is shameful and to lose money is to be a fool.

The downside to all of this is that I have repeatedly become in-volved with men who are dreamers and dilettantes when it comes to money—I guess you could call it a self-fulfilling prophecy. In my last relationship my partner repeatedly resisted whenever I at-tempted to clarify agreements about asset ownership. In turn, I abdicated responsibility about our finances in the mistaken belief that it would enhance the relationship. That was a two-hundred-thousand-dollar lesson.

When we draw conclusions or make assumptions about the way the world works, we tend to seek out information and ex-periences that confirm and reinforce our beliefs; this is what Vanessa was doing when she sought out men who fit the mold of her particular money script. Vanessa's experiences with ro-mantic partners also shows the subconscious yet natural draw we all have to what is familiar. Without examining our past and working through unfinished business, we're often com-pelled to re-create the same situation, or its mirror image, over and over again.

Boys struggle with the specific gender-related money les-sons they receive, too. Scripts like "A man has to be the bread-winner in the family," "You're a failure if you can't take care of your family," and "Money is the only measure of your worth" can become harmful and limiting, and often lead men to place disproportionate value on their workplace identity and income status. And indeed, it's difficult not to, because our culture values material success—especially for men—so highly. Men, no less than women, need close personal relationships to be emotionally healthy; yet if they devote all their energy to their careers, they'll never develop satisfying connections to other people. If they build their entire sense of self around their professional identity and achievements, then once they lose that, through retirement or unemployment, they're very likely to become anxious or depressed. And, with few emotional resources to deal with their distress, they can spiral down into severe emotional problems, or even suicide. During the Asian currency crisis of the late 1990s, for example, suicide rates among men rose at twice the rate as that among women. Even more alarming is the current spate of murder-suicides. After killing their families, these men facing financial disaster killed themselves because they believed they had no other options. Of course the current financial meltdown is only the trigger for these terrible crimes. The real cause is a severe emotional and psychological imbalance, combined with the men's over-investment in their identity as breadwinner.

Financial Fairy Tales—The Moral of the Story

An old woman gleefully plots to cannibalize two children she's locked up in her home. Two sisters hack off parts of their feet in a fruitless attempt to get a wealthy husband. Another old woman abducts a baby girl from her parents, keeps her isolated as she grows up, and deliberately blinds her only visitor. These are not the plots of horror films but those of the Brothers Grimm fairy tales, which are indeed grim. Yet their violence and dark themes may be part of their appeal, explaining why they've been told and retold for centuries.

Many theorists believe that just as dreams reveal the thoughts that lurk beneath a person's consciousness, folk and fairy tales represent the beliefs, fears, and values that lie underneath a culture's surface, or what Carl Jung called the collective unconscious. Jung also believed that characters (such as the wise old man or the trickster) represent archetypes, or innate and universal ideas and concepts that connected all humans; and that expression of these archetypes served an important cultural purpose. In the 1970s, child psychologist Bruno Bettelheim argued that fairy tales also serve an important function in children's emotional development, helping them understand and cope with upsetting or confusing feelings or events in their world: sibling rivalry, fear of abandonment, rage at a parent, and so on. The fairy tale, in other words, offers lessons and reassurance in a way the child is able to take in and act on. This is why children focus on specific stories, wanting to hear them over and over. Bettelheim wrote *The Uses of Enchantment* "to show how fairy stories represent in imaginative form what the process of healthy human development consists of, and how the tales make such development attractive for the child to engage in."

What does all this have to do with how you handle your finances?

We've talked about financial flashpoints, how the brain creates narratives around those moments, and how those narratives are often inaccurate, illogical, or only partially true. We've also talked about how these narratives become imprinted in the brain, to be called up in any situation resembling the original flashpoint experience, and become part of our personal history, elements of our private folklore. Just as a child finds comfort and security in having the same story read and re-read, our unconscious minds keep replaying our money scripts—which, like fairy tales, help us understand, simplify, and bring order to the complexities of the adult world. At the subconscious, animal-brain level, we organize our emotions and financial thinking and behavior around these money scripts, hoping they'll bring us the "happily ever after" we desire. And what do we do when real life fails to match the fantasy? Often, instead of questioning our underlying assumptions, we just try harder to make them fit.

Remember that money scripts can be damaging because, unless examined and challenged, they never change. Even with awareness and insight, the prospect of giving up our money scripts can fill us with fear; we're terrified of returning to the confusion and chaos we experienced before we developed those survival beliefs. Even though we are now adults, and have control, perspective, and reasoning that we didn't have as children, our animal brains cling to these scripts—or fairy tales we tell ourselves—just as they do to any other meaningful narrative.

In our work, we've learned that transforming a dysfunctional financial life just cannot happen without identifying the underlying money scripts, examining where they came from and how they have helped us and hurt us. The deliberate, thoughtful consideration of money scripts and their influence on our behavior grounds the changes we want to make. Our ability to live to our highest financial potential in our lives is determined to a large degree by our ability to identify our scripts when they creep into our minds. By shedding light on them, they lose their power to control our emotions and actions. Awareness opens us up to limitless possibilities. We can catch ourselves, stop, and start over. The first step to changing our self-defeating behaviors is changing our thinking. Thus we can become conscious and purposeful creators of our lives.

In the next section, we'll look closely at twelve common money disorders, their symptoms, their scripts (or the fairy-tale beliefs they represent), and the common financial flashpoints that are their catalysts. We also include results from a groundbreaking study we conducted that documented the lasting changes in people who successfully dealt with the underlying causes of their money disorders. The results were exciting. The individuals we studied reported significant and ongoing changes, including improvements in mood, decreased anxiety about money, and improvements in overall financial and psychological health.

By now we suspect you've already recognized some of your own beliefs and behaviors in the stories or examples told in these pages. As you continue to read, take note of which disorders or disordered behaviors resonate the *most* for you. By the end of the next section, you'll have a richer, deeper, understanding of why you act the way you do, and be well on the path to change.

Before we take a closer look at the specific money disorders, take a few moments to focus inward. Try the following exercise.

1. As best you can, recall the memorable experiences you have had with money, both joyful and painful, going as far back in your memory as you can.

2. Take a sheet of paper and write down a few words summarizing each event. You can also draw symbols representing them.

3. Go back and make a note of the emotion you attach to the event. Use words like *angry, sad, happy, afraid, hurt.*

4. Now look over everything you have written and ask yourself: "If I had to write one or two sentences to summarize my experiences with money, what would they be?" Another way to do this would be to finish this sentence: "The moral of my story is . . ."

Part Two

MONEY DISORDERS

5

What Exactly Is a Money Disorder, Anyway?

Everyone makes a poor financial decision now and again. This is normal and, to the extent we learn from our missteps, even necessary. Single, isolated, or rare financial mistakes, do not qualify as money disorders. Money disorders are persistent, predictable, often rigid *patterns* of self-destructive financial behaviors that cause significant stress, anxiety, emotional distress, and impairment in major areas of one's life. People in the grip of money disorders can't seem to shake these faulty beliefs or change their unhealthy behaviors, no matter how much chaos and misery they cause. Typically, they know they *should* change their behaviors, but they just can't seem to do it. Or, even if they're able to shift their behavior for a time, they're unable to make the changes stick. Often they feel intense shame about the behaviors and may hide them from others and even from themselves. This only postpones any resolution of the issue and further impedes change.

MOLLIE: *My husband and I struggled and fought over money matters often. Neither of us had any sort of financial map to guide us. Neither of us had savings or risk management strategies and we lived paycheck to paycheck for the most part. I struggled to figure out a way to get some kind of relief from the anxiety I felt, to learn how to manage money in my life. With my husband, I would try to control, threaten, cajole, manipulate, withdraw, argue, cry, plead, bargain, always driven by my fear regarding finances. So it was these financial issues that led us to couples' therapy over and over, but the focus was seldom about the financial issues that had become a wedge between my husband and me.*

Hurricane Katrina blew the lid off of things, so to speak. Our home was flooded and our investment property was destroyed. My business was temporarily lost—I hoped it was temporary—so my income was at a standstill. My community was devastated and so many things I counted on for security—my income, my spiritual community, my neighborhood structure, my local friends and family, even my faith—all of those were challenged. Though I had a great marriage in so many ways, my money issues reared up like a dragon. It demanded healing or I knew I would lose more than a lot of material things—I would lose my marriage.

Mollie and her husband did slay the dragon and their marriage was saved. But like most of us, they didn't take that step until things were at a crisis point. They limped along, struggling with money issues without ever actually dealing with them. This created more stress, which put the animal brain ever more in charge. By now you're well aware that when your animal brain is activated, you will automatically default to using your money scripts to guide you in your financial decision making. To the degree that those scripts are faulty or incomplete, your decision making will be, too. That's at the core of money disorders.

As we've discussed, money disorders stem from family dysfunction, emotional difficulties, coping strategies gone awry, profound painful childhood experiences, or—most often—a combination of these factors. Similar to other compulsive or addictive behaviors, money disorders are symptoms of unfinished business related to a troubled past. The self-medicating aspects of these disorders may help us temporarily avoid difficult feelings and psychic pain. However, the relief this offers is only temporary, and it comes with its own set of emotional, relational, and financial side effects. Symptoms of money disorders may include any or all of the following.

- Anxiety, worry, or despair about one's financial situation
- A lack of savings
- Excessive debt
- Bankruptcy, loan defaults, or both
- Conflict with family, friends, or colleagues around money
- An inability to sustain changes in financial behaviors

What does financial wellness look like? We agree with researchers Dr. So-Hyun Joo and Dr. John Grable who list several factors contributing to a healthy financial life.

- Maintaining reasonable and low debt
- Having an active savings plan
- Having and following a conscious spending plan
- Lack of conflict with family/partner around money
- Experiencing high levels of financial satisfaction
- Experiencing low levels of financial stress

As we've learned, even the most irrational money behaviors make perfect sense when we discover their underlying money scripts and the context from which they arose. Still, when these problematic behaviors become habitual they can lead to significant problems in relationships, work, psychological health, and general—not to mention financial—well-being.

While unresolved childhood issues, financial traumas, and other early flashpoint experiences make up the backdrop of all financial disorders, the disorders themselves take many forms. And it's important to note this: Like money scripts, these disorders are not mutually exclusive. We can show signs of more than one, in varying degrees, in varying situations, and at varying times in our lives. These disorders may be persistent but they are not static. And while the scripts that underlie them rarely change (at least not without conscious effort and hard work) the ways in which the disorders manifest themselves are prone to morphing over time. And of course, because no two people are identical, because we all have wildly different backgrounds, experiences, family histories, and ways of seeing the world, these disorders don't look exactly the same from person to person.

So as you read these descriptions and real-life examples, look for overall similarities to your issues, behaviors, and thinking patterns, knowing that while you may not find a perfect description of yourself and your money difficulties in a single disorder, you may see many glimpses of yourself throughout. We also invite you to visit our website at www.YourMentalWealth.com to take a free money disorders diagnostic test. You will need to use the code at the back of the book to access your assessment and see your results.

In the following chapters, we've grouped twelve common disorders that we have seen in our practice into three clusters. The first cluster consists of disorders in which money, or dealing with money, is systematically avoided: financial denial, financial rejection, excessive risk aversion, and underspending. In the second cluster are those disorders in which people are overly obsessed with spending or with having money or things: compulsive hoarding, workaholism, unreasonable risk taking (and its extreme version, pathological gambling), and over-spending (as well as its extreme form, compulsive buying). In the last cluster are disorders that are tangled up in one's relationships with others: financial infidelity, financial incest, financial enabling, and financial dependence. As you'll see, each of these disorders stems from specific patterns of thinking and acting—and they aren't that difficult to spot, once you know what to look for.

6

Money-Avoidance Disorders

The disorders discussed in this chapter all involve a systematic rejection or avoidance of money. These stem from scripts that equate money with negative emotions or painful events—in other words, the belief that money is bad. To extend the fairy-tale metaphor we introduced in chapter 4, these scripts are what we think of as "big bad wolf" scripts.

What do we mean? Well, every good fairy tale needs a villain, right? In *Cinderella,* it's her stepmother and stepsisters, who abuse the poor girl terribly. In *Sleeping Beauty,* it's the vain and sinister queen, who tries to have her rival killed. In *Little Red Riding Hood,* it's the Big Bad Wolf, who tries to consume the heroine for dinner. When money is a force that stirs up fear and anxiety, it becomes the villain. This leads to a cycle of avoidance; instead of dealing with our money issues, we do what so many fairy-tale characters do—we run away from them. The disorders that fall into this category are financial denial, financial rejection, excessive risk aversion, and underspending. Scripts common to these disorders include the following.

COMMON MONEY-AVOIDANCE MONEY SCRIPTS

If I'm in the right place, doing the right things, for the right reasons, then the money stuff will take care of itself.

It's wrong to have more money than others in the family.

Money I haven't earned isn't really mine.

God has his eye on the sparrow. If they don't have to worry, why should I?

There is virtue in living with less money.

Most rich people don't deserve their money.

Having money separates you from people you care about.

I don't deserve to have money.

Enjoying an inheritance or insurance settlement is the same as saying that I'm glad someone died.

Money corrupts people.

Money will change me and make me into the type of person I will despise.

Good people shouldn't care about money.

Being wealthy means that you can't be sure whether someone loves you or your money.

It is not okay to have more than you need.

Having money or working for it consciously would "contaminate" one's work.

People become rich by taking advantage of others.

Money is the root of all evil.

You can have love or money, but not both.

It's extravagant to spend money on yourself.

You should never trust anyone else with your money.

As we've studied the financial beliefs of clients with money avoidance issues, we found an interesting paradox. The people who indicated that they avoid accumulating wealth, that they are paid less than they are worth and feel guilty about getting paid for the work they do, often also carry the two following seemingly contradictory money scripts.

My self-worth equals my net worth.

Things would get better if I had more money.

Even though people with these scripts may avoid wealth (however consciously or unconsciously), many also have some underlying resentment about their financial situation and believe that they would feel better about their lives if they had more money. It is also common for them to blame their financial condition on some outside authority: the school system they work for, an unappreciative company, a corrupt government, an ungrateful community. This is an excellent example of the duality of problem money behaviors, the fact that it's not uncommon for one's desires, values, behaviors, and beliefs to be in conflict with each other. When our beliefs and behaviors are at odds, we are prone to sabotaging ourselves, making it very difficult to accumulate wealth.

Financial Denial

Denial is a classic defense mechanism, designed to reduce anxiety and shame over our troubles. So financial denial is when we minimize our money problems or try our best to avoid thinking about them altogether rather than face our financial reality. People in the throes of financial denial often won't look at their bank statements or credit card bills. They won't negotiate for raises. They won't talk to their partners about money. They avoid saving or accumulating wealth. They just don't want to think about money *at all*. But like most defense mechanisms, financial denial almost always backfires, because by ignoring our problems, all we're really doing is allowing them to persist and worsen. Someone who avoids opening bills or statements so they don't have to face their reality, for example, is essentially inviting late fees and overdraft charges, digging themselves further and further into debt.

Then, to relieve any tension that arises, people who live in a state of denial rationalize their avoidant behavior, which only makes it harder to see the truth. As a result, they will likely just keep avoiding or denying the symptoms rather than trying to cure the problem, which serves only to reinforce the denial and further entrench the behavior. Soon the avoidance becomes hardwired, unconscious, and automatic. It's the classic definition of a vicious cycle. In other words, denial works well in the short term but leads to disaster in the long run.

Often, financial denial can be rooted in confusion, or lack of understanding, about money. This confusion can result from any number of flashpoint experiences—receiving mixed messages about money, being told that money issues are none of our business, being shamed when we do something involving finances—usually in childhood. Consider Harris's story.

HARRIS: *I remember watching my mother and stepdad and how they handled finances. They alternated between being very frightened about where they were financially and then being very loose and carefree with money. They'd spend a lot, and then they'd panic. They'd resolve not to do it anymore, and then they'd do it again. It became confusing as a kid. It taught me that resolving to change your financial habits is pointless and impossible because you end up just going back to your impulses anyway.*

At first I followed them on the roller coaster of feeling tense and worried and then free and relaxed. But as I caught on, I became more and more confused. There were all these weird messages: "You should have exactly what you want" and also "You can't have what you want," and none of it was quite tied to financial reality. I went back and forth in terms of what was right and wrong. Then I moved to the place of not feeling anything, refusing to get caught up in their drama. I just didn't pay much attention when they got worried and I didn't get too excited when they were feeling flush. I decided to not get upset, to not buy into any emotions at all about the money.

To this day it's really difficult for me to sit down and make a budget and say, "Do we actually have this much money? What's the plan? Buying this doesn't fit our plans; therefore we can't get it. Or it does and therefore we can." To this day I really don't know how to do that very well, although I am getting better.

I have to say, not worrying about money is a fun way to live. Ninety-five percent of the time you're able to put all concerns out of your head and just trust that everything's going to work out. I like the trust concept, but trust without actual work or attention doesn't work so well. But not worrying about money, not thinking about it, was an easier way to live. It let me avoid a lot of work that goes into actually thinking things through, money-wise. In some ways it served me by helping me avoid the tension that sometimes comes with full awareness. Awareness of, "Holy cow, my parents are on a crash trajectory. I have to jump off this train before they kill me along with themselves." All in all, it basically served to reduce tension. But it sure set up a bunch of bad habits. In many ways, though it was supposed to relieve tension, it ended up creating a lot more.

Harris received a lot of mixed messages about money from his parents yet no real training in how to handle it. Sometimes his parents spent freely; at other times, they seemed to resent spending, and there didn't seem to be any recognizable pattern to the responses. They also intertwined financial and nonfinancial transactions, like buying him a car to get him to agree to exercise more. This only caused further confusion.

To reduce anxiety, make sense of the wildly conflicting money messages he received, and deal with the associated roller-coaster ride of emotions, Harris concluded that money was just not important and he was better off disconnecting himself from it. So he simply avoided dealing with it at all. While this may have been a useful adaptive response in his childhood, this avoidance followed him into adulthood and kept him in denial about adult financial issues. As he points out, denial does relieve the immediate tension around money. But in the long run, it only serves to compound our financial problems.

Allison, too, received emotionally charged and conflicting messages from her parents about money.

ALLISON: *There was a lot of drama around money when I was growing up and I was always conflicted about what the truth really was—my mom's "the sky is falling" speeches versus her wild shopping sprees. My response to those things was always to act like they weren't happening, because I had no tools to deal with them. I just went about my business as if nothing was wrong. But something was really wrong and I knew it.*

Another form of financial denial occurs when one partner pays little or no attention to family finances while the other takes care of everything related to money. If the uninvolved partner is left on their own for some reason, such as separation, divorce, or death, the resulting financial ignorance can add a great deal of unnecessary stress to an already painful situation. In the case of a divorce, the spouse who doesn't know anything about the couple's finances is vulnerable to being manipulated or taken advantage of.

In its extreme form, financial denial can take the form of dissociation. A common reaction to trauma, dissociation is essentially an extreme form of the "freeze" response. When removing oneself physically from whatever is upsetting or threatening is difficult or impossible, dissociative states allow people to escape by "going away," or removing themselves emotionally and mentally. When the chaos and emotional

upheaval is too much to tolerate, we psychologically discon-
nect from the situation—it's an extreme way of denying that
the problem exists. It leads to emotional numbness, loss of a
sense of self, and problems with memory storage and retrieval.
For instance, a question even loosely related to money, even
something as simple as "What would you like for your birthday?" can trigger a moment of dissociation—the person will go
totally blank and be unable to form a thought to answer the
question. Pretty much any question regarding their personal
relationship with money—"What do you think a fair salary
would be for you?" or "How could I support you financially?"—
can be met with the same reaction. It isn't that the person
doesn't want or need anything. It isn't that she doesn't have
any ideas about what a fair salary would be. It isn't that he
doesn't know what kind of support he needs. It's that their denial is so pronounced, in the moment when these people are
forced to articulate those needs, they "shut down."

Disassociation is a common response to intense and overwhelming emotional experiences. As with so many coping
mechanisms, disassociation works well in extreme situations
(for example, for soldiers in the midst of battle, who dissociate
from the surrounding violence so they can perform their duties, it can be a valuable and lifesaving defense mechanism).
However, in most contexts, the dissociative response long out-
lives its usefulness, and can be very destructive when it becomes habitual and is generalized to non-life-threatening
events. Being emotionally present is critical to healthy financial decision making and good mental health in general.

Financial Rejection

This is a surprisingly common disorder, given how much our
society values money. Ironically, while we all want money, at
the same time, many of us also seem programmed to feel guilt

over having it. This is where the problems begin. People whose self-esteem has been beaten down are prone to this disorder; they feel they are unworthy or undeserving of anything good in life, including money.

MIKE: *My father left me a lot of money and I couldn't get rid of it fast enough. I bought a new car every six months for five years. Whenever I saw the money in my checking account, I was angry. It wasn't mine. It seemed like Dad was saying, "You couldn't make it on your own, so I had to leave you something." It wasn't mine, it was his. I didn't deserve it or want it.*

MARGARET: *When my dad died I inherited his company which was valued at over thirty million dollars. I refused to accept it. I never wanted to be one seen by people in my town as one of "those rich people." I purposely had lived a very simple frugal life, even though I lived in the same town as my parents who owned the largest factory and was the largest employer in the county. My parents were very good with their money, but they didn't mind driving fancy cars and taking exotic vacations. I knew how people had talked about my mom and dad when they were alive and I didn't want to be talked about like that. After their death, I flat-out refused to accept responsibility for the company. I wouldn't show up at meetings. I ignored requests from my attorney to meet. The way I saw it, owning the company was just an unfortunate accident of fate and I wanted no part of it. Unfortunately, other relatives didn't have that same problem and their behaviors were threatening the survival of the company. The lawsuit that they filed finally got my attention.*

Mike and Margaret illustrate a common dynamic among those who reject money. For them, the meaning of money is connected to unfinished emotional business related to painful associations—in this case, their relationships with their parents. Believing that money goes only to those who "deserve it" either through earning it or being "good enough," they were unable to enjoy their resources, and in some cases, squandered them. This is also a common dynamic in people who receive death benefits.

An especially striking example of rejecting money is Kathy Trant's story. Her husband, Dan, was a stockbroker killed in the 9/11 attack on the World Trade Center. Over the months following the tragedy, Kathy received almost five million dollars in settlements and donations. By June 2005, she had five hundred thousand dollars left. Where did it all go? She paid for extensive renovations she didn't need on the home she and Dan had shared, tripling its square footage. She bought a whole new wardrobe; the shoes alone cost a total of half a million dollars. Unable to sleep, she'd stay up through the night and order things from catalogs. Kathy gave her maid fifteen thousand dollars to buy property in her native El Salvador, and she tipped a Las Vegas masseuse several thousand dollars to pay for breast implants. She treated several of her friends to a Super Bowl vacation that cost seventy thousand dollars. She spent the money in a frenzy she didn't fully understand. "I want my husband back," Kathy said. The settlement was "blood money that I don't want."

Rejection of money can express itself in several forms: squandering sudden money (like Kathy), taking an unconscious "vow of poverty," and avoiding the acquisition of wealth. These are often rooted in the script that "money is bad." If you believe to any degree that money is bad, then it follows that people who have money are bad. If those beliefs are guiding your behavior with money, it's perfectly logical that you aren't going to allow yourself to accumulate wealth or enjoy financial prosperity, even if it "accidentally" comes your way.

The following story perfectly demonstrates this "Money is bad" script.

NEIL: *When my parents got a divorce we went from living a middle-class lifestyle to being a lower-class and "broken" home. Divorced families were not as prevalent then as today. I could tell we had less than others just by the pencils, pens, and erasers the other kids brought to school and by how many pairs of pants they wore. We never had more than two pairs.*

So I grew up thinking that there were two kinds of people: us . . . and them. Being "them" meant you had life too easy. Growing up, hearing about missionaries and how they suffered, I was taught only the good, tough people could do that. In other words, hard work equals good, money equals bad. I knew I was tough and as an adult, at some level I've always felt guilty for making money, because I really was supposed to be a missionary. And even today, my wife and I work in the helping professions, and there seems to be a negative stigma if you're interested in making more money than you need to exist while you help people.

As a child, Neil learned that having money means that one is not really experiencing the important things in life, that the greatest virtue lies in poverty and suffering. So as an adult, Neil felt extremely guilty about having money. When we met him he was acting out a laundry list of self-sabotaging financial behaviors: squandering money, not saving for the future, missing opportunities, and overall repelling wealth.

Sometimes, our rejection of money comes out of a subconscious desire to stay in the socioeconomic setting in which we are most comfortable, our financial comfort zone, which is usually determined by the environment we grew up in. If we're suddenly moved to a different zone—either coming into or losing a large amount of money—with different rules, expectations, and responsibilities, we become intensely uncomfortable. If we don't make a conscious effort to adjust to those new

surroundings, the old impulses will determine our decisions—
often to our financial detriment.

A classic example: professional athletes who blow through
millions of dollars and end up bankrupt. Most professional
athletes grow up under modest circumstances and then find
themselves multimillionaires overnight. Yet almost 80 percent
of NFL players are either bankrupt or in serious financial
straits within two years of retirement; about 60 percent of
NBA players are broke within five. They squandered their
money because they didn't make the adjustment to face their
discomfort and anxiety over the new questions and responsibilities that wealth brings.

One former pro football player said, "I once had a meeting with J.P. Morgan and it was literally like listening to
Charlie Brown's teacher. I was so busy focusing on football
that the first year was suddenly over. I'd started with this
$4 million base salary, but then I looked at my bank state-
ment, and I just went, What the . . . ?" It was practically all
gone. Social and family pressures, combined with a lack of
knowledge about how to handle money, lands these young
men right back where they started. Other people who receive sudden windfalls—lottery winners, recipients of settlements or inheritances—often show similar money-rejecting
behaviors.

One form financial rejection can take is a vow of poverty, common for people who work in the helping professions. For
example, in one of our studies we found that social workers
and educators were more likely to hold negative views about
money and the rich compared to people in other professions.
Remember Paul, from the introduction, whose newborn
brother died in the delivery room while the wealthy doctor was

out playing golf? Is it any wonder that he grew up to both devote his life to helping others, and to shun money?

> PAUL: *I've always had a really hard time with my fee structure. I'd
> think, "I don't deserve that much. Other people have so much
> less. I should give it all away to them." So it stayed on the low
> end, compared to other therapists in town.*
>
> *Well, after I worked on my money scripts, I took another look
> at my fees.*
>
> *I didn't really change them much but now the level is not
> based on the idea that I'm not worth more. In fact, I think I'm
> worth more than any therapist in town. Keeping the fee structure
> I have was a conscious decision I made, because of the type of
> person I want to work with. They're mostly recovering addicts and
> alcoholics and most of them really scrape to be able to pay my
> fees. If I were to raise them much, I'd turn that market off. I
> might be able to attract a different market but I'm not so sure I
> really want to work with a different market. I like the market I'm
> working with now.*
>
> *The big, big difference is that all of these are conscious deci-
> sions. That is totally different than the way it used to be.*

Paul's story shows the importance of making money scripts
conscious. This allows us to heal emotional wounds which, in
turn, enables us to *choose* how to behave after careful consideration, as opposed to reacting unconsciously and automatically.
Even if the behavior doesn't change, the emotions around it are
much healthier, and will result in better, sounder financial decision making, rather than disordered money behaviors.

Kristen, whom we met in chapter 3, is a perfect example of the
unhealthy pendulum-swing response that's common in money

disorders. You may remember that Kristen grew up in an extremely wealthy but unhappy home, and she felt acute shame and embarrassment over her family's wealth. As a result, she vehemently rejected money, later in life, because she made an erroneous causal association between money and isolation or rejection.

> KRISTEN: *The worst thing someone could call me was a rich bitch. So I went to the other extreme. In high school my parents insisted that we wear nice clothes. I would leave the house dressed as I was supposed to be, but I'd change into a pair of ratty overalls before school started. All I wanted to wear was overalls. I had all these negative ideas about money. Since I felt guilty about having money, I was unconsciously giving it away. I did good with it and it felt so good to give it away, almost like a cleansing.*

Ellen, on the other hand, avoided wealth for an entirely different reason. You read some of Ellen's story earlier, when she described her mother's "by any means necessary" approach to getting money for herself and her children. Unfortunately, those means included not only hard work, but scamming whoever would befriend her, stealing from employers, defaulting on loans—and repeatedly getting caught. She seldom had a job lasting more than a few months. Losing jobs meant that the family seldom lived in one place more than three or four months at a time. Her mom cheated the welfare system and Ellen, as the oldest, was coached to lie to authorities to keep the money coming in. These behaviors caused her daughter a great deal of shame, and as an adult, Ellen has associated money—asking for it, having it, or receiving it—with dishonesty or being a hustler. So Ellen rejects money so that no one will ever think she's getting it dishonestly. In her eyes, the worst thing that could ever happen to her is to be accused of being dishonest.

> ELLEN: *One time I rejected payment for a job that I did because I wanted to support a colleague's effort and didn't want to "appear" poor, as if I needed the money. I'm sure that others who were working on the project were offered payment too and I doubt that any of them turned it down. Later, when I realized what I had done, I was furious with myself.*
>
> *But overall, I am improving. I work with low-income clients and I am always tempted to give my services away. I have a very fair sliding scale but I would often end up canceling the outstanding balance for some clients. This year, I have stood firm on my fees, doing pro bono work in a way that works for me but doesn't leave me feeling abused. My clients appreciate the boundaries and I am enjoying my work more.*

The behaviors of people who repel wealth are often similar to the actions of those who have taken vows of poverty. They may create their own self-imposed glass ceilings in their careers, either failing to pursue or actively turning down opportunities for promotions or growth that would take them outside their financial comfort zones. They may stay in low-paying jobs for which they are overqualified. They may achieve some success in the form of a well-paying job, then sabotage themselves to the point that they lose it. They may unconsciously choose not to use their talents to the fullest because underneath they are afraid of the success and the monetary gains that might follow. Lynne provides another powerful example.

> LYNNE: *As a little girl, the one thing I remember about my mom and dad was their constant fighting about money. They would*

come to blows over it. It scared me so much as a kid that I wanted nothing to do with it. They both died very young and my sister and I ended up with nothing. We had to be cared for by my aunt and grandmother who lived together. They never mentioned money, we seemed to always have just enough. They were both killed quite tragically in a car accident when I was in my midtwenties. You can imagine the shock of learning that they had left my sister and me 1.5 million after-tax dollars to split.

I panicked. All of a sudden I had money. All of a sudden I knew that I would end up with a life just like my mom and dad's. Fighting about the money with someone. Watching it destroy friendships and relationships. Fearing I would become like those evil rich people, I immediately began an unconscious campaign to get rid of it. I became my own personal nonprofit. If you had a good cause, I made a donation. I went through my share of the inheritance, all $750,000, within six years. My sister kept and invested hers. We have not spoken in thirty years. I just didn't want to be around anyone who had money. I'm now fifty-five years old. I have nothing. I'm highly educated, with a Ph.D., and I'm a gross underearner. I volunteer my services. I undercharge. If something doesn't change, I'll need to work until the day that I die. At this point, I just hope that I can work until the day I die.

Here, Lynne's feelings about money were tied up in the pain she felt after losing her family members. She felt guilty for profiting over their tragic death, and that lingering guilt led her to later also reject the money she earned.

When we pay attention to media coverage of the antics of a few wealthy celebrities, the belief that "rich people are bad" is reinforced. Seeing the children and grandchildren of billionaires squander their money and apparently their lives on self-indulgent excess can give the rest of us a sense of superiority about our own modest circumstances. It can help justify our resentment of the mega-rich and reassure ourselves that we are better off not having wealth. Of course, what we don't see are the stories of children and grandchildren of the wealthy who live full, meaningful, fulfilling lives. It's true that these stories are not publicized as often, but it's also true that we don't look for them. Why? Because they contradict the script "Wealth ruins relationships and people." The benefit of this belief is that it helps us feel content with what we have. The down side is that it is a distorted conclusion that feeds our ego and our sense of moral superiority, and limits our ability to acquire and enjoy wealth.

Underspending

In our nation of overspenders and debtors, it might seem odd to see "underspending" described as a self-destructive financial behavior. After all, spending less than you take in is a fundamental principle of financial health, right? Technically, yes, but underspending, taken to the extreme, can keep you just as poor as overspending can. Unlike overspenders, those who underspend may have plenty of savings. Yet, they keep themselves *emotionally* poor by refusing to use and enjoy what they do have.

The kind of underspending that creates problems is not the same thing as making a conscious decision to live a modest lifestyle. Choosing to be thrifty is a matter of managing your resources well to make the most of what you have. But the key word here is *choosing*. Underspending is unhealthy because, like rejecting money, it is often based on irrational subconscious feelings of fear or anxiety, a sense of guilt or of being undeserving of good fortune, or a compulsive need to be self-sacrificing.

GWEN: *I grew up in a small town and we had a family company, with our name on all the delivery vehicles. I never quite knew if somebody was my friend because of me or because of my name.*

One of my first memories is being with my mom at our bank and the teller saying, "Oh, you'd be a great person to file a lawsuit against." There were many, many instances like that, where people made comments about our family's money. Their message was essentially, "You have money. Your life must be easy." From my perspective, it didn't feel that way at all.

I think the belief I assimilated around money was that it exposes you and you have to keep it hidden. I still tend not to buy showy things. I don't buy fancy cars, take fancy trips, because if I were showing off my money in some ostentatious way, then there is this overriding sense that would make me a vulnerable target and the money would be taken from me. The rest of what I make up about that is if that happened, I would have no one to blame but myself.

Gwen's story is an example of the "paranoia of the wealthy." Often, people who grow up with a lot of money have a lingering uncertainty about their relationships: "Do people like me because of me or my family's money?" So they'll underspend in order to hide what they have, depriving themselves of things like nice clothes and fancy cars, for fear of being seen as a "show off." Her sense of vulnerability also highlights a common pattern in financial flashpoints and money scripts—the longing for safety. The rich learn that money doesn't keep you safe and the poor learn that a lack of money is no protection either. Like so many other money scripts, both are true and both are false. It all depends on the context.

Underspenders are unable to use their resources to enhance their own life or the lives of others. Many stories have been told about people who lived like paupers, inhabiting ramshackle homes, wearing shabby clothes, going without the dental or medical care they need—only to leave estates worth millions. Those are underspenders.

Ebenezer Scrooge, from Charles Dickens's *A Christmas Carol,* is the iconic example. Although he had significant wealth, he lived his life as if he were poor. Dickens wrote, "Darkness is cheap, and Scrooge liked it." Scrooge lived in a sparse, dreary home that he did not heat, ate meager meals, and deprived himself of basic comforts. Like overspending, underspending has its origins in a painful past. Dickens showed us some of Scrooge's financial flashpoints: an abusive father, a childhood of want, loneliness, and lack. To escape this experience, Scrooge became a miser, investing all his emotional capital in monetary capital. He was able to accumulate wealth but contrived a life of poverty, refusing to spend money on the simplest of daily necessities. For him, parting with money was like losing a friend. No amount of money could ever give Scrooge relief from a painful childhood; it took a visit to his past to free him. (Our first book, *The Financial Wisdom of Ebenezer Scrooge: 5 Principles to Transform Your Relationship with Money,* coauthored with financial planner Rick Kahler, CFP, used the old miser, his nephew, and the three ghosts as an extended metaphor to illustrate many of the principles you're reading about here.)

Excessive Risk Aversion

Another disorder that involves a measure of financial avoidance is excessive risk aversion, or an irrational unwillingness to take any risks with one's money. Just as opening a credit card statement is terrifying for someone in financial denial, a person in the grip of risk avoidance reacts to any risk, however slight, with enormous anxiety. Even something as innocuous as putting their money into a government-insured savings account may feel too scary. While being financially conservative is generally a good thing (especially when it stems from a conscious decision to be conservative, rather than paralyzing fear of risk), these people are conservative to a fault. They have often learned it is better to do nothing than to lose anything, and they're locked into a perpetual freeze response. As such, they may miss many opportunities that come their way.

On a global level, the first few years of this century were a time of excessive risk taking and speculation (in other words, gambling) on complicated financial instruments such as derivatives and credit swap defaults. (In his annual letter to Berkshire Hathaway stockholders, Warren Buffett called derivatives "financial weapons of mass destruction, carrying dangers that, while now latent, are potentially lethal." He pointed this out in *early 2003*.) Then, in the wake of the subprime mortgage collapse, the markets swung to the other extreme of excessive risk-aversion, where lenders were too frightened to loan money to even the most fiscally fit borrowers. The result? Our economy came to a grinding halt.

GWEN: *I grew up with lots of fear and worry around money. I was often present for discussions between my mom and dad where they would also talk about the difficulties with the business, the potential legal exposure, things like that. My parents would often have that kind of conversation at the dinner table and we were told that children didn't interject into adult conversation. I think it bothered me, but I didn't feel as though I was in a position to change it.*

What I carried with me from that early exposure was a keen awareness of the legal issues revolving around my business. I tend to be super-compliant, which is good, but I also tend to play it safe and not to take risks, and that means I've lost some opportunities. I think I also have tended to charge less than I'm worth, thinking that if I don't charge as much, then they won't expect as much and I'm not exposing myself to as much risk of being sued.

Like the other unhealthy behaviors we've talked about, excessive risk avoidance is linked to anxieties that we pick up, as children, by observing the adults in our life. Here, Gwen unwittingly internalized her parents' irrational fears about being sued, fears she then generalized to any kind of risk-taking behavior. People who witnessed a family member experience a huge loss from a bad investment, or a failed business venture, may become excessively risk averse (another example of the "pendulum swing" we've talked about) as a result. Many children of pathological gamblers become risk averse; they have seen, firsthand, what risk taking can do to a family, so they gravitate to the opposite extreme.

7

Money-Worshiping Disorders

These are the disorders that place a disproportionate amount of importance on money: earning it, saving it, spending it. They share a common thread in that they all arise from scripts that equate money with safety, self-worth, and/or happiness. To revisit the fairy-tale metaphor, these can be thought of as "fairy godmother" scripts. Think about the fairy godmother in the Cinderella story. With a wave of her wand, she transformed a pumpkin into a luxurious coach, rags into a splendid gown. These scripts treat money as something just as magical, special, and transformative. They are rooted in a core belief that regardless of our personal behaviors, liabilities, or limitations, with the wave of a magic wand, a pile of cash will appear and solve all our problems. It's a child's understanding of money, investing it with fantastic power instead of looking at it as a tool that can be used well or poorly. Because just like Cinderella's coach and gown, which turned back to pumpkin and rags at midnight, the sense of safety and security we get from money is fleeting—and just as illusory. When we focus on money alone as a solution and convince ourselves that "more money will make things better," all we're doing is temporarily masking our underlying problems.

SALLY: *At the end of every month, my mother, my siblings, and I would go to my father's office to pick up the payday check. He always had cookies and chocolates and we got to eat as many as we wanted. The people who worked there were always friendly and I remember feeling happy and safe. I guess it had to do with the happiness and safety my mother felt that day. That day was the day she got to have the money to plan for the next month. Though, according to her, there was never enough—she always said that she had to perform miracles to feed a family of six with that money—that day was always a day to celebrate.*

Later, in my adolescent years, my dad lost his job. He kept telling us that he'd figure things out, that we shouldn't worry. I believed him, but I still worried. Sure enough, things were okay in terms of our schooling, food, and home. However, we had times of high stress, times when there was a lack of money, and then times of abundance.

It was during these years that my mother emotionally abandoned us. My father began being unfaithful and she was totally preoccupied with that. Our family began to fall apart. My father became very distant. He had rage outbursts that seemed to come out of nowhere and it felt as if we lived with a monster in the house. There was a constant tension.

When my grandmother died, Mom inherited her money and belongings. Until then my mother never had enough money to act on her own. She'd always been economically dependent on my father, and even though their relationship had deteriorated she had to stay. When she got her own money, she built her own house and lived independently, making her own choices about how to use her money and she seemed pretty safe. She still lives there.

A sudden money event—receiving a sizable inheritance—allowed Sally's mother to leave a dissatisfying marriage and gain financial independence. Sally also experienced her father's paydays as times when the whole family was happy and celebrating. It's no surprise that Sally's animal brain would conclude that "more money makes things better." As an adult, that fantasy kept her unconsciously waiting to be saved by a sudden influx of money the way her mother was. "Sometimes I still wish someone could just save me so I could stop worrying," she says. "But fairy tales never come true."

Sally's story shows how easily money can become mentally linked to happiness (even though research shows that this just isn't the case). This money script, left unexamined, can create a life of hoarding, workaholism, and/or a dogged pursuit of money and/or people who have it, above all other things.

COMMON MONEY-WORSHIPING MONEY SCRIPTS
More money/things will make me happier.
You can't trust people about money.
There will never be enough.
It takes money to make money.
Security is boring.
Life is short; live a little.
Somebody has to win, and it might as well be me.
If I just keep trying, my day will come.
I'm just lucky—a winner.
I have to work hard to be sure I have enough money.
If I don't work hard, people will think I am lazy.
My self-worth equals my net worth.
I will never be able to afford the things I really want in life.
It is okay to keep secrets from my partner about money.
Spending money on someone is how you show love.

On March 21, 1947, New York City police received a report of a dead body at 2078 Fifth Avenue at 128th Street. The address was already known to police and neighbors as the residence of "the Hermits of Harlem," elderly brothers Homer and Langley Collyer. The Collyer family had moved into the four-story mansion in 1909, when Harlem was an up-and-coming neighborhood for the white upper-middle class. Homer worked briefly as a lawyer and Langley performed as a concert pianist, but neither brother spent much time in the outside world. After their parents died and as the neighborhood changed around them, the brothers remained in the house, slowly filling all four floors with random, rotting junk. The heaps of trash were mined with elaborate booby traps (some armed with chunks of concrete and jars of urine and excrement) to ward off intruders. By this spring morning, Homer had been blind and bedridden for years; Langley dosed him with hundreds of oranges to restore his sight and saved heaps of newspapers so that Homer could catch up on the news when that happy day arrived. Most nights, Langley ventured out in tattered rags, dragging a box on a rope, in search of new treasures to haul home. Neighborhood kids called him "Ghosty Man."

The officers responding to the call knocked on the door and got no answer. Finally, they chopped a hole in the heavy wooden door. "Fumes foul with age and mildew billowed forth. The police peered into a solid wall of rotting junk amassed over the decades: shattered sawhorses and fractured frying pans, crushed umbrellas and rusted cycles, broken baby carriages and smashed Christmas trees, chipped chandeliers and tattered toys. . . ." Homer's body was found in his bed, but Langley was nowhere to be seen.

A team of professional movers was hired to clear out the tons of debris. They found, among other things, several pianos and an entire disassembled automobile. As they slowly cleared away the piles, the workers noticed an especially unpleasant odor among all the other smells. Sixteen days after his brother's body was found, Langley's corpse was discovered under a pile of newspapers—the apparent victim of a newspaper avalanche.

The Collyer mansion was razed not long afterward; today a tiny park occupies the site. But the brothers' legacy lives on. When New York firefighters get a call to a cluttered, trash-filled apartment, they refer to it as "going out on a Collyer."

Hoarding

The animal kingdom gives us many metaphors for human hoarding, including "squirreling things away." But squirrels often lose track of just where those treasures are buried and so we at least get new, nut-bearing trees out of the deal. Human hoarding has few such benefits.

Compulsive hoarding is another example of an otherwise positive behavior—saving—taken to unhealthy extremes. It's good to save money, but it's also necessary to spend it. It's also good to have extra toilet paper on hand but not stacked to the ceiling. Hoarding behavior can take various forms. For some it is enough to simply hoard money; others have a compulsion to hoard various—and oftentimes bizarre—objects.

Some compulsive hoarders are overspenders or compulsive buyers, but the key difference is that it is the accumulation of the stockpile, not the *act* of buying or spending, that provides the hoarders with safety, security, and relief of anxiety. No matter how useless the objects seem to others, compulsive hoarders are emotionally attached to their possessions— be they magazines, hundred-dollar bills, or Mickey Mouse figurines—and become anxious or overwhelmed at the thought of getting rid of them. If you know a hoarder, you probably know how hard it is to get them to throw or give anything away. Even while the clutter and out-of-control accumulation may cause embarrassment and shame—since hoarders are aware that their anxiety and hoarding behaviors are unreasonable— the accumulated objects become stand-ins for love, affection, or whatever is missing in that person's life. This is why hoarders feel such irrational attachment to their possessions. For the hoarder, these are not just things. They have emotional meaning.

Hoarders may protect their possessions by creating "secret stashes" hidden from family, or they may refuse to allow anyone inside the house to see—and judge—the mess. Hoarders also feel a kind of responsibility toward their objects, believing that simply throwing the stuff away would be an act of treachery. In the hoarder's home, the clutter intrudes on the simple actions of daily living. At its extreme, hoarding makes a home unsafe and unusable: beds and chairs inaccessible, doorways blocked, floors entirely covered.

It's difficult to pinpoint a definitive cause of compulsive hoarding. There's some evidence that it has a genetic component, and can be a symptom of obsessive-compulsive personality disorder. Among the people we see in our practice, hoarders often have a history of childhood scarcity, childhood abandonment or betrayal, or both. For instance, hoarding behavior is common in foster children who come into their foster or adoptive homes from situations of extreme deprivation. We have worked with many foster and adoptive children who kept food hidden in their room, despite having unhindered access to full refrigerators and pantries. Their early experiences taught them that there was never enough to eat, so they developed anxieties over running out and going hungry—anxieties that persisted even after this was no longer a rational worry.

One child had a more unusual hoarding compulsion. He collected and stole over a dozen cell phones from friends and family members and hid them in his room. Many of the phones were broken and none were activated; they were useless to him as phones, but in his mind they were extremely important nonetheless.

Remember Bridget from the introduction? Abandoned by her mother, she was adopted into a loving but unstable family. As a child, she demonstrated classic hoarding behavior.

BRIDGET: *As a small child I would hide money in places around my room. If I got money as Christmas presents or birthday presents, it was always a very small amount and I would squirrel it away. I became very miserlike in my dealings with money. At the same time, I became very suspicious of people who had money. My parents were always very critical of people who had money. They would assert that those people got their money by some less than desirable means. They would make comments like "They can act that way because they have money." Or "Oh, the only reason you'd want to be friends with that person is because they have money and you don't."*

Bridget outgrew her childhood hoarding behavior, as many children do. But even though she was no longer compelled to keep a stash of hidden coins, her emotional relationship with money remained troubled; she associated money with both security and shame.

Like financial disorders in general, hoarding behavior can be triggered by events far less dramatic than parental abandonment. Lewis had a privileged upbringing, yet he often felt emotionally distant from his parents. As a child, he learned that he could connect with them through their interest in collecting. As an adult, this comforting emotional association with objects continued. Lewis's collecting soon outdid his parents', to the point that his friends and family teased him about it. He collected everything: art, sculpture, old sinks, old mirrors, used furniture, used pots and pans, walking sticks, newspapers—*everything*.

LEWIS: *Mother and Daddy collected things. They took me with them out into the country or antique shops and I was a little bitty boy, pretty rambunctious, and so they started me collecting little glass jars that mustard used to come in. They sold for a nickel or a dime. That gave me something in the store to look for and kept me busy and out of trouble. It always felt relaxing to me as an adult to go collecting things. It was a good way to unwind. So I took collecting to an abnormal level.*

I believe that stems too from my father being sort of a hoarder. During World War II there were things that were hard to find, sugar or canned pineapple, things like that. Throughout my life my father always bought things in bulk, toilet paper, canned goods, and that type of thing. He never talked about running out. His behaviors were just accepted, though other people in the family would make fun of his habits behind his back. Just like my family made fun of mine. I think I learned some of those behaviors from him.

Though Lewis himself didn't experience the tumultuous and economically strained years of economic collapse and wartime scarcity, he was still influenced by those times, since he observed and imitated his father's behavior. As we discussed in chapter 4, the economic experiences of childhood form the financial habits we cling to into adulthood. The Great Depression and the wartime shortages that followed created many compulsive hoarders: people who washed and saved used aluminum foil, stashed hundred-dollar bills in coffee cans hidden all over the house, and mistrusted and avoided financial institutions for decades. Let's hope the current financial situation doesn't end up creating another generation, or more, of compulsive hoarders.

Unreasonable Risk Taking

Betting on the horses or playing roulette is risk taking for entertainment, and within reason there's nothing wrong with that. But when risk taking becomes excessive, it can be very damaging. Here, we're defining excessive as putting one's financial well-being at unnecessary risk in the pursuit of large, but unlikely, gains—like taking your rent money or your child's college fund to the race track, or the broker's office.

But there are many other forms of unreasonable risk taking besides what is conventionally thought of as gambling. Trying to time the stock market through day trading is one; another is investing in high-risk "double your money" schemes. There are also even less obvious ways of taking unnecessary risks with your money and your financial well-being. You might write large checks before the money to cover them is in the bank, or you might spend an anticipated bonus or salary increase before you actually receive it. These are gambles of sorts, too, in that you could find yourself in trouble if for some unforeseen reason that check you're owed, or bonus or salary increase you're promised doesn't come about. Whether it's at the black-jack table or the mall, it's incredibly risky to spend money you don't actually have in your possession, period.

People are prone to taking excessive risks for many reasons. Some are trying to make up for lost time or previous market losses. Others risk more than is prudent following a lucky streak, overestimating the odds of ongoing good fortune. Iron-ically, risk taking can also be the result of pessimistic or fatal-istic thinking: "I'll probably lose what I've got anyway so why not risk it all?" Many others use excessive risk taking to self-medicate and reduce feelings of emptiness, depression, or anxiety; the adrenaline high they get from the experience helps them temporarily feel energized, connected, and whole.

You'll remember from chapter 2 that our brains tend to see patterns or connections where none exist, which causes us to overestimate the impact our actions have on a particular event or outcome. Many excessive risk takers take this to extremes, interpreting one big win as evidence of their skill or savvy rather that what it is—luck. As a result, they'll continue to take one risk after another, believing that they are smarter than the market or have what it takes to beat the odds. These overconfident risk takers are *sure* they're right, that their next big investment will be the one that hits. Most have a story they love to tell about the guy they know who risked it all and won big. They are sensation seekers addicted to the thrill of the chase, excited about the next big scheme. This isn't the only motivation for excessive risk taking but it's a very common one. Certainly it was a big part of what drove Stuart's behavior.

STUART: *Though my mom would say, "Money doesn't grow on trees," it did for me as an adolescent and young adult. By this time Dad was doing pretty well and I didn't have to live in the real world, financially. Dad paid off a car I couldn't afford and shouldn't have purchased. While I was in college, Mom would send me care packages that would include hundred-dollar bills. So, emotionally, the financial roller-coaster ride that my family was on didn't seem to be a big deal for me at the time.*

I went to Wall Street straight from college and made a ton of money. When my company consolidated with another I got a big payout. As a stock analyst I made a lot more money. All that is gone now, a result of a number of bad, high-leveraged investments. Without realizing it, I was repeating my dad's experience.

As an adult, until recently, I still lived my mom and dad's arguments. I would say, "I know it looks bad but we'll make it, just you watch," and my wife would say, "No, we're not. Please, no more risks." I would ignore her and just go make some more investments.

Perhaps the most crippling and destructive of these scripts has been that "money comes easy if you're smarter than the next guy." That made me overconfident. I believed I knew how it all worked. My belief was that by looking ahead, I could see the turn in the road before the next guy could. I was very, very wrong, but I didn't know it yet.

Though the family lived in modest circumstances when he was a child, Stuart was protected from financial reality later in life, after his father became very successful. Emulating his father's drive, Stuart soon became overconfident, attributing his successes solely to his own ability instead of crediting the long bull market. Many studies in behavioral economics have shown that this is a common reaction, and that overconfident traders initiate more trades than their more restrained, realistic counterparts, which can create the illusion that they are beating the market. But in reality this volatility tends to reduce their profits in the long run.

Pathological Gambling

Pathological gambling is excessive risk taking exaggerated to an especially destructive extreme. For pathological gamblers, gambling becomes like an addictive drug. They gamble to make themselves feel better or escape from their problems and, like an alcoholic who needs more and more alcohol to feel drunk, they need to gamble with more and more money to keep it exciting. They often hide their gambling from others and may engage in illegal acts to help fund their gambling. As much as 5 percent of the population experiences gambling problems at some time in their lives and up to 2 percent become pathological gamblers.

Research has shown that a trauma history and symptoms of posttraumatic stress are strong predictors of pathological gambling and that trauma treatment can result in a significant decrease in pathological gambling behaviors. Financial flashpoints reported by the gamblers we have worked with typically include a time when they first witnessed or experienced the thrill of winning. Often, it starts with small lucky streaks, although they did not see it as luck; they were convinced they had some innate sense of how to beat the system. They become addicted to that feeling of being successful, which also provides temporary emotional relief from feelings of anxiety, and are convinced they can repeat their successes. And so, no matter how much they lose, they keep on trying.

AARON: *I will never forget my first slot machine experience. It was Super Bowl Sunday and there were very few people in the slot area of the casino. I had never been to Las Vegas and a friend took me to a famous casino on the strip. He showed me how the slot machines worked and wandered off. I started with ten dollars worth of quarters. I'd lost about two dollars when the machine locked up when I pulled it. There were buzzers going off, alarms ringing, and I was freaked out. I considered slowly walking away, because I figured the machine had registered a "slug," a fake coin. I looked around and my friend was nowhere to be seen. Other people were staring at me. I knew that they had video cameras in the ceiling so they would catch me if I ran away, so I just stayed still and hoped that everything would die down. Then a security guard came up to me and said, "You know what you've just done, don't you?"*

I said "Officer, it's not what you think! I was just using the coins from the roll of quarters a friend of mine gave me."

The guard said, "Where is this friend of yours?" I said I didn't know, and the guard looked at me as if I was lying. He asked me again if I knew what I had done, and I assured him that I didn't. He said, "Well, we have a problem here."

I was shaking in my boots. I figured they believed I was trying to cheat them and, having just recently watched the movie Casino, *I was afraid I'd end up dead somewhere in the desert. The guard did something to the machine that produced a piece of paper and shut the machine down and said, "Come with me." Everyone was staring at me while I walked in front of him toward a cagelike area. He conferred with a guy behind the counter, handed him the slip of paper, and then motioned for me to walk up to the window and said, "You've just won the jackpot; this man will give you your money." The clerk just nodded and started counting out hundred-dollar bills, twelve of them. Twelve hundred dollars, from spending two. Unbelievable. I was hooked.*

I eventually found my friend and told him about the jackpot, and he started treating me like I knew what I was doing. Over time I became known as the guy who had luck with the slot machines. I actually thought I knew how they worked, which ones would be "hot," which casinos paid off the best. That's how my gambling addiction got started.

Pathological gambling is one of the more self-destructive disorders discussed in this book. If you think you might be at risk for pathological gambling, we highly recommend that you seek the help of a mental health professional and check out the 12-step recovery program Gamblers Anonymous (www.gamblers anonymous.org).

Workaholism

Workaholism is one of the few addictions that our society values and that people are quick to claim, even take pride in. Yet it is just as damaging as any other out-of-control habit. Workaholics are so immersed in work they have little time to invest in family life, child rearing, leisure, and even sleep; as a result, they experience more marital discord, anxiety, depression, job stress, job dissatisfaction, and health problems.

Workaholism can stem from another fairy godmother script, the belief that more money will make you and your family happier, prove your self-worth, make you a valuable, capable, lovable human being. But this is a fool's errand. Just as money is no guarantee of happiness or safety, it's also no measure of one's worth as a human being. If you're depending on money to satisfy this kind of deep emotional need, you will never earn enough or have enough. You'll get stuck on an endless treadmill, working harder and harder to make more and more money to achieve happiness as it falls further and further out of reach. Devoting your life exclusively to work and monetary success is *not* a way to achieve happiness. As we've mentioned, decades of social science research have demonstrated that once your income lifts you above poverty, there is absolutely no direct correlation between money and happiness; those who earn fifty thousand dollars a year per household are not necessarily any less or any more happy than those who earn five million dollars a year.

Pursuit of money, however, is only one aspect of workaholism—and often not the primary one. If you are a workaholic, the chances are that you feel better about yourself at work than you do in any other part of your life. You probably have better-quality relationships there, and feel more competent, in control, successful, comfortable, and more a part of things at work than anywhere else. Workaholics often have an unconscious belief that they have to be productive in order to have any value, so the more they work, the more valuable they feel. They believe that the best way to be responsible to their loved ones is to work hard and sacrifice themselves to work, when in fact the opposite is true; their families often end up resenting the fact that they put work first.

Like any other addict, workaholics use work to cope with feelings of emotional pain and inadequacy. They get adrenaline highs from work binges and then they crash from exhaustion, leading to feelings of irritability, low self-esteem, anxiety, and depression. To cope with these feelings, they then fall into another cycle of excessive devotion to work. Much like any other addictive substance, work becomes the only thing that can calm them, quiet their inner demons.

Workaholism is often a family disease (as you read about in our own family history), because workaholics tend to pass down—deliberately or otherwise—their unrealistic and unattainable perfectionist standards to their children with comments like

"Five A's and one B? What's the B about?" As a result, their children feel like failures. They grow up convinced they are inadequate, that they are valuable only to the degree that they can be successful and productive, and so they may attempt to compensate for these feelings by losing themselves in work or some other addictive substance or behavior.

But like so many other disorders, workaholism can also be the result of a reaction to the opposite extreme: a parent or other influential adult who didn't work enough. A child who, consciously or not, develops resentment or contempt for a lazy parent may swing to the other extreme of overworking.

> LESLIE: *My mom and dad divorced when I was very young. My dad worked hard when he worked, but he'd always take voluntary layoffs. Though he'd tell me that there wasn't enough money to pay for whatever I needed, he would take a layoff and be pretty much free to do whatever he wanted to do. My mom was on welfare. I lived with her for a brief period of time and decided that I didn't really want to live that life either.*
>
> *I decided I wasn't going to be like my parents. I was going to be successful and look successful. I worked hard; at one moment in time I had both a full-time job and a part-time job, I was going to college full time, and I was managing an apartment building. I was a good worker. But I worked too hard. Because it was hard to trust people, I didn't have a lot of friends, so I gave up myself for whoever I was working for. I'd put in sixty hours a week and do whatever they asked me to do, even if it compromised my beliefs. Once while working for a public company, I was asked to sign a document in someone else's name, commit forgery, and I did it. There weren't many boundaries.*

In her pursuit of financial security and success, Leslie abandoned her true self. She had few friends and poured all her desire for connection into her work and her colleagues.

This also led her to violate the standards of right and wrong—her own and society's at large. Instead of improving her self-worth by increasing her net worth, Leslie's unbalanced approach to building wealth by working herself to the ground did just the opposite.

Our client Paul, whose baby brother died at birth, grew up hating and resenting rich people and money itself; at the same time, he keenly felt the shame of being poor and was determined that his own family would never experience it. So "work harder" became his response to every situation.

PAUL: *At one time I worked one full-time and five part-time jobs. I'd say, "I think I want that thing for my wife and kids. I'll work harder." Rather than working smarter, I just kept working harder and harder.*

The cost of all this—and I certainly didn't know it at the time—was that I wasn't really available, physically or emotionally, for my wife and my children. I was constantly going, working, doing; not taking care of myself; not being there for my first wife and my kids. All that frantic working to attain monetary success cheated me in the relationships I could have had with them. I don't know if it would have made a lot of difference with my first wife, but I am certain it would have with the kids. I picked up that driven-ness from my father and unfortunately my son has picked it up from me. He's got gobs of money but I see that drive of "I gotta be doin', I gotta be doin', I gotta be doin' " playing out in his life, too, and sadly I see what that is costing my grandchildren and daughter-in-law.

Overspending

In the years preceding the current economic downturn, Americans' average savings rate dropped as low as *negative* 0.5 percent, the lowest since the Great Depression. We were actually spending more than we earned, and so of course we carried more debt per household than ever before. In the past few decades, we have become a nation of overspenders; overspending has become the American way of life, both individually and collectively, and we're paying the price now. These days, many of us who have debt are slaves to it; we're caught in a cycle we desperately need to break. Recently, savings rates in the United States have seen an increase, a hopeful sign that many Americans may have hit a financial bottom and are ready to take an honest look at their overspending and make some positive changes.

Overspenders are trying to achieve feelings of safety, comfort, affection, and wholeness by spending excessively on themselves and others. In our work with overspenders, many report financial flashpoints where giving or receiving a present seemed to transform a relationship. Another common flashpoint is having experienced deprivation, or a time in their childhood when not having a particular item made an emotional impact; they were teased and bullied for not having the "right" clothing, or they convinced themselves that if they'd only received the one possession they craved, they finally would've been happy. Many overspending clients say, "Then and there, I decided that I would do whatever I had to do to get those things." People who overspend on their children tell us, "I resolved to never have my children feel the way I did that day."

Often, extreme confusion about money can result in overspending.

> ALLISON: *I got so many conflicting messages about what money is, how it works, and whether or not I should fear it. I was always afraid of having money, as if its presence was an issue. But the flip side was the other belief, that I had to have money or I'd live in fear. I worked incredibly hard, to the point of missing out on a*

lot of life, to have money. The fear of not having money was a real motivator. I so desperately wanted my own independence that I worked really hard to get the money I associated with that. But then I couldn't stand having it. I'd blow it all on clothes or new furniture, or treating everyone to an expensive dinner, or a week-end trip somewhere. Or I'd just give it away—anything so that I wouldn't have to deal with it. I got so tired of being a slave to my debt. I'd hear friends my age talk about their nest eggs and their futures, and I didn't have those things and didn't know how to get them. I had no idea that the cycle I was in was something I could break.

Overspenders like Allison have confused and confusing re-lationships with money. On one hand, they're convinced that money and the things it can buy will make them happy; yet they are often broke because they can't control their spending, then full of anxiety because of their financial problems. You read earlier about Allison's family history, with their extreme back-and-forths between ignoring and obsessing over money. This is a common background for overspenders.

Other overspenders simply convince themselves that money is unimportant, so why not spend it freely? Consider Stephanie, who also grew up with mixed messages about money. After a divorce, she became poverty stricken and homeless, but once she got back on her feet she began to spend uncontrollably.

STEPHANIE: *Another thing that impacted my financial views was that a colleague who had inherited quite a bit of money would often say, "It's only money." I liked this statement and took it to heart. It gave me a false sense of freedom. I wanted to believe that money was something I could always get more of. That state-ment gave me permission to toss money around in a too-careless way. My feeling was, I had finally come through a rough, rough*

*time, and now I could let down my guard. My colleague never
told me her whole money situation, but I know that she had inherited a large sum, which was not my situation at all. All I knew
was that I wanted to be like her and have no worries.*

Stephanie's "Money is not important" script may have
helped her feel better about her financial situation in the short
term, but in the long run it only encouraged her overspending
and prevented her from coming up with a reasonable financial
plan for her future. There's also an element of "magical thinking" about her behavior, as if by adopting her colleague's
motto, she could become like the colleague, complete with a
sizable inheritance.

One sign of an overspender is the emphasis that's placed on
the *act* of spending. Overspenders often use the process of
buying and shopping to feel connected to others and themselves. Spenders often have a "community" that connects
around the activity of shopping: favorite stores and the people
who work there, shopping buddies, or online social groups focused on shopping. Overspenders may also build rituals
around shopping, such as eating lunch at a certain place or
visiting stores in a certain order. Some feel like the clerks at
their favorite stores are their friends. After all, the clerks know
them on a first-name basis and make special personal calls
with early notice of special deals, just as a friend would. When
favored clients arrive at the store, they're greeted with smiles
and special attention. Their good taste is reinforced. They
hold special "gold" or "platinum" cards or status, and they see
that their purchases make the people at the stores happy. They
feel special, important, and loved.

Online spending can be just as addictive. It may not have as
many personal interactions but it does have one big advantage:
It's available twenty-four hours a day. And it's not entirely without rewarding one-on-one experiences. We had one client who

did her shopping almost exclusively online. So the UPS and FedEx couriers came to her house on a regular basis, and she considered them her friends. She joked—accurately—that day to day, she saw more of them and had more friendly inter-actions and longer conversations with them than with her husband.

Overspending can become a vicious cycle. Overspenders experience an irresistible impulse to spend; they lose control over their spending, and then, to ease the anxiety over having lost control, continue to buy. If left unchecked, overspenders are at risk for developing compulsive buying disorder.

Compulsive Buying Disorder

Compulsive buying disorder is overspending on steroids. If overspenders are often worried about money, compulsive shoppers are constantly consumed by their money worries. Ironically, one of their only escapes is the act of shopping itself and so they obsess about it, experience irresistible impulses to do it, and lose control of their spending. Often, early in their lives, compulsive buyers learned that the ritual of shopping provides a temporary escape, whether from a traumatic past, depression, dissatisfaction with their relationship or life, or feelings of emptiness. To fill the emotional void, shopping be-comes like a drug, just as work is for workaholics. When com-pulsive buyers think about and anticipate the pleasure they will feel when they shop, dopamine, a "feel good" chemical, floods their brains—only to wear off quickly, leaving them craving another fix. Shopping can offer such a tremendous thrill for them, they literally get the sensation of being high. Soon after, however, they feel the inevitable emotional crash, which usually comes in the form of low self-esteem and buyer's remorse. When left untreated, compulsive buying can lead to excessive debt, financial strain, bankruptcy, relationship problems, divorce, problems concentrating at work, and in some cases, legal complications.

Unfortunately, in our consumer-oriented culture, compulsive buying is a relatively common problem. It afflicts one in twenty people in the United States (approximately the same rate as clinical depression) and over 75 percent of compulsive shoppers are women. The prevalence of compulsive buying also appears to be on the rise, especially among adolescents; a recent study of high school students found that 44 percent met some of the criteria for compulsive buying.

We should note here that in some cases compulsive buying takes a surprising twist: The shopper seldom actually buys anything. The problem here is not the spending but the inordinate amount of time and energy expended in the process of shopping (at the expense of jobs, relationships, and other productive activities), whether it be going to actual stores, looking through catalogs, watching the home shopping channels, cruising the Internet, or some combination.

Compulsive buying, like most other addictive and compulsive disorders, has been successfully treated with a variety of approaches including psychotherapy, psychotropic medications, and support groups such as Debtors Anonymous.

If you're having difficulty controlling your spending, insert some space between your impulse to buy and your buying behavior. Let's say that you realize that you're trying to fulfill an emotional need by making the purchase. What then? Try brainstorming healthier ways to meet that goal, such as talking to a friend, journaling about your thoughts and feelings, or having a good cry. Whenever you do go shopping, leave the credit cards at home and take cash. Research shows we spend approximately 30 percent less when we buy with cash instead of credit cards or gift cards.

8

Relational Money Disorders

The disorders in this category—financial infidelity, financial incest, financial enabling, and financial dependency—claim multiple victims. In other words, people suffering from them often wreak havoc on the emotional and financial lives of others, in addition to their own, through their disordered behavior. These disorders are also very much tangled up in relationships—and emotions over one's relationships—with others. People with these disorders are often secretive or dishonest about money, even with their loved ones.

In keeping with the fairy-tale theme, these are what we think of as "locked room scripts," from the old French fairy tale of Bluebeard. In the story, Bluebeard is a rich but nasty nobleman with a frightening blue beard. He's brought six wives home to his castle, but one after another, each wife disappears without a trace. Finally he marries a local girl, giving her parents a sack of gold. She has the run of the castle, except for one room behind a heavy locked door. Bluebeard forbids her from ever entering the room or even asking about it;

of course, she's overcome with curiosity. Soon, Bluebeard goes away on a trip, leaving his young wife with the keys to the castle. He warns her not to unlock the door to the secret room. She tries to resist, but soon enough she unlocks the door to find the bloody bodies of her six predecessors. Bluebeard catches her and tries to kill her, too, but her brothers hear her cries and come to her defense, killing the violent Bluebeard instead. Stories like this (another is the myth of Pandora's box) reinforce the notion that we all have dangerous or shameful secrets, things that those close to us are better off not knowing.

Two relational money disorders—enabling and dependency— also incorporate elements of the "Prince Charming" fairy tales by investing money with a transformative power to control or rescue oneself or others. Yet they also share in the "locked box" theme of the powerful, even fearsome, secrecy surrounding money. Enablers promote and dependents absorb a sense of money as a mysterious and pervasive influence, and both are prone to hiding the extent of their giving and receiving from others out of a sense of shame or guilt.

For many people money is a deep source of shame and secrecy, so much so that talking about it is one of the last taboos in our society. You probably know people who feel comfortable telling you, in great detail, about their sex lives or digestive problems, and yet they huff, "That's none of your business!" if you ask how much money they make.

Very often the secrets persist even within families. We've worked with many people who, even as adults, have no idea how much their parents make or made. While parents shouldn't burden their young children with details and difficulties of the family finances, it's equally unhealthy to treat money as such a shameful secret that it can't even be mentioned. The money scripts that result are some of the most common ones, and they can exert great influence not only on us but on those close to us, at great cost. Consider these stories:

CAROLE: *I felt that definitely money was a secret. I witnessed my sister being severely disciplined, actually slapped in the face by our mom and sent to her room, after she came home from a high school economics class and asked, "How much money does Dad make?" I had never seen my mother that angry.*

Once, when I was twenty-three, I had to sign a legal document regarding the insurance for a fund my father had set up. I was trying to learn about finances and I wanted information. I was curious and I asked what something meant. My father was furious. He said, "It means sign this or you'll have a bear on your hands." I later learned from my sister, who had found out from her husband, that I had an option to not sign the paper and then I could cash in a certain amount, because I was over twenty-one. And my father was angrily assuming that that's what I wanted to do.

The lesson I learned from all this is "Don't talk about money. It's a secret." And then, "Ask about money and you'll be seen as a greedy person." As a result, I stopped asking anything about money.

Despite her attempts to teach herself about financial matters, Carole never became comfortable handling, discussing, or even thinking about money. Once she was living on her own, she wasted a great deal of her inheritance and at one point ended up declaring bankruptcy. Aimee, too, was confronted with a wall of silence when she tried to inform herself about the family's finances.

AIMEE: *My parents never told me how much money we had. The answer to that question was always, "Enough." When I was six-*

teen and applying for scholarships, I asked my father for help with filling out the forms and he said, "Don't bother; I make too much money."

"How much is too much, Dad?"

"Just . . . too much."

So what I learned very early is that you should keep secrets about money, even within the family.

If a child grows up with the idea that money is something that can't be talked about, then is it any wonder that as an adult he or she will be secretive or dishonest about it, even with loved ones? This is part of the real damage that comes from surrounding the issue of money in silence and shame, even within the family.

Relational money disorders can also arise when money is used as a means to control others. This happens most often in families; sadly, parents trying to control their children by bestowing or withholding money is an all too common phenomenon.

Because money is such a powerful influence in modern society, it can easily become an instrument of abuse. We heard a heart-wrenching story from a woman named Rita, who grew up with a mother who suffered from severe and untreated mental illness. Rita's mother was paranoid and manipulative and often used money to try to control her only daughter.

RITA: *As a child, I always knew my mother wasn't like other mothers. She never hugged anyone or said "I love you," and she would sometimes go entire days without saying a word to me or my father. She was paranoid about everything—someone was always trying to steal from her or take advantage of her. And she was incredibly controlling, demanding to know where I was and who I was with at all times, even though I was a good kid and was usually alone, at the library or anywhere else I could think of to go just to get out of the house.*

Growing up in Israel in the '60s, we didn't have a whole lot of money—no one did, then—but we had enough to get by. Of course, my mother insisted on being in charge of the family finances, and she guarded every penny like it was Fort Knox. She knew that if I didn't have any money, I couldn't go to movies or cafés with friends, and she could control where I went and what I did at all times. The first time I ever remember her giving me any money was when my father got sick with terminal brain cancer, and she gave me bus fare to go visit him in the hospital. I'd never had any spending money before, though, and I couldn't bear to waste it just on taking the bus. So I would walk to the hospital and spend the money on treats for myself—like used books or a stick of sugarcane. (Such a wonderfully rare treat! I can still taste the grainy sweetness.) The only problem was that it was a good three or four miles to the hospital and took close to an hour to walk, which meant that I barely had any time to spend with my father. Looking back, I realize how many of his last precious minutes I wasted walking back and forth just to have a little pocket change, and I can't forgive myself. I was about thirteen or fourteen years old at the time.

COMMON RELATIONAL MONEY-DISORDER MONEY SCRIPTS

Take care of your children now and they'll take care of you later.

You can tell how much someone loves you by how much they spend on you.

If you hold others financially responsible, they will reject you.

Spending money on others gives my life meaning.

One of the ways to keep friends and family close is to give them gifts and loan them money.

There will always be someone I can turn to for money.

I'm not competent enough to take care of myself financially.

I don't need to learn how to manage money.

It's my duty to take care of less fortunate family members.

Financial Infidelity

Given our complex relationships with money, it is not surprising that people keep secrets about it. In fact, many couples avoid talking about money *because* it is such an emotionally loaded issue. When secrecy or dishonesty over money persists in a relationship, it can become the disorder we call financial infidelity: deliberately and surreptitiously keeping a major secret about one's spending or finances from one's partner. When we talk about financial infidelity, we mean keeping significant financial secrets, such as making purchases outside an agreed-upon budget or lying about the cost of a big-ticket item. Some people even take out a second mortgage, cash out a 401(k), or make risky investments without their partners' approval or awareness. These are all cases of financial infidelity.

When financial infidelity is discovered, it rocks the very foundation of the relationship, eroding any semblance of trust. When a person's lies about secret money behaviors come to light, the other partner will inevitably ask him or herself, consciously and unconsciously, "If they're lying to me about this behavior, what else are they lying about?" And even if the financial infidelity isn't discovered, it's unhealthy to live a life full of secrecy and deceit.

Often, financial infidelity stems from the fact that trust is already absent in the relationship, for reasons having nothing to do with money. We knew one woman, for example, who suspected her husband might be cheating on her, though she had no evidence to support it. Worried about what might happen to her financially if he were to leave or divorce her, she opened up a secret checking account in her name only. For years, she squirreled away any extra money she got her hands on into this account—including a fairly sizable inheritance from a deceased aunt that she neglected to tell her husband about. She never spent any of the money, and her husband probably never would have found out about the account, if the IRS hadn't come knocking. Turns out, she hadn't been paying taxes on the interest or on the inherited money, and when the family was audited she was forced to come clean. Her husband was understandably furious at what he saw as an enormous betrayal of trust, and the rift took years to mend.

Ironically, the fact that money is the number one area of conflict in relationships is one reason why financial infidelity is alarmingly common. In our practice, we've seen many instances of financial infidelity. One woman deliberately scratched up the soles of her new shoes so that when her husband asked, "Did you just buy those?" she could simply show him the scuffed soles and say, "Do these look new to you?" She rationalized this as "not really lying" since she didn't actually deny that the shoes were new. Another woman hid the cost of her purchases by paying partially in cash; her husband saw the checks for the false, smaller amounts and was fooled into thinking she bought only bargain items. One man forged his wife's signature on fraudulent tax returns, and another lied to his fiancée about his disastrous financial condition until after they were married. Yet another secretly took out credit cards and had the statements mailed to a coconspirator's address.

These people demonstrated classic gender patterns in their acts of financial infidelity. In a survey of 1,001 people commissioned by *Money* magazine, 40 percent of the respondents, both men and women, admitted that they have told their partner that they paid less for a purchase than they actually did, and 16 percent confessed to buying something that they did not want their spouse to know about. But while both men and woman admitted to financial dishonesty, their methods were different. Women were more likely to tell their husbands that they paid less than they actually did for clothing and gifts, while men lied about their spending on cars, entertainment, and sporting events. Almost twice as many men admitted that they had spent over a thousand dollars without their wife's knowledge, while women were more likely to say that the most they had spent without telling their husbands was one hundred dollars.

If, as we have seen, lying or being deceitful about money causes so many problems, why do so many people continue to do it? For many, the behavior stems from trust issues rooted in childhood. This was the case with the woman with the secret bank account; growing up, her mother was secretive and untrustworthy, and as a result she had profound difficulties trusting those closest to her. In other cases, the behavior is a result of poor communication skills, a history of betrayal in adulthood, or the desire to avoid conflict. Forty-five percent of those who admitted being deceitful around spending stated that they were not honest about their spending in order to avoid their partner's anticipated anger, disapproval, or lecturing.

Financial deception doesn't only happen between spouses or partners. We know of a young man in college who was totally self-supporting. When he finally applied for a grant, at age twenty-four, he found out that he didn't qualify because his father was still claiming him as a dependent, and his father's income was far too high. He was understandably deeply hurt, and the incident drove a huge wedge between him and his father.

Financial infidelity is such a common issue in our work with couples that we developed a four-step process for addressing it. It uses the acronym SAFE.

S: *Speak your truth.* We've discussed the taboos and the shame that often short-circuit any conversation about money. That makes it all the more important that you resist your temptation to avoid discussing money issues. The first step to establishing financial safety in your relationship is to sit down with your partner and talk openly about money—what it means to you, your early money experiences, your preferred spending/saving style, and your financial goals.

A: *Agree to a plan.* Many acts of financial infidelity occur among couples who lack explicit agreed-upon strategies of spending and saving. A spending plan is an essential component of a healthy financial relationship. It is helpful for couples to agree on the amount of money that each can spend on a single purchase or recurring purchase (like groceries) without needing to consult with their partner. When a potential purchase goes above the agreed-upon amount, the couple should agree to consult with each other prior to making it.

F: *Follow the agreement.* It sounds obvious, but this is the hardest part. An agreement is only as good as a couple's commitment to honoring it. It is helpful in the beginning to set up a trial period of thirty to sixty days. After the agreed-upon period of time, the couple should meet and answer these three questions: Is the plan working for me? Is it working for you? Is it working for our relationship? If either person answers no to any of these questions, the couple should renegotiate their plan, and form an alternative one that they can stick to.

E: *Establish an emergency response plan.* If couples find that they can't talk about money without fighting, can't come to an agreement, or can't *keep* their agreements about money, they may be in trouble—and not just financially. As such, it is important to have an emergency response plan for when these types of difficulties arise. This plan should identify, ahead of time, what the couple will do if they arrive at an impasse or cannot arrive at or adhere to a plan. For example, the emergency response plan might include an agreement to seek help from a psychologist, pastor, social worker, counselor, or marriage and family therapist.

With money being the number one cause of marital conflict and the number one cause of divorce in the early years of marriage, couples simply cannot afford to be financially unfaithful. Even if you're not currently having these kinds of issues with your partner, it can't hurt to use the SAFE process to establish an agreement around money to ensure you maintain financial fidelity in your relationship.

If you are the partner of someone who has engaged in acts of financial infidelity, it's important to look at your own behaviors as well. Many times, financial cheaters feel the need to lie about or hide perfectly reasonable expenditures because they are married to a financial bully—someone who uses money to control and intimidate his or her partner. While the financial cheater must take responsibility for his or her lack of integrity, the financial bully must also take responsibility for helping create an environment that encourages it. There is nothing to be gained from playing the victim, and it may be useful for you to take a long hard look at the relationship. Consider whether you might have done something to contribute to or exacerbate the erosion of trust. Be mindful of your own actions and whether or not you may be unintentionally encouraging dishonesty in the relationship. In our experience, it's extremely rare that all the blame lies on one side.

Financial Incest

Yes, the term is shocking—and so are the consequences. *Financial incest* is a phrase we've coined for describing what we've seen in a significant number of clients: using money to control or manipulate one's child or to satisfy some adult need. The word *incest*, of course, connotes sexual abuse and while financial incest is neither sexual nor physical, it is psychologically abusive, and it can be extremely emotionally scarring and damaging for the child. Consider the following example.

> KRISTEN: *Mother never forgave me for this. My mother bought me a horse, against my father's wishes and without his permission, and she made me swear I wouldn't tell him about it. I loved this horse. I used to go out to the farm where it was kept and ride and play with my friends who also had horses.*
>
> *One day I was sitting at the dinner table, because now we were old enough to start having dinners with our parents. When we were little, we never ate with our parents, but when we were twelve or thirteen sometimes we'd have dinners with them. One evening I remembered I had to go feed my horse. I said, "Can I be excused? I have to go feed my horse." In that moment, I had forgotten I wasn't supposed to tell. My dad said, "What horse?" My mother and I got into big trouble. My dad was really upset and he gave my mother a hard time for months. Eventually, he relented, but I was between them on that one. I probably thought I could protect my mom from dad's wrath. To this day, fifty years later, my mom has not forgiven me for telling him about the horse. She still brings it up, though Dad passed away five years ago.*

In this case, Kristen's mother compounded financial infidelity—making a purchase she knew her husband wouldn't approve of—with financial incest—enlisting her young daughter in a conspiracy to keep the purchase secret. She inappropriately involved Kristen in emotional and financial issues that should have been dealt with between the two adults. Another example of financial incest is when parents use their children as human shields when bill collectors come calling, telling them to answer the phone or door with lies about where the adults are. Another all too common example is when parents use a child as a messenger to negotiate financial situations. This is a frequent experience in families where high-conflict divorces have taken place. Consider Colin's story.

> COLIN: *I gave up asking for anything as a kid because when I wanted to do anything, take skating lessons, for example, I would ask my mom. She'd say, "Go ask your dad; his child support isn't enough to pay for extra stuff like that." I would go ask Dad, and he'd say, "Tell your mom that she'd have enough money to pay for your lessons if she didn't spend it on new clothes for herself." I was eight years old.*

Financial incest arises when a parent can't adequately distinguish between his or her needs and those of the child. Kristen's mother felt neglected by her father and resented his spending constraints; instead of discussing the situation with her husband, she acted out and drew in her daughter for emotional support. Instead of answering Colin with "Your mother and I will talk about that later," his parents were unable to resist venting their anger at each other, with him as the innocent bystander who's injured the most.

So why would a parent use a child in such a manner? It's not always conscious; financial incest is often triggered when an adult has unfinished business of their own, perhaps owing to a blurring of parent–child boundaries in their own childhood. It can also occur when a parent doesn't feel that they have a satisfying adult connection to their partner, so they compensate by making the child their confidant.

Like other forms of emotional abuse, being forced as a child to take on an adult role in handling finances can have very painful long-term effects. Remember that children develop erroneous or damaging beliefs and assumptions about money in their struggle to make sense of the frightening and confusing adult world; therefore, the more confusing adult experiences or responsibilities a child is forced to confront, the more unhealthy scripts and behaviors he or she is likely to develop. A common effect is difficulty recognizing or meeting one's own needs; the role of caretaker comes much more naturally. It is not uncommon for children who have some "success" in the caretaker role to develop a sense of extraordinary financial responsibility for their families for the rest of their lives. Another is a deep-seated feeling of inadequacy, the sense that you'll never be able to do enough, which means you'll never *be* enough. And, as with other forms of abuse, adults who've experienced financial incest are more likely to reenact it with their own children.

If you have slipped into financial incest with one of your children, it is not too late to make things right. Typically it is a sign that you are overwhelmed and do not have an adequate support system. Take your worries, anxieties, frustrations, and financial stress to a therapist or adviser, and avoid involving your children in issues that you have not resolved yourself. If your child is old enough, it's appropriate to say something to the effect of "You know, I involved you in my money stuff in a way that isn't right, and I am sorry. If you ever feel that I'm doing that again, please let me know." Tell a trusted friend, family member, or adviser that you're trying to change this behavior and have them serve as an accountability partner.

Financial Enabling

Financial enabling involves an irrational need to give money to others, whether you can afford it or not, and even when it is not in the other's long-term best interest; having trouble or finding it impossible to say no to requests for money; and/or perhaps even sacrificing your own financial well-being for the sake of others. The classic example is parents financially taking care of their adult children who should be able to support themselves, often to the detriment of both parents and children. This seems to be a growing issue, in part because the baby boomers have more disposable wealth than earlier generations, and in part because we live in a society where a prolonged adolescence is becoming more and more common.

Financial enabling often results from scripts that equate money with love. Financial enablers use money in an attempt to assuage guilt over past wrongs or slights, to feel close to others, and to continue feeling important and useful. They use money to keep loved ones close, sometimes to keep them beholden, to stay in control. More often than not, their intentions are good, but the results are not. Like someone who buys an alcoholic a drink to help his buddy's hand stop trembling, the financial enabler may relieve an immediate problem only to worsen the more significant one underlying it. This attempt to help only serves to extend the suffering of the person they are trying to help—the financial dependent—and make the inevitable crash much harder. The longer an adult child is buffered or supported financially by his or her parents, the more difficult it will be for him or her to develop their own financial coping skills—he or she will become stunted, both financially and emotionally.

Some financial enablers grew up in poverty, and promised themselves that they would not let their children go without. Other financial enablers were spoiled as children themselves. Because their parents taught them that money equals love, they don't know how to express love to their own children other than by buying it. Often, their parents shielded them from any money troubles and made them feel like they'd always be taken care of, no matter what.

Lewis, who we met earlier, grew up in a privileged environment, but he keenly felt the lack of any teaching about money; in fact, he felt that his parents had deliberately protected him from learning anything about money, its uses, and how to handle it. He was determined to do better with his children. But despite his best intentions, he fell back into old familiar patterns.

LEWIS: *Over the years, I realized that I had developed a money relationship with my kids, which was a lot like what I had grown up with. I felt like I needed to support and subsidize their lifestyles, and they were all too happy to let me. I did it with all four of them.*

Then when I retired and my wife and I were living on a fixed income, we ended up spending down our nest egg to support our children. We were making mortgage payments for two of them. We were paying for our grandchildren's private schooling. We were even helping pay their utilities and food costs. They were all unemployed, because they couldn't find a job that "suited" them. When I would try to say no, my wife would secretly slip them money, and I was doing the same thing when she would say no to them. We were paying out tens of thousands of dollars a month, every month. We knew if we didn't do something we would burn through our retirement funds.

They had learned that in times of crisis they could always come to the Bank of Mom and Dad and receive interest-free loans that they would never have to repay. I realized I was creating the very same thing that my mother and father had with my sisters and myself, with disastrous results.

The source of this couple's struggle? Lewis and his wife were carrying a lot of guilt and shame for not being better parents throughout the years and, like so many other financial enablers, used money in a well-meaning, yet unsuccessful, attempt to "buy" forgiveness from those they believed they had neglected or harmed.

Financial enablers aren't always parents; we've seen many cases of people who consistently enable their partners, spouses, friends, or even acquaintances. They believe, consciously or not, that lavishing or spending money on others will give their life meaning, or earn them respect and love.

CAROLE: *When I graduated from college, I had excellent credit because my father had paid all the bills, and paid them on time. I got several credit card offers and the silence around money I had grown up with led to me opening one with a very high limit. I felt empowered buying all kinds of supplies for my art studio. I bought supplies for other artists, too. I felt like I was an important person in their lives. They treated me that way. Looking back, I realize I was acting as their personal banker. When they could, they would pay me back in cash, which I kept and used as walking-around money instead of paying down the credit card bills. I started paying just the minimum and piling up debt. I never thought about when or how I would pay it all off. I was not talking about it.*

By the time I was twenty-five, I was about six thousand dollars in debt. I realized that I needed to take responsibility for it and began working with a debt management company. Then I moved in with my boyfriend, and together we went totally out of control financially. I later found out he had a cocaine habit. After two years I owed seventeen thousand dollars on credit cards. I was terrified. I took the advice of a woman who called herself a psychic healer, filed for bankruptcy, and moved into my van.

It's a universal search: What is the meaning of my life? What's my place in the world? How can I get people to like and respect me? The healthiest answers, the ones most likely to make us happy, have to do with relationships and service to others. But for financial enablers, relationships are so tangled up in money, they confuse emotional investments with actual currency. Like many people from wealthy backgrounds, Carole enjoyed the power and the sense of importance she got from playing banker to her circle of friends. But as financial enabling tends to do, it backfired, and she ended up losing her friends, her boyfriend, *and* her money.

Financial enabling can sometimes be linked with financial infidelity, as enablers often lie or deceive their partners about the amount of money they are secretly giving to their friends or adult children. Remember the woman with the secret bank account that her husband discovered when the family was audited? Turns out she had also been paying her adult son an "allowance" from the secret account so her husband wouldn't find out about it.

In hard times, financial enabling becomes more and more common. In fact, in the wake of the recent economic meltdown, the number of adults in their twenties and even thirties moving back in with their parents has been steadily on the rise. But this has serious effects on both the enabler and dependent and can be very damaging to the parent–child relationship. One financial planner we work with explains why.

RUSSELL: *We're trying to give our clients the message that the people who are tethered to your financial life raft are living in significant risk, and they're putting you at risk. They're like very heavy boat anchors attached to your life raft. If and when their anchor gets dropped overboard, if it's tethered to your little life raft, you're going to get flipped upside down. For example, we've had two clients whose adult children have lost their homes to foreclosure, and one adult son has moved back in with the parent. That's where we probe, trying to find our clients' risk factors that have nothing to do with investments. These are risk factors of*

family, close friends, and causes. We need to help them figure out
how to address, in an appropriate fashion, the issues of sustain-
ability for their tethered loved ones.

Admittedly, it's hard to say no when someone you care
about, and are used to caring for, asks you for money, particularly in hard times. We knew of a woman in her forties who
lost half her savings in the market crash. Tragically, her husband had just been stricken with cancer, and she wanted
nothing more in the world than for him to live out the rest of
his days at home. However, for this to be possible he would
need professional home care, which cost close to twenty thousand dollars a month. She no longer had that kind of money, so
she appealed to a well-off uncle for help. He wrestled with the
decision for months. On one hand, it was the right thing to do.
On the other hand, if he gave her money once, when would
the requests end? Plus, while it was true that he had the
money, he was also nearing retirement, and he had worked
hard and saved wisely all his life so that he could retire in luxury. Ultimately, he gave her a onetime gift—a sizable amount
of money—but always feared that she would be back when it
ran out.

If you realize you're a financial enabler, the first thing to do
is acknowledge that your behavior is doing more harm than
good. If your financial gifts were enough to prod someone to
growth, inspiration, and independence, chances are it would
have already happened. Sure, it's never easy to say no to a
friend or loved one when they come to you for help—especially
in a tragic situation like the one above. But it becomes easier
when you remind yourself that saying no, gently, is the only
way to break the cycle of dependence and enabling. Remind
yourself that you're not being stingy or callous. You're merely
doing what's best for them and for yourself. And it will relieve
you of the sense of powerlessness over the situation. As Lewis

put it, "The most important thing I learned was that I had more control over the situation than I thought I did. My kids had their part in it certainly, but if something was going to change, I was going to have to take responsibility for changing it."

Financial Dependency

The prince searched high and low, throughout the kingdom, until he found Cinderella and swept her away to a wonderful new life. "Prince Charming" money scripts, which we introduced when we talked about the role of gender in shaping our money scripts, are rooted in the belief that a "higher power"— be it a knight in shining armor, the government, the lottery, or a benevolent universe—will swoop in and save the day. But leaving our financial well-being in the hands of another person, entity, or the Fates can be disastrous. Even so, many people choose to remain financially dependent on others because it protects them from having to take on their own financial education, preparedness, and planning.

The financial dependent is the dance partner to the financial enabler. Even though the enabler might subconsciously be trying to strengthen the relationship, in fact financial dependence is associated with increased parent–child conflict. It can happen no matter what one's financial situation; we've seen it in second- or third-generation families stuck on welfare, and in wealthy beneficiaries of trust funds. In all cases, financial dependence saps people's ambition and sense of autonomy and can leave them feeling lost and helpless in the world. Mollie's is a classic case.

MOLLIE: *The summer before my senior year in high school, I wanted to get a job. Many of my friends were working and it seemed exciting. My father said that none of the women in his house would ever work for pay. But he didn't seem opposed to me doing volunteer work so I volunteered with the Head Start pro-*

gram. My father came out and took pictures of me and the chil-
dren and gave each of the children a picture, which was beyond
anything they had experienced.

The following year, I called up my father from college quite
frustrated because I couldn't balance my checkbook. That was a
very new experience for me. He tried to help for a few minutes
and then he said, "Do you have enough money in your account?"
I replied yes and he said, "Then you don't have to worry about
it." I never put much effort into balancing a checkbook ever
again. Close was good enough.

I learned that women are to be respected and part of what that
means is that they will be taken care of financially by men. A be-
lief which might have been okay, if my father hadn't died at age
forty-one, with no insurance and no planning for the future. This
manifested itself in my adult life by holding my husband to a
standard that suggested the degree of his love was measurable by
how well he could provide for me financially. He could never
earn enough to make me feel that he loved me enough, and we
fought about money all the time.

Mollie's experience is an all too common one, and a good illustration of the contextual nature of money scripts. When circumstances are stable, the money script isn't necessarily
damaging; if Mollie's father had lived forever, continuing to
take care of her, perhaps she wouldn't have ever had a reason
to learn how to balance her checkbook. However, when circumstances change—and they always do—then automatic,
rigid adherence to the money script can inflict tremendous
damage. When the role of breadwinner, holder of the family's
financial knowledge, and financial power are all carried by just
one member of a family or a domestic partnership, everyone's
financial health is at risk. It is not a matter of *if* a financial crisis will emerge, but *when*.

Unfortunately, given the gender roles that still to some extent prevail in our society, most cases of financial dependence are in women. Worse is the fact that adherence to the Prince Charming fairy tale puts women at a significant risk for other difficulties, including such things as workplace discrimination, domestic abuse, career self-sabotage, and an inability to provide for oneself and one's children. In fact, financial dependence is also a major reason women decide to stay in abusive relationships. In one study, almost half of domestic violence victims reported a lack of money as being a significant reason for them to return to their abusers.

There's also a great deal of evidence to link economic distress and instability with domestic violence. A recent study, which drew on data from a national survey, revealed that for couples where the male was always employed, the rate of domestic violence was 4.7 percent. When the male experienced one episode of unemployment, the rate rose to 7.5 percent; with two or more periods of the male's unemployment, the rate for domestic violence rose to 12.3 percent. And a three-year study in Illinois showed that women who experienced domestic violence had more uneven employment histories and worked less outside the home compared to women in similar situations minus the violence.

Often a terrible feedback loop is established. With economic instability comes a narrowing of choices; women in abusive relationships may decide that the partner's financial support, however erratic, outweighs the risk of violence. And recently we've seen very extreme cases of domestic violence related to money, in which men have "solved" the problems of job loss and overwhelming debt by murdering their family and killing themselves.

People who suffer from financial dependency live in a childlike world where the normal rules of finances are irrelevant. They have no real sense of how money works in the everyday world, nor do they feel they need to know. When they need money the person they are dependent on gives it to them. If they overspend, it is covered by the Bank of Mom and Dad, Bank of Spouse, or Bank of Trust Fund. Those who are financially dependent often equate love with money, just as the enabler does. At the same time, they may resent, to some degree, the price they have to pay to get their stipend; often the "gifts" from the enabler come with strings attached: "You can have this money only if you use it to go to law school" or "If you take this money, I get to dictate when you come visit me." Enablers often act as though they have a right and duty to involve themselves in the financially dependent's life in other areas as well.

Being shielded by one's parents from having to worry or think about money can lead to issues both psychological and financial in future relationships. Consider Martha, who developed problems with overspending and financial fidelity.

MARTHA: *I was raised by parents who modeled a great deal of healthy behavior around money. They worked together as partners around budgeting and spending. They saved money. They used credit cards the way they're meant to be used: They'd charge something only if they could pay off the balance in full each month. They started IRA accounts and planned for their retirement. They took good care of me. All the things that financially healthy people do.*

The only problem was they never sat me down and taught me how to do these things or why those things were important. My parents never discussed our family's financial situation around me, and to this day I couldn't tell you how much money they made. I remember, as a teenager, asking if we were "middle class" or "upper middle class" and being told that was inappropriate to even ask.

So I grew up not worrying about, not even thinking about, money. I went away to college, which was paid for by my parents, and given an allowance to live on. My freshman year I met my first husband who was seven years older than me. We married when I was twenty and I willingly let him handle all of our finances. I enjoyed being taken care of and I was thankful I didn't have to worry about money in any way. We enjoyed the good life: traveling, dining out, shopping, partying. We ran up huge credit card debt. Ten years later, I was divorced and filing for bankruptcy.

My second husband and I started our marriage with tons of debt and obligations from our previous marriages. We struggled from the very beginning. I let him handle all our finances, but soon I became resentful. I felt like I was being treated as a child. He would make rules about spending and budgeting, but he would break those rules himself. He would blame me for our financial problems but not take responsibility for any of his behaviors. I became very passive-aggressive about my spending. I would hide purchases or use our children as an excuse to spend because they "really needed" something. I justified my overspending because I was buying for the children. Somehow, because I wasn't buying things for myself, overspending was okay. I applied for credit cards in my name only without his knowledge, I lied about my spending, and I was dishonest in every way possible. I was betraying him with money, just as if I was having a physical affair with someone. My behaviors were exactly the same: secretive, dishonest, hurtful.

Martha's experience is a poignant example of how well-meaning parents can set a child up for future financial difficulties. Ironically, it was her parents' financial effectiveness, in part, that led to her belief that she didn't need to worry about money. But while they modeled healthy financial behaviors and a balanced distribution of financial knowledge and responsibility, they failed to pass on critical financial information to their daughter. And since her parents never taught her the skills they demonstrated, she assumed they weren't important for her to know. It became natural for her to believe she would always be taken care of. As is common among people raised financially dependent, Martha attracted partners into her life who shared the same set of beliefs—that the man should be in charge of the finances. It felt so comfortable for Martha, so right. However, her willingness to put her financial health exclusively in someone else's hands ended in disaster, twice.

This is the price of the "big taboo" around talking about money; even positive habits are not passed down. But when parents don't know how to talk about money, or recognize that it's important to do so, how will their children learn to communicate about it in a healthy way? In a later chapter we'll talk about ways to involve children in the household finances in healthy, age-appropriate ways.

One thing is certain, though. Spoiling one's children is *not* a good way to teach them about the value and meaning of money. Phyllis and Catherine are good examples.

PHYLLIS: *I was the firstborn grandchild to both my maternal and paternal grandparents. My mother suffered four miscarriages before I was born and she was bedridden for five months when pregnant with me. So, as you can imagine, I was spoiled.*

When I started eating solid food, my favorite thing was bacon. That's all I wanted to eat. This was during World War II, and meat was rationed. Everyone got a very limited number of meat coupons a month, to buy a certain amount of meat. I've heard stories how my grandparents and neighborhood friends would stand in line for hours at the butcher shop and use all their meat coupons to get bacon for me, Little Phyllis. Times were bad for most people, but there was abundance for me. I loved it.

My maternal grandparents lived upstairs over us. My maternal grandmother was an angel in my life in many, many ways. She

gave me everything I wanted or needed, or what she thought I
needed. I grew up knowing that I was special, and I'd never lack
for anything.

It turns out that monetary indulgence was one of the few signs of love in Phyllis's tumultuous childhood. She launched herself into the world at an early age, expecting to be taken care of. Though she learned, on a logical level, that spending money on someone wasn't the only measure of love, she still held tight to that money script and acted on it, and it wreaked havoc on her finances. Because she associated love and feeling special with money (and food and other "goodies"), she couldn't stop herself from showering presents and spending money on her husband, her children, her grandchildren, friends, colleagues—even when she couldn't really afford the expense. She had a hard time believing they'd want her presence without the accompanying presents.

CATHERINE: *My father always worried about money. One year*
he did really well. I said to him, "Oh, gosh, I guess you're feeling
good about that." He said, "Well, yes, but now there are the taxes
I'll have to pay." So what I learned was there was no way to ever
feel good about what you had. There was always an emphasis on
the downside. You can never relax about money.

For me, growing up, I was never really responsible for dealing
with money or paying my own way. When I did do anything in-
volving money, a big drama usually ensued. One time I sent my
car off to the filling station. This was when they'd come get your
car, so I'd sent it off to be washed and have the oil changed. When
my father found out, he just went berserk because I'd spent that
money frivolously. I learned that there were consequences to
being spontaneous around anything that involved money. He al-
ways called my mother a spendthrift, always criticized her for
that. I tried to do whatever I had to do to make sure he didn't put

me *in that same category, and in this case I knew I had ended up there.*

At the same time, my grandmother had lots of money and we could always go to her. Our whole family depended on her financially. So rather than deal with my father, I'd go to my grandmother.

What I lived with, then, were the extremes around money. What I learned from that is that I always had to depend on somebody else to take care of me and provide for me, to be the limitless supply of money.

The belief that others will take care of you financially comes at a high cost; it often goes hand in hand with a sense that one is incapable of taking care of oneself at all. Not only did Catherine take on her father's fear and anxiety around money—in good times and bad—she also learned that she was powerless to change the situation. In Catherine's case, this came at a very high price indeed; she ended up getting stuck in a cycle of domestic abuse.

The driving force behind financial dependence and its related problems is often a learned helplessness, which makes it even harder to break the cycle of dependency: "I can't possibly take care of myself, so why try? I have to find someone who can." But as we've seen, Prince Charming isn't coming. Even if the prince (or princess) turns out to be a hardworking provider, relying on him or her entirely isn't a wise decision. This is particularly true for women. As we've mentioned, given today's high divorce rates and the fact that men die almost a decade earlier than women, *all* women need to be prepared to take care of themselves financially.

Next Steps

As you can see, we gain tremendous power from becoming students of the life events that created our financial flashpoint experiences, the subsequent automatic and habitual money scripts, and the unaddressed emotions that keep them locked in place. As we become more and more skilled at engaging our inner scientist, especially in the midst of intense emotions such as fear, anger, or excitement, we can learn to benefit from the instinctual gifts of the crocodile and the emotional and social wisdom of the monkey. We can make conscious choices about our money, learn from our mistakes, and step into a world of expanded possibility. We can develop a relationship with money that fits our values and goals. True, many of these money scripts will always be with us and they'll continue to pop into our heads in both times of stress and calm. However, we can learn to recognize them for what they are: partial truths that stem from our past, which may or may not be helpful today. Then we can make the shifts in thinking necessary to correct and change them. *How* to go about this is the focus of the next section.

But first, think about the experiences and behaviors you just read about. Which were most resonant or familiar to you? If you haven't already, take our free money disorder assessment at www.yourmentalwealth.com. Think about what made those experiences so emotionally compelling. Looking back on it now, how do you see things differently? What have you learned? Now that you better understand why you behave the way you do, and why you should stop beating yourself up for it, what do you commit to doing differently?

Part Three

BEATING YOUR MONEY DISORDERS

9

Resolving That Unfinished Business

All the people you've read about in the earlier chapters have what we call *unfinished business* around their financial flashpoint experiences; this is the phrase therapists use to describe the emotions and memories surrounding past experiences that a person has avoided, repressed, or left unresolved. When the feelings around the event are not fully processed or resolved at the time they originally occurred, often because they are too overwhelming or traumatic, they linger in the background of our hearts and minds. The residue of these events keeps us trapped in the past, unable to fully embrace the present and limiting our ability to create an optimal future. When not appropriately expressed, the sadness, grief, fear, anger, anxiety, mistrust, or terror associated with these events carry over into our present lives where they interfere with our ability to be emotionally in control.

Unfinished emotional business and the behavior adaptations it creates can be remarkably resistant to change, unless it is dealt with, as the following story shows. Carole's painful memories of asking her father for money are still impacting her life; and they will continue to do so, until she comes to terms with them.

> CAROLE: *When I was in college and for a few years after, I went home every two months. The whole week before the trip, I'd be anxious, with terrible knots in my stomach, and the knots just got worse through the weekend of the visit itself. On Sunday evening, I would always be summoned into my father's office after dinner, and my father would go on and on about how he never bought expensive autos or extravagant luxuries for himself, and then he would write me a check. With the check, he was paying my tuition, room, board and utilities, no matter where I lived or how much it cost. I have no recollection, at all, of what things cost during college because the event of going to that room for the lecture and the check was so oppressive and uncomfortable, I just shut down. I couldn't focus on the nuts and bolts of a monthly budget. Just the other day, someone asked how much dues for my sorority were and I had no idea because that bill, and all the others, went directly to Dad.*
>
> *I felt like such a burden to him. I felt like the biggest, most expensive problem a person could possibly have. To this day, I have trouble asking for what I need around money, and pretty much anything else, unless it's something to do with my art. However, I just spent the past month waiting too long for checks people owed. That happens too often—there's some resistance to someone paying me once we've struck a deal, and it's difficult for me to go get what is owed me.*

Think about how your body responds to stress: your muscles knot, your stomach churns, your hand clenches into a fist. That clenched fist is a lot like your brain in the grip of unfinished business. Both are in a defensive posture; both are closed off and unavailable for more useful activities. Unfinished business limits our capacity to connect with ourselves and others. Research has shown that unfinished business is associated with anxiety, depression, and interpersonal problems.

Money disorders arise from unfinished business related to past painful events and relationships connected directly or indirectly to money. If you're suffering from a money disorder, lasting change must include resolving unfinished business related to the traumatic event or events you experienced. This resolution will not only allow you to make good use of sound financial advice and planning, but it will also help you to rewrite the scripts from your past to live more fully in the present. We detail some of the strategies for doing this later in the book.

How can events from the past have such powerful influences on our present? That's one aspect of the time paradox.

The Past Becomes the Future

In *The Time Paradox: The New Psychology of Time That Will Change Your Life,* behavioral psychologist Dr. Philip Zimbardo (with collaborator and coauthor Dr. John Boyd) analyzes the unique relationship time plays in our thinking and behavior. The "paradox" referred to in the title is really several interlocking ones. To name three:

- Time plays a crucial role in our lives but we're almost completely unaware of its effects.
- Though time is a universal experience, there is no universal way of experiencing it; instead, there are several general patterns, each of which has both benefits and drawbacks.
- Time is experienced individually yet it's also a force that influences the fate of cultures and nations.

Through decades of research, Dr. Zimbardo has developed and refined the Zimbardo Time Perspective Inventory (ZTPI), which measures an individual's attitudes toward time. In analyzing the results of ZTPI testing, Zimbardo and Boyd discovered that five general time frames emerge most consistently: future orientation, present-hedonistic orientation, present-fatalistic orientation, past-positive orientation, and past-negative orientation. (You can take the ZTPI yourself online: http://www.the timeparadox.com/surveys/. The test takes just a few minutes to complete and you'll receive your scores immediately.)

Each of us is very likely to have certain aspects of all five types, with the accompanying behaviors and beliefs. It's a very rare person who fits squarely into one frame and thus expresses that frame's aspects almost exclusively. Even so, our attitudes about time can tell us a lot about how we experience our unfinished financial business and what sort of disordered financial behaviors we are most prone to exhibit.

Present-Hedonistic (Pr-H) Person: This frame indicates a focus on sensory experiences and immediate gratification. Not surprisingly, Pr-H people are lively and fun loving, often described as "the life of the party"—if a bit volatile and moody. They enjoy intense experiences and activities with a payoff in the present, such as sports and sex. A Pr-H person is likely to be vulnerable to addictions of all kinds. All this means that for a Pr-H person, unfinished business related to money can easily lead to money disorders such as overspending, excessive risk taking, and compulsive gambling.

Present-Fatalistic (Pr-F) Person: These people believe that they have so little control over their lives that it's pointless to plan for the future. Pr-F people are likely to do poorly at school and in the workplace because of their self-fulfilling prophecies of their own failure. Believing that outcomes aren't determined by their behavior, they're also prone to excessive risk taking; in other words, they are motivated by "If I can't control the outcome, anyway, I might as well go out with a bang!" scripts. One of the major causes of the Pr-F frame seems to be negative early-life experiences, which result in a kind of learned helplessness, the belief that one is powerless to improve one's life and therefore there's no use in trying to. This, as we've discussed, is a pattern of thinking often associated with financial dependence, and "Prince Charming" money scripts. Obviously, addressing such losses therapeutically could help such a person resolve their unfinished business and shift their thinking to a healthier, less pessimistic, and more empowered frame of mind.

Future-Oriented (F-O) Person: Unlike the previous two groups, people with future-oriented frames make decisions and organize their lives by weighing the potential outcomes of various actions. "Delayed gratification" is their middle name, and they're very good at problem solving and planning. However, taken too far, someone with an F-O frame may become overly focused on the future, never allowing themselves to enjoy the present. In financial terms, this can cause enormous anxiety about one's future finances, lead to overcontrolling behavior (like bullying one's spouse about money), underspending, and workaholism. People with future orientations may be focusing so much on the future in a subconscious attempt to avoid the difficult memories and feelings of the past.

Past-Positive (P-P) Person: Individuals with this time frame tend to be homebodies, centered on family and close friends, prizing a sense of rootedness and continuity. They often focus on the past, "what's worked before," in making decisions.

Taken to excess, this frame can lead to risk aversion, under-spending, and hoarding.

Past-Negative (P-N) Person: When the past in question is traumatic, P-N framing can lead people to become, as Dr. Zimbardo puts it, "Smithsonians of trauma, failure, and frustration, endlessly recycling the non-modifiable past despite current good times." Any unfinished financial business can easily become a wing of that museum. Like their P-P fellows, the past weighs heavily in P-Ns's decision making; however, for P-Ns, the past becomes a model for what to avoid.

Again, we suspect that you've recognized something of yourself in one or more of these descriptions. Whatever category you fall into, the point is that when we have unfinished business, the past invades our present and affects our future. Think of it this way. You only have two feet. Let's say your left foot is on a nice, smooth sidewalk. If your right foot is mired in quicksand, you're not really able to stand securely on that sidewalk, and you certainly can't follow it where it leads. Similarly, to truly occupy your present life and effectively move toward a future you desire, you must pull yourself out of the quicksand; you must address and resolve unfinished business from the past.

Obviously, not every troubling experience results in unfinished business; otherwise, our psyches would be enormous bundles of nothing else. So why do some painful or unsettling experiences stick with us, while others don't? And, more important, how do we wrap up our unfinished business and free ourselves from its grip? It all comes back to the nature of trauma.

The Origin of Unfinished Business

Trauma is energy—emotional energy. Just as an overloaded electrical circuit can short out if not discharged through a circuit breaker, our traumatic energy can turn destructive if it's not discharged safely. Animals have a natural process for releasing this energy—in fact, animals in their natural environment may do this many times a day. Picture a doe standing in a meadow. With a flick of her tail she lowers her head to munch on some clover, and she raises her head while she chews, scanning the bushes. All of a sudden, she hears some rustling in the leaves. Her entire body flinches instantly, as she braces herself to run. She looks toward the noise and sees a squirrel. She determines that there's no threat. Her body then twitches for a few seconds, and she goes back to eating calmly.

Two ducks are in a pond. One duck veers into the other's territory, and the first duck attacks. They bite and quack and splash; then they separate and, with a flap of their wings, go their separate ways.

In each case, the fight-or-flight energy generated was released and dissipated, leaving no harmful remnants. However, when the built-up energy has no natural outlet, posttraumatic stress responses are more likely to occur as unresolved trauma locks the brain into survival mode. This is no less true for people than it is for other animals. By releasing the energy around the traumatic event, either through physical or emotional outlets, we are able to find resolution and move forward. In other words, we need a mental or emotional catharsis to acknowledge and release built-up energy, allowing our systems to return to normal.

Children instinctively know how to deal with difficult feelings by crying or screaming. However, parents and society at large often admonish the upset child for showing fear, anger, and other intense emotions. As a result, the child may take in the message that *all* forms of emotional release are *always* unacceptable. Or, if encouraged to "just get over" the fear, sadness, or anger, the child may come to believe that strong emotions themselves are not okay. When that child grows up, he or she will likely push aside these feelings or avoid anything likely to elicit them, simply because the prospect of experiencing them while not being able to express them is so frightening.

Our culture places a huge taboo on expressing our intense emotions; just think about how others would respond if you threw yourself on the floor of the office and started weeping and wailing after being passed over for a promotion, or if you started screaming in frustration in the middle of the airport after being told a flight was delayed for *another* hour. A large part of our socialization involves learning to suppress our most intense emotions. As a result, we've become experts at finding ways to avoid uncomfortable feelings or dial down their intensity. There are healthy ways to do this, but all too often we resort to self-destructive activities such as alcohol abuse, smoking, compulsive eating, compulsive spending, overworking, and so on, to keep unexpressed emotions at bay. However, these avoidance techniques only help in the short-term and end up adding to our problems. They also limit our ability to be in the present moment, to see the reality of our situation and make rational, clear-headed decisions.

Remember the split-brain experiment and the overactive explanatory mechanism mentioned earlier? That aspect of the brain comes into play when we have unfinished business. As we've seen, our beliefs and conclusions about an event are often incomplete or inaccurate, as our brains scramble to make sense of things, latching onto a "logical" conclusion. The more complicated the situation, the more susceptible we are to drawing incomplete or false conclusions. And the more emotionally intense the situation, the more likely we are to re-spond as if it's a threat to our very survival, and the more re-sistant we will be to relinquishing our beliefs that have kept us going so far. As always, the key is to turn to our innate re-sources and consciously train ourselves to deal with our fears in more productive ways.

Forty years ago, Swiss physician Dr. Elisabeth Kübler-Ross developed a new way of looking at the grief felt by those suffering from terminal illness. At a time when very few people were willing to face their feelings about death di-rectly and honestly, Kübler-Ross changed the very way people thought about grieving. Her first book, *On Death and Dying,* outlined the five stages we must go through in order to come to terms with and ultimately heal from our grief. In our work, we've come to understand that her model applies to any up-setting or traumatic event: divorce, job loss, financial set-backs, and so on.

- *Denial:* In an effort to escape an inevitable loss, we try to pretend it's not really happening. "There must be some mistake." "This will blow over."
- *Anger:* As the reality of our situation begins to sink in, we lash out in fury and resentment. "It's not fair!" "Why me?" "I don't deserve this!"
- *Bargaining:* Once the anger burns out, we try to negotiate with a higher power or the universe at large for a different outcome. "Just fix it this once and I'll never do it again." "All I'm asking for is six more months."
- *Depression:* When we finally realize that we can't avoid or escape the negative results or consequences, we lose all hope. "There's no point in doing anything." "I give up." "Why bother?"
- *Acceptance:* At last, we come to terms with the reality of our situation and handle it realistically and with some

grace. "Overall, I'm proud of what I've accomplished." "There are still a few things I can do."

Progressing through these five stages can provide us with the emotional release necessary to overcome our fear, anxiety, or sadness, and ultimately feel at peace. Of course, not everyone proceeds through the stages at the same rate, in the same order, or in a linear fashion, and it's possible to get stuck at a particular stage or stages. But these five stages do seem to be universal, and as you face the long-buried emotions connected to your unfinished business, you may find yourself going through this cycle. It may be painful but it helps to recognize that it is a normal, healthy response to trauma, and that your distress is temporary.

Changing Your Mind

But who wants to dredge up the past, especially the painful parts? After all, you can't change the past, can you? Shouldn't we just let bygones be bygones? This would be fine if we could just banish the past painful events from our memories. But it doesn't work that way. Ironically, while we have a tendency to avoid painful memories, the effects on our life persist until we face the issue and deal with any built-up, unexpressed feelings.

Many people think of memory as something like a DVD that can be played over and over, with the images and events remaining the same every time. But quite the contrary: Our memories change all the time. Psychologist Dr. Elizabeth Loftus has done groundbreaking work on just how flexible—and fallible—our memories are.

Loftus and other researchers have shown that our recollections of actual events are often distorted by *information taken in every time we call up the memory.* What's more, one of Loftus's experiments showed that it's possible to implant entirely new memories of an event that never happened. In one experiment, older family members were coached to tell a subject about an incident when he or she was either lost in a mall for several hours or narrowly rescued from a shark attack. Neither incident ever happened, but after a credible source had described it, the subject not only "remembered" it but later added details and embellishments.

What all this means in the context of resolving financial trauma is that you *can* change your financial flashpoint memories—not erase them, but profoundly alter their meaning and emotional impact on your life. Think about how you feel when you recall an upsetting incident. You first feel the original emotions, with something close to the original intensity, right? But if you're able to get past that first flood of emotion and apply your adult perspective and knowledge, you can create a more realistic and even helpful interpretation of the memory. This may include recognizing that the experience taught you some very valuable lessons and perhaps even saved you future problems.

One way to do this is through role reversal: Imagine the incident from the point of view of the other person or people involved. What were they thinking? Where was their motivation or intention? Knowing what you know now about that person's background and what he or she was dealing with at the time of the incident, can you better understand what might have prompted their behavior? For example, let's say your memory is of a huge fight you recalled your parents having about money. Knowing what you know now as an adult about the emotional heft financial issues can have in a relationship, might their actions seem more understandable?

POSTTRAUMATIC GROWTH

In the past few decades, the field of psychology has expanded to not only include an emphasis on restoring people to emotional health after experiencing a traumatic event but also to study how crisis and human suffering can be the precursor to psychological growth. Psychologists Richard Tedeschi and Lawrence Calhoun have found that these changes can include greater appreciation of life, enhanced personal strength and spiritual growth, improved relationships, and an emphasis on new possibilities in one's life.

The idea here is not to absolve anyone of their actions, or attempt to justify or condone what was done, or transfer the blame to anyone else. The goal is simply to help you by reducing the anxiety produced by these memories, and a fuller understanding of everyone's motivation helps. It takes you out of the role of powerless victim and restores a sense of volition. It can also help you determine what parts of the event you could not control (which in childhood is pretty much everything), so you can stop blaming yourself.

Another method of healing involves identifying the beneficial growth and learning that accompanied a traumatic event. Ask yourself what the experience might have taught you. You can do this through introspection, meditation, or psychotherapy; the more spiritual among us might even find it helpful to "ask" their higher power. Whatever your method, if you identify a higher purpose, learning, or psychological benefit that came from the original incident and attach that to the memory and feelings associated with it, the memories will lose their hold on you.

The emotional, intellectual, and spiritual benefits of having survived a traumatic experience are just beginning to be acknowledged and studied by the new field of "posttraumatic growth." This is an area of psychology focused on helping people achieve emotional and spiritual growth in the wake of a traumatic experience. One just has to recall the lives of men such as Nelson Mandela, Mahatma Gandhi, and Thich Nhat Hanh and others to understand that many of our greatest inspirational and spiritual leaders have transcended histories of remarkable suffering and deprivation. This is no coincidence. Just like intense fire and heat—when handled correctly—can burn out iron's impurities and result in hardened steel, so can the fire of trauma and tribulation result in a strengthening of character, spirit, and human potential.

Calling up and acknowledging our memories and their associated emotions—and learning how to actually feel them without becoming overwhelmed—helps us become more productive in dealing with them and more resilient in the long run. This is a critical element in the treatment of trauma and anxiety, one that underpins all psychotherapeutic methods and principles. It explains why such different forms of psychotherapy can be useful: insight-oriented therapy (identifying and analyzing the issues), behavioral therapy (engaging in the feared activity), cognitive therapy (exploring, examining, and changing anxiety-producing thoughts), and experiential therapy (reenacting aspects of the event to call up and express the uncomfortable or repressed emotions).

Besides therapy, there are many other avenues for addressing these feelings, including journaling, support groups, pastoral counseling, or talking with a close friend. These are all places where we are allowed and encouraged to release trauma energy and talk about the experience, which is exactly what we need. By confronting our internal realities in a safe place—whether it's with a counselor or a trusted friend, or in your favorite chair with a cup of tea—and experiencing a full range of emotions, we allow those emotions to burn themselves out until they reach manageable level of intensity.

When we access these old memories, we are able to supplement them with new information and insights and thus change the hold they have on our lives. Resolving unfinished business requires both being in touch with our emotions and engaging the rational brain to help us bring in new insights and understandings. And examining our experiences from an adult perspective and with adult insight helps us release the past's power on our present lives and future directions. This is the beginning of deep healing and lasting behavioral change. This is how one client puts it:

> STUART: *What is helpful is that I can now notice when some of my old money scripts show up. I know them. I know what they are. I know what to do with them. I sit them down and listen to them and then show them the door.*

Resolving Unfinished Business: An Exercise

As we've seen, when we have a strong emotional attachment to an unfinished piece of business in our lives, it takes up psychic energy and space and keeps us trapped in the past. Resolving unfinished business results in a release of energy, relief, and an ability to be more present in the moment. To see how this feels for yourself, try this experiment. Make a list of two or three items of unfinished business in your life. Start with the simpler stuff—that e-mail from your mother-in-law you haven't responded to or that call from your son's principal you've been avoiding returning. Okay, now put this book down and get on it. Send the e-mail. Make the call. No time like the present.

How does it feel to check off those items on your list? Like a weight has lifted, right? When we are able to take action to resolve our deep-seated unfinished emotional business, the energy release and relief is even more profound. In a later chapter, we'll have more intensive exercises to help you get there.

Money Secrets Among the Professionals

Even though we've both been psychotherapists for years, it wasn't until relatively recently, when we had to deal with our own money problems, that we realized how entrenched the money taboo is. Even among the healing professions, very few therapists and counselors are comfortable addressing financial issues with their clients, and fewer still have received any training to do so. This, despite the fact that money is most people's number one source of stress, and surely affects our family relationships as well as all others. Conversely, financial advisers often aren't comfortable talking about squishy things like "emotions" and don't have the training to help an anxious client drill down to expose and deal with unfinished business.

That's one reason we teamed with a financial advisor to create an intensive course to heal money issues. It teaches many of the therapeutic techniques we've described above, as well as others, along with practical financial planning and counseling. One of the most important things we do is help people overcome their deep shame around their relationships with money. We help them see that there's a distinction between their messy, disordered money behaviors and their core self. They learn that their disordered money behaviors make perfect sense given their histories. And they also learn how to take the first steps toward reorganizing their financial lives—just as you will have, by the time you're finished reading this book.

Recently we conducted a study of the program's participants to determine how effective our methods were at reducing financial anxiety and fostering financial health. The study was published in *Psychological Services,* a peer-reviewed journal of the American Psychological Association, and was featured in the *New York Times.* What it found was that after completing the program, the participants reported immediate improvement in several areas related to their psychological and financial health: fewer intrusive thoughts, lowered feelings of inadequacy and inferiority, increased sense of belonging and hope, less anxiety around money, and fewer episodes of stress-related symptoms, such as panic attacks.

Most exciting was the fact that these changes were stable three months later, when people reported continued improvements in their financial health and money attitudes. Specifically, they reported reductions in their belief that money is a symbol of success, less use of money to impress or influence others, and a greater focus on the present in dealing with money. Overall, they placed less value on the importance of status seeking, acquisition, competition, and external recognition. Most encouraging, they reported significant reductions in anxiety caused by money, and less worry generally around money and financial situations. Many of the stories you have been reading in this book come from interviews we conducted with program participants. Most of these people attended the program years ago and they continue to report positive progress today. They've described the effect as life-changing and long lasting, even during these challenging financial times.

Stuart is a financial planner who believes that he began working with us just in time to save himself from serious losses, even though he was unaware of the risks he was facing.

STUART: *As a financial planner, the whole idea of psychology and money behavior intrigued me. I signed up for the workshop be-*

*cause of that and because I wanted to be a better and more suc-
cessful financial planner. My curiosity saved my life as I know it.
I had no idea that my thinking and behavior were "broken." I ran
headlong into my greed, which had been driving all my personal
financial decisions. I was shocked by that awareness. I realized
that I was addicted to getting more and more, and I realized I had
driven our family into the ditch financially—just as my wife had
been trying to tell me. What I learned during the program turned
my life around. I believe it saved my marriage. I believe I would
be divorced and bankrupt today if I had not learned those lessons.*

*My old money scripts have morphed into ones that work bet-
ter. "Leave me alone; I know what I'm doing" has turned into "My
wife has a good 'read' on financial situations. I need to listen to
her feelings about financial decisions before we act." That's a new
concept, too—we acting, instead of I.*

*"I am my net worth" has turned into "I'm okay right where
I am." I have learned that I can enjoy life today, with what I
have, without pushing to get more. "More is better" is now "More
can be a burden." I feel more at peace, living in today. I feel more
balanced.*

Our work with clients provides the basis of this book. So
now we'd like to share with you some of the specific exercises
we use in our program, in the hopes that we can help you
achieve some of the same results that we've seen among our
clients.

Exercise: The Money Atom

The Money Atom is an exercise we adapted from the field of
psychodrama—a psychotherapeutic approach in which participants explore internal conflicts by acting out unresolved emotions and interpersonal interactions. The Money Atom is

designed to help you gain a better understanding of the unfinished business impacting your financial life—beliefs, issues,
and attitudes about money that stem from your childhood. As
we said earlier, you may feel some resistance as you go through
this exercise, as well as fear or anxiety. That's okay—in fact, facing and working through that resistance is an important step
toward achieving the emotional release you want. Just notice
the uncomfortable feelings and remind yourself that they
won't last forever. If something pops into your head that seems
especially significant, make a note and go over it later with a
therapist, a counselor, or a trusted friend.

1. Think back to the family system you grew up in. In addition to parents and siblings, this can include grandparents,
neighbors, cousins, teachers, clergy—anyone who was a significant presence in your life. Recall the people, their person-
alities and relationships, in as much detail as you can. In this
exercise, you'll draw a chart or diagram of your "family" as it
was when you were a child.

2. Take a sheet of paper—the biggest you can find, but at
least eight and a half by eleven inches. The paper will represent the scope of your family system, so draw a square on the
paper to represent where you feel you fit in your family when
you were a child. The size and position of the square should
reflect your perception of the status and/or position you held
in the system.

3. Draw a triangle to represent each significant male in your
family system: father, father figure, brother, uncle, grandfather, and so on. Again, the size and position of the triangles
can represent the influence and position the person holds in
the environment and in relation to you. Try beginning with the

most significant male and then position others. So you can keep track, put each man's initials inside "his" triangle.

4. Do the same thing with significant female figures, this time using a circle to represent each one.

5. Think about experiences that influenced your childhood. These could be anything from the death of a beloved pet, to a family member's serious illness, to physical abuse, workaholism, alcoholism, bankruptcy, or divorce. Don't forget societal influences outside the family: religion, war, sexism, racism. What we grew up with automatically seems "normal" to us, so try imagining your childhood as an outsider might see it. Use rectangles to represent each of these. Again, use their size and location on the paper in relation to you and others to represent how they influenced you.

6. Every family is affected by people and events no longer present: a grandfather who died young and left his family in poverty, chronic illness, tragic loss, or the lingering effects of some societal event, like war, natural disasters, or the Great Depression. We call these unseen influences "ghosts." Some of these ghosts might have been moments of great fortune as well as misfortune. Add your family's ghosts, using the same shapes you did before (triangles for males, circles for females, rectangles for nonhuman factors), but draw them with dotted lines.

7. Think about each of the people represented on your chart and his or her relationship to money. For each person, draw a dollar sign inside the circle or triangle to illustrate that relationship. Use your imagination to alter each dollar sign to symbolize the relationship: for example, a small one might

represent an avoidance or rejection of money while a large one might signify a focus on it; a dollar sign with an X through it could represent secrecy around money, perhaps multiple dollar signs to represent lots of money or obsession with money, and so on.

8. Draw arrows to represent how money circulated within the family. Who brought it in? Which directions did it flow? Who spent it? Did they have to consult other members? Don't worry about having a perfect graphic representation; the point is to get you thinking about the family dynamics concerning money.

9. Take a look at what you've drawn and think about the underlying relationships. What kind of money scripts would this family hold to? Take a separate sheet of paper and, along the right side, mark four columns. (You'll label these and fill them in later.) Now write down all the scripts this family would be likely to produce, leaving plenty of space after each.

10. Read each money script carefully. Think about how deeply you've taken on each one as your own, acting on it reflexively. Draw several stars or asterisks by the ones you've deeply internalized, draw a line through the ones you've left behind. Now think about your own money scripts that you identified from reading part 2. Are there scripts that appear on both lists? Underline those and pay attention to any patterns that emerge. Also pay attention to the scripts marked with several stars.

11. Label the four columns on the right as Emotional, Relational, Occupational, and Financial. Under each script, draw two rows and label them Costs and Payoffs.

12. Reflect on the good things these beliefs have brought you. Even the most destructive beliefs have a payoff of some kind—even if it's ultimately an undesirable one—or we wouldn't hold on to it. Often, the payoffs can be expressed as avoiding something: anxiety, isolation, risk. Write these down in the appropriate boxes.

13. Do the same with the costs. Let yourself really think about your painful financial experiences and try to relate them to the money scripts you've identified here. Consider how they've contributed to your financial difficulties as an adult.

14. Take a look at the balance sheet. Which money scripts have cost you more than they've brought you? Which ones would you like to rewrite? Which ones are serving you well?

Once you get to step 9, you may feel like you've hit a wall. Don't think that you're doing anything wrong, or the exercise isn't worth doing. Make notes of the thoughts that occur to you and put them away along with your diagram. Later, show them to a trusted friend, therapist or adviser.

Exercise: Money Egg

While the Money Atom is designed to facilitate awareness and insight, the Money Egg can help unlock the emotional component to our memories and experiences around money. Because we're trying to get to deep-seated emotions, this is one time when you shouldn't let your rational brain take over. To help avoid that, do this exercise quickly, going with the first thing that comes to mind. Don't spend more than about ten minutes total on the first three steps.

First find a place that's quiet and private to do this exercise; don't try to squeeze it into a break at work. Why? Because you may experience feelings surfacing during this exercise. Don't suppress them or push them away. Let yourself feel them and express them safely. There can be enormous healing power in letting yourself cry (even though you've been told for years that only weak people cry).

1. On a blank sheet of paper, draw a large egg-shaped oval.

2. Think back to the earliest time in your life you can re-member. What is the very earliest painful, pleasurable, or oth-erwise notable experience around money that you can think of? Pick up your pen or pencil in your nondominant hand (that is, if you're right-handed use your left hand and vice versa). This helps suppress your rational brain and encourages input from your animal brain. Think of your earliest financial flashpoint experience and draw symbols or a simple scene to represent this event. Box it in with lines that make it a seg-ment of the inside of the egg.

3. Think of the next money experience you can remember that was pleasurable, painful, or otherwise notable and draw it the same way you did the first one. (Remember to use your nondominant hand!) As you keep drawing and boxing in the symbols, your egg will start to look like a patchwork quilt. Fi-nally, at the top of the egg, draw the most recent memory you've decided to illustrate. It can, but doesn't have to be, something in your present life. You should at least go up through your early adulthood.

4. Go back to the bottom of the egg with the earliest mem-ories and look at each section. Recall with greater detail the situation and events. Using your dominant hand this time, write down a word or phrase that sums up the emotions you feel in response to each one. If you just feel kind of blank,

imagine the scene with someone you love in your place. Write down the feelings that come up for you as you watch it happen to that person.

5. Beginning at the bottom of the egg again, create a list of "lessons" that you learned about money based on these experiences. You'll likely notice some money scripts you have previously identified and perhaps even some new ones.

6. Looking at the entire picture, quickly complete this sentence: "The moral of the story about money in this person's life is . . ."

These exercises are designed to help you identify and begin to come to terms with your self-limiting or destructive money scripts. In chapters 10 and 11, we'll talk about how you can build on these changes and carry them forward into the future.

10

Financial Therapy

At one point in the not-so-distant past, the brain was believed to be a static organ, and once everything was in place, it wasn't changeable. Like a brick building, once the electrical and plumbing systems were installed, that's the way it stayed. Recently, through new imaging devices and technologies, scientists have discovered that the brain is actually amazingly flexible—what neuroscientists call plastic—and that it is able to reshape and rebuild itself. This new research has exploded popular myths about what is possible in terms of learning, changing, and growing emotionally throughout our lives.

For instance, you've probably heard that adults have all the brain cells they're ever going to have. Cutting-edge research shows that reality is a bit more complicated. Researchers at the Picower Institute for Learning and Memory recently discovered that brain cells, or neurons, in a particular area of what we're calling the rational brain, can actually regenerate, which opens up a whole new world of possibilities in terms of our cognition and perception. As well as generating new neurons, the brain can also create new associations and connections among them. When we engage in a repetitive activity—such as training or meditation—the brain creates new, robust pathways between neurons used in the activity, while other connections grow feebler. This capability shows enormous promise for *un*learning problematic behaviors and replacing them with better ones. (We'll discuss this in more detail later in the chapter.)

But even though the brain may be able to change its structure, the brain can't do this all on its own; it needs some help from you. In our work, we have found that sustained change—rewiring those neural pathways—often begins by examining our past, our personal and problematic histories; Sigmund Freud, the father of psychoanalysis, likened the process to archaeology. This book is essentially a "dig" into the traces and relics of your own past. By now, if you've completed some of our exercises, you've already identified some of your financial flashpoints and the money scripts they've led to. So at this point you likely have a good bit of insight into how your past has helped shape your present and may be limiting your potential. Now we're going to share some additional tools designed to help you hone in on the emotions and beliefs surrounding these events so you can beat that money disorder, once and for all.

Remember: Your self-limiting money behaviors did not develop in a vacuum. We believe they can't be changed in a vacuum, either. You didn't get into this mess alone, so don't be surprised if you can't get out of it by yourself. Social support, encouragement, feedback, accountability to others, professional facilitation, and advice all can be crucial to changing your financial behaviors. For this reason, support groups like Debtors Anonymous can be very helpful, even if your problem isn't specifically related to out-of-control debt. Other useful tools are reputable credit counseling, financial therapy, financial self-help/education, coaching, and financial advice from a qualified professional. We encourage you to engage these resources along your journey to financial health, and we'll give you some tips on how to select advisers. But first, and always, change begins with you.

Overcoming shame is an important aspect of moving towards financial health. To learn to separate your self-worth from your mistakes, and distinguish feelings of shame from feelings of guilt, consider taking the following steps.

Step 1. Accept responsibility for your behaviors. No excuses! Owning up to our actions is part of healthy emotional functioning.

Step 2. Seek to understand. Without excusing your actions, ask yourself: Did I intend to do harm? Did I do the best I could with the knowledge I had at the time? What would I do differently, knowing what I now know, if I found myself in a similar situation?

Step 3. Make a confession. Share with someone you trust the full details of your actions. Explore the context from which your actions or inactions arose. Allow yourself to express your feelings of sadness, regret, frustration, or anger.

Step 4. Make a repair plan. The advice of a mentor, psychologist, or clergy member may be helpful. Be careful not to do more harm in the process of trying to make things right.

Step 5. Take reparative action. Make apologies with the intent of making the other person feel better, not you. Do not apologize expecting your apology to be accepted.

Step 6. Don't do it again. If you make the same mistake, see step 1. If you find yourself repeating the behavior and feel you can't stop, seek help.

Face Your Fears

Denial is a powerful obstacle to growth. To right our off-course financial trajectory, we first have to get real about our financial situation and the consequences of our financial behaviors. This can be especially challenging with money, something that prompts significant shame in many of us. Adaptive in times of extreme stress, denial insulates us from feelings of shame and anxiety and keeps us from feeling overwhelmed and paralyzed. However, if we chronically avoid being honest with ourselves and others about our financial reality, we're robbing ourselves of the adaptive, useful aspects of stress. Like physical pain, distress is a signal that something's wrong. Ignoring or denying these signals keeps us from taking the steps needed to change those destructive and self-limiting behaviors that cause the stress in the first place.

Ironically, the most effective treatment for anxiety and fear is controlled exposure to the thing we fear. Avoidance feeds fear and keeps us from growing beyond our self-imposed limitations. The fact is, we'll never transcend our fear if we don't allow ourselves to directly face the feared stimulus. Once we realize we have the ability to cope with whatever we're dreading—and this is often the most difficult step—we realize that our problems are not insurmountable and our anxiety dissipates.

TED: *Talking about dealing with unfinished business, I'm reminded of how my daughter Brenda dealt with her own daughter's first visit to a dentist. Morgan was showing some anxiety about the upcoming event, so Brenda found a book about going to the dentist and some toy dental tools. After they read the book together, Brenda asked, "Do you want to play dentist with me?" First Brenda pretended to be the dentist, then Morgan got to practice using the tools on Mom. The subsequent visit to the dentist went very smoothly. (And no cavities!)*

By handling her daughter's fears in this way, Brenda did what she could to ensure Morgan would have no unfinished business around dental visits. But by using the same principle of "playing out" your anxieties around your unfinished business, you can go a long way toward putting it aside for good.

Identify Your Triggers

As you can see from the many stories you've read in this book, our most destructive financial habits often follow predictable patterns. Each of us has certain *triggers,* those emotions, situations, or events that precede and prompt our unhealthy behaviors. Common triggers for unhealthy financial behaviors follow the HALT acronym popular in 12-step circles: hungry, angry, lonely, or tired. To those four, we would add afraid. What this means is that the greater the degree to which we are experiencing one or more of these conditions, the more likely we are to get ourselves involved in self-defeating behaviors. You should always be on the lookout for these triggers, so you can stop them before they strike. Triggers can also be highly idiosyncratic, related to the details of a specific traumatic incident and tied directly to your own history.

Most of us are unaware of our triggers, until we make the conscious effort to identify them. But whether we are aware of them or not, they're there. Identifying and cultivating a real-time awareness of them is critical, so we can learn to avoid the places, situations, and people that are likely to bring on the behaviors we're trying to extinguish. If exposure to a trigger is unavoidable, we can prepare ourselves to recognize and counteract our automatic responses. Then we can learn how to transcend them. Here's an example:

STEPHANIE: *Recently when I heard about people losing their homes because of the mortgage crisis, it triggered all my worst fears. I felt like I was about to spin off into a panic state, fearing I would lose my home and everything I had worked hard for—even though I'm not anywhere near being in that situation again. I had to keep reminding myself that the fear came from old stuff, not anything in the present, and I could just set it aside.*

Through our work with Stephanie, she learned what her triggers were and exactly where they came from, and she was able to release some unresolved emotions attached to her early financial flashpoints. She began to use her adult consciousness to become a student of her inner dialogue and impulses, rather than being a victim of them. Distance and perspective allowed her to notice her triggers and counteract them. She has developed an emotional "pause" button that she can press when she feels triggered. During the pause, she uses tools to reduce her anxiety so that her rational brain stays in play.

Knowing your triggers is also essential for *relapse prevention,* or preventing undesirable behaviors from reoccurring after you have made successful changes. When we're distracted, when we're at our weakest, we become vulnerable to our triggers. The exercise below can help you identify what situations and issues are particularly problematic for you.

IDENTIFYING YOUR TRIGGERS

1. Take a sheet of paper and draw a two-inch circle in the middle.

2. Draw a four-inch circle that surrounds the first circle.

3. Draw a six-inch circle that surrounds the other two circles. What you've drawn should now look like a target.

4. In the smallest circle, list all your self-defeating and self-destructive financial behaviors. For example: "I don't follow a spending plan," "I make purchases on impulse," "I hide spending from my partner."

5. Within the next circle, list all the people, places, things, beliefs, attitudes, behaviors, situations, and feelings that you experience just before you engage in the behaviors found in the inner circle. For example: "When I go shopping with Mary," "Right after I make our monthly payment to our credit card company," "When I know I'll be challenged on what I

want to buy," "When I'm feeling unappreciated by my partner," "When I feel lonely," "When I think of my granddaughter," "When I am tired", "When my partner and I have fought," "When I feel underappreciated," and so on. These are your triggers.

6. In the largest circle list all the people, places, things, beliefs, attitudes, behaviors, situations, and feelings that help you (or could help you) avoid the triggers themselves or, if that's not possible, resist the triggered impulses. For example: "Meet Mary for other activities," "Call Susan before I go shopping and let her know what I am shopping for, and call her when I return to let her know what I bought," "Ask my partner to do some communication skills training with me."

Identify Your Emotions and Come Back to Your Body

"What?" you're thinking. "Come back to my body? I'm in my body all the time! And why should I 'identify' my feelings? I *know* what I'm feeling!" The fact is, we may *think* we know what we're feeling but often we don't. What we think of as anger may actually be fear, and what feels like depression may actually be anger. Remember, the animal brain deals mainly with emotions, while the rational brain labels and assigns logic and "causes" to them—interpretations that are not always accurate. The rational brain tends to focus on language, while the animal brain communicates through bodily sensations. It's vital that you become attuned to your body so you can "read" what your animal brain is trying to tell you. The following techniques will help you focus on what's *really* going on so you can deal with the actual emotions, not the assumed ones.

Belly breathing: Because of the feedback systems between our body and brain, one of the quickest ways we can calm ourselves is by paying attention to and adjusting our breathing.

When we're stressed, anxious, or afraid, our breathing becomes shallow. This shallow breathing—called chest breathing—doesn't bring adequate oxygen into our lungs and interferes with our ability to think clearly. Belly breathing, on the other hand, is how we breathe in our natural and stress-free state. If you've ever seen the way sleeping babies breathe, you'll have noticed that their chests are relatively still while their bellies do most of the moving. That's what we want you to imitate. Try this:

- Put one hand on your chest and the other on your belly. Inhale as deeply as you can. Pay attention to which hand moves the most. If your chest moves more, gently shift your breathing to your belly, feeling it expand when you inhale and contract when you exhale. Sometimes it helps to exaggerate the inhale and exhale to lock in what it feels like to breathe with the belly expansion.
- After you inhale, hold the breath for a second or two.
- Exhale, taking as long as you did to inhale.
- Repeat several times.

In times of stress or excitement, try putting five or ten deep belly breaths between a thought or impulse and your action in response. This can be extremely effective in bringing the rational brain back online, and that will help you identify your emotions and avoid doing something you'll later regret. There is some evidence that suggests that any "urge" we have diminishes in intensity by up to 50 percent within the first minute after it shows up. We're much more likely to make wise decisions if we're able to simply sit with the urge, breathe deeply, and allow the impulse to dissipate.

Listening to music: In his recent book *Musicophilia,* neurologist Dr. Oliver Sacks describes how music can liberate people immobilized by Parkinson's disease, return language to stroke patients, and soothe those whose memories have been lost to disease or injury. There's lots of research to show that music in certain pitches, scales, and rhythms has calming effects. In our work, we frequently use music to help clients get in touch with and express pent-up emotions. Music seems to bypass our rational brain and go directly to our emotional centers, which is why it's quite common to tear up or become excited while listening to music. If you feel emotions and stress beginning to build up, try taking a fifteen-minute break to listen to music that you find calming and nurturing. What you choose is largely a matter of taste, but we've found that instrumentals by such artists like Enya and Yanni, lullaby instrumentals, or recorded nature sounds can help initiate a relaxation response.

Mindfulness meditation: In our financial therapy work with clients, we encourage the development of a mindfulness meditation practice. One of the most effective ways to get in touch with our bodies and know what we're feeling is to use meditation techniques, which have the effect of calming and quieting the "monkey mind," thus allowing us to separate ourselves from endless interior chatter. When we listen to it carefully, we find that the background chatter is often made up of negative messages from our past, which can call up difficult feelings which, in turn, lead us to make unwise financial decisions in an attempt to quiet those feelings. Mindfulness meditation also enhances body awareness, which helps reduce anxiety and produce a feeling of connection and "wholeness." When people feel more connected to their bodies, more aware of their presence in the world, they are in better touch with their emotions. They also experience fewer feelings of emptiness and less temptation to act out, financially or otherwise, in a vain attempt to fill that void. Most of our suffering, anxiety, and worry comes from fretting about the past or dreading the future. Meditation trains us to live in and appreciate the present.

In 2004, neuroscientist Dr. Richard Davidson of the University of Wisconsin–Madison enlisted Buddhist monks in a study to examine the effects of meditation on brain activity. Each of the monks had accumulated at least ten thousand hours of practice in meditation focusing on compassion, a generalized feeling of loving kindness toward all beings. The control group was made up of people with no previous experience in meditation who were taught similar techniques and practiced them for a week before the experiment. The results were dramatic. During meditation, the monks showed large increases in a kind of brain activity called gamma waves, which indicate that different parts of the brain are working together to coordinate a higher-order mental activity. The control group showed modest increases in gamma wave activity, but the monks' levels were, at that point, unprecedented in neurological research. According to Davidson, "This pattern of gamma-signal activity is seen during focused attention and other kinds of specific perceptual tasks. However, previously it was observed only for very short periods of time, less than one second. In these practitioners, we saw it displayed for minutes." Since then, Davidson has continued his research and his findings indicate that compassion meditation changes the structure of the brain to strengthen the areas linked to emotions such as altruism and empathy.

Another of Davidson's studies investigated concentration meditation, in which the meditator focuses intently on something, such as his own breathing or a knot in the grain of a wooden chair leg. When experienced and novice meditators were tested on attention and memory, they all showed improvement postmeditation. However, the people who'd been meditating longer and more intensively demonstrated greater improvement, and functional magnetic resonance imaging readings showed that their brain structures were working more efficiently.

Davidson's overarching focus is happiness, which he defines as "a state, a trait, and a skill." He's convinced that meditation can reshape the brain toward happiness, in a way that the pursuit of money can't.

You don't need special clothing or equipment to start a meditation practice, just some time to yourself and a comfortable place to sit. To get started, try setting an alarm for five minutes. Close your eyes and observe what's going on in your mind. At first, it'll probably be a jumble of thoughts and worries. Don't try to push them away or shut them out. Just act as a quiet, objective observer might. Say, "Oh, there's that thought," let it go, and bring your attention back to your breathing. As you become more and more aware of it, your breathing will change. If it's too fast, your awareness will slow it down. Continue until the alarm goes off.

Do this at least once a day, if possible, and slowly increase your meditation time. If you'd like to learn more about mindfulness meditation, we recommend books by Thich Nat Han, Jack Kornfield, and Jon Kabat-Zinn to help incorporate this type of meditation into your life. For others, contemplative prayer serves the same purpose. Still others have found that yoga, tai chi, self-hypnosis, and other such disciplines give them the same "quieting the mind" effect.

Gather More Information

When unfinished business is resolved, energy is released, which gives us mental and emotional space to expand our thinking. The events may be old news, but the memories are forever changed when we bring new insight and understanding to them. You can use this opportunity to gain clarity about where you are in your emotional life compared to where you want to be. The exercises below are designed to help you gather more information about your money scripts, so you can begin to rewrite them.

The Apple Tree Exercise: Your Financial Family Tree

Just as a genealogical family tree traces your origins, a financial family tree can help you discover the origins of your ideas about money.

1. Bring to mind an image of your mother or whomever you consider your most important mother figure. On a sheet of paper, list three or more adjectives that would describe her behaviors around money: generous, impulsive, stingy, for example. Next list three or more things you can remember hearing her say about money and how it worked: "Nothing's too good for you," "It's only money," "Mind the pennies and the dollars will take care of themselves." Write down some of the beliefs you know she had about money by the way she lived her life, which may be somewhat different than the things she said. Looking at what you've written down and what you know now about her background and upbringing, think about the overall money scripts that she lived, both through actions and words, for example: "Money can be used to show love and to exert control," "Money's less important than having fun and enjoying life," "Money means safety and security and nothing's more important than that."

2. Do the same with your father and/or father figures.

3. Imagine what each of them would say to the other about money, if they were completely open and honest. Write that down. Next, write down what you recall that they actually said to each other.

4. Write down what you can remember each of them saying to you or other family members about money.

5. Do the same for any other significant adult whose presence and behaviors influenced the family while you were growing up, such as a grandparent, sibling, neighbor, boss, or a close family friend.

6. Go back to the lists and circle any of those words or phrases that *you* believe are true about you. Use an asterisk (*) to identify any of those words or phrases you can remember using to describe yourself or passing on to others.

7. Put a rectangle around any of those words or phrases that you can recall *others* have used to describe you. If you're prepared for honest feedback, ask your significant other or close friends to read the list and circle which of your family's money messages *they* believe you've inherited.

We call this the Apple Tree exercise because many people discover that a surprising number of their current thoughts and beliefs represent financial "apples" that didn't fall very far from the family tree. Take us, for example.

BRAD: *My father likes to begin his speeches by saying, "My message comes from my own mess." When we present together, I follow up by saying, "My message comes from his mess, too!"*

While I can't blame my father for my financial behaviors in adulthood, his mess did set the stage for mine. That became clear for me one afternoon, as I sat in a financial workshop and first heard my father talk honestly about his relationship with work. During a sharing portion of the workshop, he told his story much as you read it on page 103. When I heard him say, "I always felt lazy compared to my father," my jaw dropped. My wife elbowed me in the side and whispered, "You say the very same thing about yourself!" My lifelong compulsion to stay busy and be productive, my lifelong feelings of insecurity, and my lifelong fear that some-

one might see me as lazy—in that moment, I understood that none of that was really mine! Instead I was playing out a family story that spanned at least four generations. This awareness has allowed me to have a much healthier relationship with work. Now, when the "you're lazy" chatter starts up, I have a choice to listen or not. I know whose voice it is, and it isn't mine. It is one of those generational "gifts" that never quits giving. I notice it and I can let it go. This insight about the origins of the voice has allowed me to replace it with self-talk that's more accurate and more consistent with my true goals and values.

Exercise: Understanding Your Money Story

While you've been reading the stories of those who've shared their financial journey, you've probably been thinking a lot about your own story. Now it's time to put everything together and get it down on paper. This exercise is a little different than the previous ones, and it's designed to help you build a stronger sense of your personal history with money. We believe that the more complete and coherent your awareness of your history, the more conscious control you'll have over your financial life.

To get started, pick a time when you're not likely to be interrupted for at least twenty or thirty minutes. Get a pen and paper, find a comfortable place with good light, and get started.

1. In the middle of the paper, starting at the very left edge, draw a "life line" extending left to right across the paper, edge to edge. The far left side of the line will represent your birth and the far right side, your age right now. Starting at the left edge, bring up your first memory of money, how it was used, when you first became aware that money existed and what it meant. If it was a positive or joyful memory, put a symbol or a

simple drawing to indicate that (a smiley face, perhaps) above the line. If it was negative or painful, put a symbol indicating those feelings below the line. The greater the joy or pain, the higher or lower from the life line the object or symbol would be. If it was a neutral experience, put the symbol right on the line. Continue writing down your most memorable money experiences (aka financial flashpoints)—as many as you can remember. These money experiences don't have to be anything that an outside observer would necessarily regard as significant. The only thing that's important is how the events affected you at the time. Remember that experiences of poverty and wealth are highly subjective and relative. Don't dismiss an event that had a major effect on you because you think that it shouldn't have mattered. If it caused you pain or happiness, it *did* matter. The important thing is to identify and record as many of the events that you can that stand out in your mind.

2. After you've reached the present on your lifeline, go back to each incident and identify a few words that describe how you felt at that moment: angry, frustrated, sad, embarrassed, happy, excited, joyful, ashamed, hurt, distressed, confused, or scared, for example. If you can't remember what you felt, imagine someone else that age experiencing something similar, and guess what they might have felt in that moment. Or ask a trusted friend or adviser to help.

3. Looking through everything you've put down on the paper, write one or two sentences that summarize the lessons you learned about money as you journeyed through life. Here, the chronology is important, because it will help you understand how you built assumptions on top of others, and how your scripts formed over time. Keep in mind that a child's thinking often polarizes or dramatizes events.

4. Complete one of the following sentences: "The moral of my money story is . . ." or "Overall, based on my experiences, the lessons I've learned about money are . . ."

If you've engaged in this exercise fully, and gotten assistance if you found yourself stuck, you'll now have a clearer picture of your mental mind-set around money and how it developed. Once we look back at our history, our financial behaviors, especially our struggles will make total, logical sense. And knowing the story by which we've been living our lives is the first step to creating a new one.

Deal with Past Betrayal

Because many financial flashpoints involve feelings of betrayal, one of the most common money scripts is "You can't trust people around money." Like all money scripts, this belief made sense in context, because it helped you rationalize and explain the betrayal you experienced. If you want to rewrite that script, it's important that you first learn to let go of any resentment or regret that still lingers.

Think back to a time you felt financially betrayed. Maybe you were promised something and didn't get it. Perhaps someone lied to you or kept secrets from you. Maybe someone took advantage of your generosity or your innocence, or perhaps something of value was stolen from you. The experience probably left you feeling used, ashamed, angry, betrayed, ignored, or wronged. You might have been left with a strong feeling that you need to get even. Perhaps you said to yourself, "Never again."

Write down what happened. Note how you felt about it. Then list the lessons you learned from the experience. These lessons might have helped you to cope at the time but may not have served you well since. If you can remember more than one experience of this type, write separately about each one. When you're finished, compare the experiences and look for common patterns. Is this an experience you have found yourself having over and over again?

Next, examine your current life. Are you placing yourself in similar situations with similar people? Are you with safe and trustworthy people but still operating from a place of fear and mistrust? Are you once again putting yourself at risk and ignoring the warning signs? Or has your mistrust led to others feeling betrayed or mistreated by you? If so, what changes are you committed to making?

As you sort through, evaluate, and come to terms with your financial betrayals, don't forget the power of empathy and forgiveness, for yourself and for others. Just as your financial behaviors make sense within the context of your history, so will the actions of others when you take *their* history into consideration.

> CAROLE: *My father is now somewhat ill and much more vulnerable and open, and so I've learned much more about him and his history. I learned that during my childhood he was providing for my grandmother and one of his brothers, who had eight children. He secretly paid for his sister's wedding and to this day she doesn't know, because my grandmother was so ashamed she couldn't afford it herself. He had his own practice as a physician and he accepted quilts, handmade dolls for me, artwork—all sorts of things in trade from uninsured, underprivileged patients. He was the only achiever in an immigrant family. These were all things I was completely unaware of when I was a young girl.*
>
> *I've developed a lot of compassion for my father and his inability to love himself and put himself first. I know that what occurred in my childhood runs deep in me. But I believe that forgiveness clears the way for fulfillment and true prosperity, and so I work hard on that part.*

Keep the Good, Lose the Bad:
Rewriting Your Money Scripts

Paul, whose story you've read much of in this book, grew up with very rigid, black-and-white money scripts: "Rich people are bad. Rich people cheat poor people; that's how they become rich." As a result, his animal brain made sure he'd never accumulate much money, never become someone he or anyone in his circle would consider well off. However, with help, he was able to moderate those money scripts, taking what was useful and discarding the rest.

> PAUL: *I was able to see that I can find a middle ground, something that makes more sense for me, that gives me more clarity around the whole issue of money. It didn't have to be an either-or thing. I could think about money, accumulate it and evaluate it and understand it without betraying some of the very basic beliefs I have about the human condition and about life in general. That was very helpful. It made it easier for me to hear a financial planner's advice without just going blank. I found I'm no longer having to constantly defend against what I am hearing from them, as I used to do.*
>
> *That's been tested sometimes, watching what's going on in our world right now. Not just the housing market, but also what's happening on Wall Street, watching the crooks that stole billions from people. It throws me back to, "Well, my dad and I were right. There's that doctor in his T-bird again." Now it's a little easier to have the corollary message follow that says, "Yeah, of course there are rich people who are crooks. There are people who take advantage of others to be found in every income group, but many rich people are also compassionate, ethical people dedicated to helping other people."*

Your money scripts made sense when you first created them. They helped you impose some order in a confusing situation and deal with painful emotions. They may still be somewhat accurate and useful, in certain circumstances, or they may even be tied to your deepest values. That's why, however problematic your money scripts are, it's a good idea to rewrite them instead of trying to get rid of them altogether. That kind of all-or-nothing response is rarely the best approach. It's another example of the animal brain's black-and-white thinking, when what we really need is shades of gray.

Write down all the money scripts you've identified in the previous exercises. To see what, if anything, of these scripts is worth keeping, ask yourself the following three questions about each script.

1. When is the script accurate? Be as specific as possible about times, places, and ways in which the script is useful. For example, let's say one of your scripts is "Money isn't important." While generally unhealthy, this script has a silver lining, particularly during tough financial times; if you believe money isn't important, you'll be more likely to find other sources of happiness and fulfillment that don't revolve around it.

2. When is it inaccurate? Again, be as specific as possible. Pay attention to your breathing and emotions; you may call up difficult memories in this part of the exercise. If you need to, take a break for some breathing exercises, meditation, or some other relaxing activity. If you just go blank at this step and stay stuck, ask a friend or counselor to help you.

3. How can I use these insights to write an expanded money script? This new script will be accurate and helpful in a full range of experiences and situations.

Let's walk through the exercise with the money script "Money isn't important." When is that statement true?

Money is less important to me than spending time with my family.

Money isn't important to me as a measure of my self-worth.

Money isn't important enough to me to make me betray my principles.

When is that statement *not* true?

Money is important because I need it to take care of myself and my family.

What's a new, expanded version of that script?

I've chosen other things that are more important to me than money, such as spending time with and taking care of my family, and I can use money to help me fulfill those values.

Going through this exercise with a number of your most dominant money scripts can be an important step in changing your financial future.

Journey to the Center of You

When our actions don't line up with our beliefs, a great deal of emotional tension and stress is created. Of course we know our behaviors should be closely aligned with our core values, but in the daily rush, small gaps can open up and grow larger without our being aware of it. And our values change over time; what was important to us at age twenty might not be as significant at age thirty-five. That's why it's a good idea to periodically check in with ourselves to see what it is we value currently and if our actions support those values.

Write down your most closely held values, the things that

are most important to you. Some examples might include the following.

Raising happy, independent children
Living a life of integrity and honesty
Building up a financial cushion for my family
Fully embracing my creative talents
Passing on what I've learned through teaching and mentoring

Here's the hard part. Be totally honest and write down everything you're doing that either conflicts with or doesn't support those values.

I tend to be overinvolved in my children's activities.
Sometimes I cut corners at work and unfairly take advantage of my colleagues.
I haven't come up with a budget that includes saving and investing.
Much of my spare time is spent watching TV or surfing the Web, instead of getting involved with others or using my talents.

For each of the conflicting behaviors you've identified, come up with one specific thing you can do to begin realigning it.

I'll let my son finish his homework on his own tonight and if he doesn't, he'll have to face the consequences at school.
Whenever I'm tempted to "cheat," I'll ask myself how I'd feel if someone else treated me this way.
This weekend, my partner and I will schedule an hour to sit down and talk about our finances.
Instead of turning on the TV as soon as I get home, I'll work on one of my projects or find a volunteering opportunity.

Now take a look at your old money scripts. How are they encouraging you to behave in ways that conflict with your values? Will your rewritten scripts support your efforts to change? If not, how can you rewrite them once again so that they do?

No More Snooze Button!

When the alarm goes off in the morning, how often do you whack the snooze button and postpone getting up just a little bit longer? Delaying the unpleasant is very tempting, which is why we often find ourselves postponing difficult changes we know we need to make. We put them off until "tomorrow," a day that never comes. For the purposes of this exercise, imagine that you have no more tomorrows at all.

Give yourself five minutes to write down your unfinished business. Think of everything you regret not having done: places you wanted to visit, skills you wanted to acquire, wounds you wanted to heal. Keep writing without stopping for the full five minutes. Don't stop to censor or edit yourself. Don't worry if you're writing nonsense; just write. If you can't think of anything, just write "I can't think of anything" until something else comes to mind.

When you're done, read over what you've written. You'll probably see some surprises there about what's truly important to you, insights that can guide you in where to put your time, energy, and money to live a more authentic life. Incorporate these into the scripts you've just rewritten. For example, if one of the things you regret not having done more of is travel, your rewritten "Money is unimportant" script might read, "It's important to use money for things that provide emotional and intellectual fulfillment, open me up to new experiences, and broaden my view of the world."

Creating a New Money Mantra

So now that you've rewritten your self-defeating money scripts, how do you make the new ones stick? This is where some of the training methods we talked about in chapter 3 come in. It isn't always easy, but you can train your brain to adopt these new beliefs and patterns of thinking; with enough practice, they'll eventually become second nature.

A mantra, a term that originated in the Vedic tradition of India, is a word or phrase that is considered capable of effecting transformation. Mantras are common components of spiritual movements; it's thought that by repeating a mantra over and over, one can divert the mind from unhealthy thoughts and replace them with healing ones. In the secular world, people think of a mantra as a personal motto—words to live by. We encourage you to create a money mantra, a motto stating your new, revised, healthy ideas about money. Then repeat your mantra to yourself when those old thoughts try to creep into your brain. As you do this, you not only banish the old thoughts, you strengthen the new ones. Here's an exercise to help you come up with your money mantra.

1. Identify a specific situation that's causing problems for you. Identify the thought that comes to mind in that situation and the resulting emotion. For example:

(Situation): When Chris and I go out with our friends Tracy and Pat, they always want to go to restaurants and clubs that are too expensive for us.
(Money script): The story I make up in my head is that Chris and I are failures for not making more money and having more stuff, like our friends.
(Feeling): It makes me feel embarrassed and ashamed.

2. Go back to the money script that underlies the feeling and rewrite several healthier, more productive versions.

> A. Chris and I don't need to measure our success by how much money we make; we are confident in our accomplishments and achievements.
>
> B. Chris and I have dreams and goals that require us to live within our means.
>
> C. Real failure for Chris and me would be measured not by how much money we do or don't have, but by failing to support each other in times of trouble.

3. Create a more accurate money script statement based on your current reality, your values, and your goals. It is important to work on this statement to make it positive rather than just a negation of the original money script. Focusing on the negative just gives it more power.

> Chris and I have chosen careers that leave us with time to spend with each other and with the children we hope to have, which is much more important than money.

4. Identify the values that underlie the new money script.

> Mutual love and support, strong family life, and responsible spending are more important than accumulating money or possessions. This is your mantra.

Once you've created your money mantra, you have a conscious statement to counter your original unconscious money script. Write it on a card and carry it with you. When thoughts, feelings, or situations trigger this money script, pull out your card and recite your money mantra. Reciting your money mantra can interrupt the automatic emotional and behavioral response to the script. It can help you identify new, healthier behaviors based on your values, such as "Instead of letting Pat and Tracy pick where we go, we can invite them to dinner at our home, or suggest other places to go that are within our budget." A mantra is a powerful reminder that you have other, healthier choices.

Financially Healthy Couples and Families

We've been fortunate enough to witness many joyous changes among the people who we have worked with, and some of the most remarkable transformations have taken place in couples' relationships. Taking away the fear and dread and emotional baggage that surrounds money eliminates a huge source of tension and conflict, freeing up energy to deal with other issues.

> MOLLIE: *What has surprised me the most in this process of becoming aware of my relationship with money is how unemotional money actually is. Stripping away the trauma imprints, rewriting the scripts leaves just dealing with financial matters. Now I feel more confident in talking, making decisions, and planning our financial future with my husband. It's like getting behind the curtain in* The Wizard of Oz. *There's not a lot to be scared about when I can clearly see what is behind my fears.*

Remember Leslie, who grew up with her parents telling her that there wasn't enough money to pay for the things she needed or wanted? Her most crushing financial flashpoint occurred when her father withdrew all her savings from the bank, telling her the money really belonged to him. Obviously, this had effects on her relationship with her husband, including distrust that created a distance between them.

LESLIE: *Now I'm able to trust my husband around money issues. Right now we're in this interesting dynamic. His salary is reduced because of the economy and I'm hearing him say, "We don't have enough money." It feels so similar to the messages I got in my childhood. I know I can trust him, but those old messages are still there. The huge difference is that I don't have to act on them, and I don't have to hide them. I can talk out loud to him about them, something I could never have done before. I know he's responsible with money and he has our best interests at heart. I know because of the work we are doing with our financial planner that we have a pretty clear picture about our finances. I'm grateful for that, being able to feel that trust in my husband and our advisors.*

Sometimes we have the opportunity to work with both partners in the relationship but more often, just one seeks help—often the one with the "problem," the one whose issues with money are more obvious. This is a good first step, but it's just a first one. When a person's disordered money behaviors are hurting the relationship, *both* people have work to do. One reason is that if the "problem" partner *is* able to make changes, it will dramatically alter the dynamic of the relationship. We've seen many cases where the other partner was initially supportive but began to show resistance once the "problem" partner started trying to change the ways things have always been done financially in the relationship. This has a lot to do with our tendency to resist change. The couple has established a system, and when one partner wants to do something different that "changes the rules," the other partner is likely to balk, even if he or she knows the change is for the better. This is natural and predictable. But if the couple can work through the initial problems, the positive changes that result often spur the other partner to take on the work as well.

MARTHA: *We did try to change our behaviors around money but we couldn't seem to do it for any length of time. One or both of us would return to our old behaviors. Then my husband went to the program. When he returned, I really couldn't stand some of the changes. But over time, it became obvious that if we were to have any healing around our financial problems, I needed to also go and do my own work. I learned to be an adult around money. I was able to listen to good solid financial information and begin to set some immediate and long-term financial priorities and goals for myself and to identify what I wanted and needed from my partner. I learned to become an equal partner in our money decisions and our financial planning.*

That's been the biggest gift, the ability to sit with my husband and each of us showing up as two adults to talk, plan, and dream around our financial wants and needs. I've become a more active participant in our monthly budgeting process and with being responsible for paying bills. When I'm willing to be an adult, it's easy to be responsible and to be honest. And it's rewarding to know that the two of us can do this as a team.

So even if you believe your partner is the one with the money issues, you might benefit from doing the exercises described in this section as well. Try some of the following exercises to connect with your partner and get on the same page in terms of money scripts and money issues.

Knees-to-Knees Exercise and Negotiation Guidelines

This exercise can help defuse tensions when you and your partner need to talk about thorny financial issues. In fact, with practice, this process can be helpful for working through any type of conflict. And these steps don't necessarily have to be done with your partner or spouse; if your money issues are getting in the way of any other relationship in your life, you can do these with that person, too.

The goal is to speak your truth, listen, negotiate, and compromise, which are the heart of any relationship. Following this process can open the door to possibilities and produce amazing new creative solutions.

In the following description, for the sake of clarity, we're calling Partner A "he" and Partner B "she."

1. Partner A identifies an issue and asks Partner B for time to discuss it. It's most productive to focus on one topic at a time, but if you need to discuss more than one issue, prioritize them ahead of time. The couple makes an appointment, negotiates how much time they'll spend talking, and agrees to ignore interruptions (in other words, turn off the phone and put away the BlackBerry). By scheduling the discussion, no one feels ambushed and each partner can think about the issue and prepare for the discussion calmly, as opposed to lashing out during a heated argument. Making an appointment is a difficult yet critical step. We can confirm that for men, the scariest four words in the English language when uttered by their wives are "We need to talk." The six scariest words are "We need to talk about money." Say them anyway.

2. Partner A and Partner B sit "knees to knees," facing each other. If we are not careful, many of our arguments become "walk-bys," where we fling comments back and forth while we're involved in other tasks. Sitting down and facing each other when talking about challenging topics helps us to give the conversation 100 percent of our attention.

3. Each partner asks himself or herself, "On a scale of 1 to 10, how intense are my feelings about this issue?" If the inten-

sity is 6 or higher for either person, the animal brain is likely to take over the discussion. Take a break for a half hour or so and reconvene. During the break, focus on calming statements and self-soothing activities. Take some deep breaths. Remind yourself that talking about issues and trying to resolve them is a good thing for your relationship.

4. Partner A spends three to five minutes describing his perspective on the issue, using "I" statements ("I feel . . ." or "I think . . ." instead of "You do . . ." or "You always . . ."). He should focus on two things: what he needs to resolve his feelings around the situation, and what he's willing to offer his partner in return.

5. Partner A asks Partner B, "Does anything I've said need to be clarified?" He's not asking whether she agrees with him; the point here is to find out if Partner B has fully understood Partner A's perspective. After any requested clarification, Partner B feeds back what she's heard to her partner, using reflective listening ("What I heard you say is . . ."). If Partner A feels Partner B has misunderstood him, he's allowed to restate what he intended to get across. This is a critical step to effective communications. Many times, the message we are sending is not what is being received, especially when the issue has intense feelings attached.

6. Once both partners fully understand what Partner A has said, they reverse roles and repeat steps 4 and 5.

7. Partner A states one thing he needs from Partner B and one thing he is willing to do to work toward resolution.

8. Again using reflective listening, Partner B listens and clarifies until the two are in agreement on what Partner A is asking for and offering.

9. Partner B has three possible responses: (a) agree to Partner A's proposal, (b) agree to part of the proposal and make a counteroffer ("What I need is . . . and what I'm willing to give is . . . "), or (c) reject the proposal and make a counteroffer. A counteroffer must always follow a rejection. "I don't think that will work for me; however, I suggest that we . . ."

10. The partners clarify what they've agreed to and write it down.

11. Steps 7 to 10 are repeated, with Partner B presenting her perspective and proposal.

12. The partners should keep repeating steps 7 to 10 until they've settled pending issues or decide to make an appointment to continue the discussion. It's a good idea to limit discussion of any one issue to fifteen minutes. If the discussion goes on much longer, it's easy for positions to become entrenched and tempers to flare. If the partners can't reach agreement on any part of the proposals, stop and make an appointment to try again later, perhaps with the help of a facilitator.

When agreements are reached, do the following.

1. Make the commitments *behavioral*—about actions, not feelings. Focus on answering such questions as "How will we know if we are keeping the agreement?" and "What behavior will we see?"

2. Set a date for *evaluating* the agreement (usually in thirty, sixty, or ninety days). At this time, the partners will review how the agreement is working and make decisions on whether to continue, revise, or cancel the agreement.

3. Develop a *backup plan* that will go into effect if either or both partners break the agreement. We strongly recommend that couples agree to seek help from an agreed-upon third party in case of unresolved difficulties or disagreements. We both have this agreement with our partners, and have sought third party help along the way. Often, the mere "threat" of our having to go sort things out with a third party has motivated us to listen and follow through when we'd rather not.

4. Consider enlisting a neutral facilitator to whom both partners agree to be *accountable*.

Here are some additional helpful hints.

- Check in with feelings whenever necessary and rate them on a scale of 1 (low) to 10 (high). Pause or take time out when feelings intensify to a level of 6 or higher. It's best to do something relaxing: Take a walk, do some deep breathing, make a cup of tea. Rather than obsessing about being stuck, each partner should spend the break thinking about what they can do or say to remove the roadblock.
- When the discussion veers off track or either partner feels confused, return to the basics: "What I hear you saying is . . ." "What I need from you is . . . " or "What I'm willing to give is . . ."
- It's easy to get defensive and fall into blaming the other partner or justifying one's own actions. If that starts happening, go back to reflective listening ("Okay, tell me again what you need, and I'll try to get clear on that").
- Celebrate your agreements and successes.

Rewrite Your Money Scripts, Rewire Your Brain

For decades, psychiatrist and professor Dr. Eric Kandel has studied, at the cellular level, how the brain learns. He was the first to discover that the real seat of learning lies not in the brain cells themselves but in the connections between them, the synapses. Early in his research, Kandel discovered something with wide-ranging implications for lifelong learning and change. Short-term memory relies on strengthening existing synapses while long-term memory requires creating *new* synapses, forging new pathways in the brain. This means that our capacity for learning is far more expansive and long lasting than conventional wisdom allows for. You can indeed teach an old (or middle-aged) dog new tricks.

That's why we've stressed exercises like consciously rewriting your money scripts and turning them into a money mantra that you repeat over and over. Repetition can actually *alter the physical structure of your brain*. The new information creates new pathways, and repetition strengthens those new pathways, just as repeated traffic across a field or lawn packs down the earth to mark a trail. Gradually, these new pathways will become stronger and dominant, while the earlier pathways laid down by your financial flashpoints and the original money scripts fade away. This allows you to change your automatic thinking and habitual behaviors, and create the life you want.

Keep in mind that because these changes can be slow, you may slip back into old habits along the way. That's normal, so don't take it as a sign of failure or an excuse to give up. Rather, identify what triggered the backsliding and think about ways to react differently when a similar situation arises in the future.

Think of Andy Dufresne, the Tim Robbins character in *The Shawshank Redemption*. First he decided that he really did want to be free. Then he took steps to get there—small, incremental steps that added up to big progress. Financial health is a process, not just a destination.

HARRIS: *It feels like I've been driving down the road with this map unfolded trying to find my way and suddenly I realize I'm holding my map upside down. To realize that my entire way of being around money has been sort of askew—that helps me navigate much better. Now I'm much clearer about when a thought doesn't sound very logical or healthy. I find myself saying, "Let's rethink what I just said to myself about this." This shift has changed a lot of behaviors in terms of my wife and me. We have started to get more organized and much more realistic about where we are. It's been a big, deep, internal shift, beginning to turn my car around and change the direction I'm going. Not only for myself, obviously, but for my wife and child.*

The hardest part about all of this is the embarrassment of realizing that I'm in Georgia when I thought I was heading to Massachusetts. I've really not been heading a direction I feel very good about, and I'm seeing that for the first time. But then I realize, "Okay, I'm in Georgia—but at least I didn't end up in Florida or the Bahamas. Thank God I got this caravan turned around when I still have plenty of time to get where I want to go."

The other part that has been hard for me, and I'm still working on it, is realizing that even when you get your map rearranged, it's a long way back. Even when you realize where you need to go, that doesn't mean you're suddenly there. There's an entire journey that you have to take, a lot of territory you have to pass through. There's a lot to learn, and there's a lot to change. I still find myself drifting off course sometimes and now I'm much more aware of it than I used to be. There really is no going back. Once you learn and grow, not doing what you know you should do becomes painful and depressing.

The easiest part has been the excitement. There's something both very painful and very alive about the truth.

Now that we've talked about specific tools to begin rewriting your money scripts and rewiring your brain, we're going to discuss ways you can find support in your journey to a better financial life.

11

Transforming Your Financial Life

In the previous chapter, we gave you the tools to help you identify and rewrite your problematic money scripts and incrementally change your disordered money behaviors. Congratulations! You're now well on your way to lasting financial health. But the journey doesn't stop there. Here we'll identify several general principles that will help you support and sustain your daily efforts.

Keep things in perspective. Many of us hold on to the erroneous belief that more money would make us happy. In fact, people who are focused on material gains at the expense of personal relationships are some of the more unhappy people around.

If your finances are seriously stressing you out, take a step back. It's important to be aware of the financial situation around you—to pay attention to important data like the housing market in *your* area or the unemployment rate in *your* industry, to remind yourself that your problems are not yours alone. But don't overdose on bad financial news. Tune in to what is going on with the country's declining retail sales and which investment bank is currently imploding, but don't obsess about it. You can't control the economy, or the bad news. You *can* control how you respond to it.

Invest in your relationships. Human beings are social creatures and much of our happiness depends on the quality of our relationships with our family and friends—so much more than on money. As such, it is important to invest time and energy in our relationships. Resist the temptation to isolate in times of stress. Take some time for yourself, but don't spend all of your free time alone. Isolation can lead to loneliness and depression. Spend time each day with loved ones who support and care for you. Meet a friend for lunch. Stay involved in family and community activities.

Focus on the present. Take a break from ruminating about your past and worrying about your future. Make an effort to spend time living in the moment. Become fully immersed in whatever you are doing. Do it right now. Take a deep breath, hold it, and let it go. When you get into the flow of life, you forget yourself and bring your focus, energy, and talents to bear to achieve your goals. We are much happier when we are actively immersed in our present activities than when we are fretting about the past or future.

Get moving. Regular exercise is one of the quickest ways to improve your mood, clear your mind, and give you energy to tackle your problems. And you don't need to become a marathon runner, either. Studies have shown that walking for twenty minutes or thirty minutes at a time gives you many of the benefits of more strenuous exercise, including relief of depression. Try making a walk part of your regular routine. Go with your significant other or a friend; we're much better at keeping up with new habits when we do them with others.

Turn off the TV. Unhappy people watch more TV than happier people. They are also more prone to develop physical and emotional problems. Instead of watching hours and hours of TV, pick up an old hobby you used to enjoy or develop a new one. Studies have shown that activities such as scrapbooking, woodworking, and playing cards can improve people's moods, while people report feeling worse after watching TV for an equivalent length of time.

Make an effort to help someone in need. Acts of generosity, such as volunteering your time for a worthy cause or engaging in community service, will have a positive effect on your mood and outlook. It helps you appreciate what you have, extends your financial comfort zone, and takes advantage of the best aspects of the human herd instinct. Dr. Daniel G. Amen, founder of Amen's Clinics, is a physician, a child and adult psychiatrist, a brain-imaging specialist, and a bestselling author. His research has shown that performing acts of kindness creates positive changes in blood flow and activity in the brain. Interestingly, when we simply reflect on things we're grateful for, the same positive changes take place. Which leads to our next suggestion:

Spend some time counting your blessings. People who take time to reflect on the positive aspects of their lives report feeling happier while people who focus on the negative aspects of their lives report less life satisfaction. Take a few minutes each day to identify three things you are grateful for, and allow yourself to truly *feel* the gratitude and appreciation, not just pay it lip service. Appreciation can be infectious; share with your partner at least one thing each day that you appreciate about him or her.

Stay positive. Ultimately, the deciding factor on how stress will impact our emotional and physical health is our attitude. Those who accept what they can't change and focus on improving the conditions that are under their control fare much better than those who believe they can do nothing to improve their situation and predict that things will never get better.

> TED: *During a recent tropical Hawaiian rainstorm, complete with double rainbow, I realized something: There was always a rainbow involved in rain showers like this, and whether or not I could enjoy it was based entirely upon my perspective. I use that metaphor to understand the possibilities during the other "rain showers" in my life.*

Embrace the opportunity for self-growth. None of us enjoys pain, yet it's an essential component of learning. Just as physical pain tells us that hot stoves should be avoided or a particular tooth needs attention, emotional pain alerts us to the fact that something is wrong. With patience and self-reflection, our most painful experiences can become our most valuable opportunities for growth. Mourn your losses; identify and forgive yourself for your mistakes; and take the opportunity to build your knowledge, improve your relationships, and bring your values in line with your goals and behaviors.

Know when to seek help. Recognize the signs that you might need professional assistance. If you're losing interest in activities you previously enjoyed, having trouble sleeping or concentrating on your tasks, showing increased irritability, or

suffering from feelings of hopelessness, worthlessness, or fa-
tigue, seek the help of a mental health professional.

Even though disordered money behaviors permeate our culture, the field of psychology hasn't caught up with that reality.
As a result, little work has been done to identify money disorders as a significant clinical issue. One exception is our study
published in *Psychological Services,* which we mentioned
earlier. The other exception is pathological gambling, and
there's some evidence to show that behavior therapy, cognitive-
behavioral interventions, self-help approaches, and medication can improve outcomes for those with this disorder.
However, pathological gambling is estimated to affect just 2 to
5 percent of the population worldwide. Given that 80 percent
of Americans cite money as the number one cause of stress in
their lives, pathological gamblers account for only a small portion of those suffering with disordered money behaviors.

Even so, the field of psychology does have tools that can
be highly effective in helping people overcome anxiety and
other self-limiting emotions, and with the recent economic
crisis a growing number of mental health professionals are
receiving training in how to apply these tools to financial
stress and trauma. Through our work with therapists and financial planners, we have developed a certification process
so that consumers can know that their therapists are trained
in dealing with money issues, and their financial advisers
have some training in working on the emotional aspects of
money. In addition to gaining access to your free money disorders test, you can learn more about our work at www.Your
MentalWealth.com.

Areas of Intervention

One thing we hope you take away from this book is the real-
ization that there is no clear-cut distinction between body and

mind, body and emotions. Thoughts, emotions, and behaviors share a complicated feedback system. There's no doubt that each influences the others but we don't always know which comes first. Everything we do is prompted by this amazingly intricate system, and in turn our actions affect that same system.

Psychiatrist Dr. Aaron Beck and his daughter, psychologist Dr. Judith Beck, have developed a model of functioning that takes into account all four aspects of human interaction with our environment: thoughts, emotions, behavior, and physiology. The Becks' treatment approach is called cognitive-behavioral therapy (CBT) and it's less concerned with chicken-and-egg questions about, for instance, whether flawed neurochemistry causes depressive thoughts, or whether depressive thoughts influence neurochemistry, or some combination of both. Instead, CBT focuses on intervening in the areas of thought and behavior, the idea being that changes in one area will lead to improvements in all others. Financial thoughts and behaviors can be addressed on all these levels, too.

Thoughts: Our core beliefs about ourselves and the world impact our mood, our behaviors, and our physiology. Negative beliefs or thoughts lead to emotions such as anger and fear, which result in physical responses, including higher blood pressure and fight/flight/freeze behaviors. On the other hand, positive thoughts create a sense of well-being, inspiring us to embark on goal-directed behaviors. By changing our internal dialogue, we can change our mood and physiology, which can in turn lead to changes in our behavior.

The first step in mastering your thoughts and their impact on your life is identifying the problematic thoughts. By completing the exercises in previous chapters, you've identified some of your core money scripts. This conscious awareness gives you the opportunity to notice when they come up so you can make a purposeful decision to accept the money script and act on it or replace it with one that is in concert with your values and goals. Interrupting an automatic thought and replacing it with a more helpful or accurate one can radically and immediately change one's feelings and resulting behaviors.

Awareness is the key. When we are able to make a distinction between ourselves and our thoughts, we are able to create new scripts to live by. CBT approaches and meditation have been shown to help people change their limiting thinking to more positive narratives.

Emotions: Our emotions, too, have a direct link to our thoughts, behaviors, and our physical health. As we've learned, when we have unfinished business, we carry unexpressed emotions from the past that can distort our current experiences. This unfinished business hampers our ability to distinguish between an emotionally charged past event or relationship and a situation or relationship occurring in the present. This decreases our effectiveness in recognizing and dealing with the real problems we face. Repressed emotions can also make themselves known in other forms, including behaviors such as overspending or hoarding, or stress-related health problems. Various forms of therapy seek to uncover repressed feelings, allowing us to acknowledge them and leave them behind. The concepts and exercises in this book are intended to help you identify and let go of the difficult emotions associated with your financial flashpoints and radically change your thoughts, behaviors, and physiology.

Our method of treating money disorders can best be described as an experiential approach. The idea is to reenact and play out the emotional climates of the family of origin, as well as other significant events and current relationships in a client's life. When successful, this leads to self-discovery, a crucial element of psychological growth. By reexperiencing events and relationships in a safe setting, we are able to view our relationships from a different, healthier perspective. This aids in the release of emotions that may have been blocked and repressed, opens the door to new insights and awareness, and helps clients learn new skills. Psychodrama, role-playing, and music are just a few of the modalities used in experiential therapies, which focus on direct experience as being the vehicle to change.

Other useful ways to access and affect your emotions are through meditation and body awareness exercises, as we described in chapter 10.

Behaviors: Have you ever noticed that when you force yourself to smile, even if you're not feeling all that smiley, your mood improves? Just as changing your thoughts and emotions can change your behavior, changing your behavior can change your internal reality. Try it now: Put a pen or pencil, lengthwise, loosely, in between your upper and lower jaws—which forces your face into a smile—and notice what happens to your thoughts. It really is pretty difficult to entertain negative thoughts while smiling. Now take the pencil or pen out of your mouth and clench your jaws. You'll most likely find it difficult to maintain that positive thinking with your muscles tightened and your lips compressed.

One of the quickest ways to change our feelings and thoughts is to take action, to do something different and replace our unthinking, automatic behaviors with new ones. Often, however, we aren't sure *what* we should do. When we're stuck like this, we find it very helpful to first create a declaration of who you want to be, for example, "I am a debt-free person." While in this frame of mind, you weigh all your decisions and actions based on this declaration. At first you may have no idea *how* to be a debt-free person, yet it is something you grow into. Just like with that smile, you fake it until you make it, learning along the way. If you keep behaving like a debt-free person, you will inevitably become one.

Physiology: On the most fundamental level, our thoughts and behaviors are chemical reactions, as brain cells take up and respond to dopamine, serotonin, and other compounds. Certain psychological conditions, such as depression, anxiety, and obsessive-compulsive disorder, seem to have a strong neurochemical component. There are many medications, and even more in the research pipeline, designed to better manage the chemical communication system between neurons. Medication can be effective in improving mood, decreasing anxiety, and reducing obsessive thoughts and compulsive behaviors. But don't be fooled into thinking that you can cure your disordered money behaviors through pharmacology alone. The right medication can help take the edge off debilitating symptoms. This allows you to more effectively address your unfinished business, interrupt unhelpful thinking patterns, and institute new behaviors, but there is still work to be done. That said, if you think you could benefit from antianxiety or antidepressant medication, you should discuss it with a mental health professional.

A promising new treatment approach worth mentioning here is that of *neurofeedback therapies.* Neurofeedback, also known as EEG biofeedback, is a technique that teaches a person to purposefully alter their brain waves. It has been used for many conditions and disabilities in which the brain is not working as well as it might and has shown some promise in the control of anxiety and depression, behavioral problems, attention deficit hyperactivity disorder, sleep disorders, epilepsy, and cognitive dysfunction resulting from head trauma, stroke, or aging. It has also been used for patients undergoing cancer treatment, because it can help reduce stress, pain and nausea, and enhance immunity. We're currently investigating the usefulness of this approach in addressing money disorders, with some very promising early results.

Research is ongoing in other areas as well. One study demonstrated that it's possible to train the brains of animals to resist fear responses—"learned safety," the counterpart to learned helplessness. Beta-blockers, a class of drugs commonly prescribed for heart problems, seem to eliminate negative emotional responses to a troubling memory without affecting the memory itself. And yet another controversial drug holds out the potential of removing the memory itself—like in the movie *Eternal Sunshine of the Spotless Mind.*

Environment: Just as our internal state impacts our environment, our environment can have a profound impact on our internal state of being. After all, most of our disordered money behaviors have an external origin, whether in money scripts we learned as children from those around us or from a financial flashpoint that we didn't initiate or create. And because the people around us are such a crucial element of our external environment, they are also powerful influences on our behavior.

If you're currently stuck in an unhealthy financial pattern, chances are that you're being supported in this pattern by someone in your life. This support can take the form of a partner or spouse who ignores your fiscally unfit behaviors, a family member or friend who continues to give you money to bail you out of trouble, or a shopping buddy who allows your secret credit card statements to be mailed to her house so your partner doesn't find out how much you're spending. But you don't want people in your life who are supporting you in your disordered money behaviors; you want people who will support you in your efforts to overcome them. In other words, to create a new financial life, you may need to change your environmental supports. Positive peer support groups can help. These are organizations such as Debtors Anonymous (www.debtorsanonymous.org), Gamblers Anonymous (www.gamblersanonymous.org), Clutterers Anonymous (www.clutterersanonymous.net), and Spenders Anonymous (www.spenders.org). Today, it seems that you can find a support group for just about any problem under the sun. And even if you can't find a group for your particular issue, it's easy to start one. You may just find out that there are more people out there struggling with what you're struggling with than you ever realized.

Finding a Therapist

At some point, you may come to the conclusion that you or a loved one could benefit from the assistance of a therapist. You might work with a clinical psychologist, social worker, counselor, marriage and family therapist, or psychiatrist. All have specialized training in mental health, with the major difference being that psychiatrists can prescribe medication. You can begin your search for a therapist by asking trusted friends and professionals for referrals or by approaching professional associations in your area. If you live in or near a city with a large university or medical school, investigate their training programs, in which students counsel patients under the guidance of experienced faculty members. This can be a good way to receive care for reduced fees. If cost is an issue, look for clinics and sole practitioners who bill clients on a sliding scale.

In some states, anyone can hang out a shingle and call themselves a counselor or a therapist. You want to make sure that your mental health provider is both licensed and a member of a reputable professional organization, such as the American Psychological Association, American Counseling Association, National Association of Social Workers, or American Association for Marriage and Family Therapy. This will help ensure that whoever you work with has the basic training and background needed to provide you with useful therapy well supported by clinical research.

The following questions will help you determine whether a therapist you're considering working with might be a good match for you.

1. "What kind of clients do you mainly work with? Do you have a specialized area of practice?"

2. "Please describe your education and training and your therapeutic approach."

3. "Are you comfortable talking about money? What is your own relationship with money like?" If this question makes the therapist uncomfortable, he or she might not be the right person to help you with your money issues.

4. "What is your fee scale?"

5. "How will we set goals for my treatment, and how will we measure my progress?"

Whatever questions you ask, do your research and trust your gut feelings. The most important thing is that you feel comfortable with your therapist. It's natural to feel a little awkward during the first few sessions, but if you're still on edge after several sessions think about what's missing and ask for a referral to someone whose approach or personality will be a better match. This is not at all unusual and you won't be insulting the therapist. If you're working with someone you like who has little training in financial matters but seems open to learning about them, he or she may find the tools and techniques in our book for financial professionals useful: *Facilitating Financial Health: Tools for Financial Planners, Coaches, and Therapists* (National Underwriter Company, 2008).

Putting Together Your Team

So let's say you've successfully dealt with the unfinished business related to your money issues, and rewritten your self-defeating money scripts, but you're still having trouble getting your finances in order. At this point, you might want to enlist the help of a financial planner, someone who can use their expertise to help you create a sound financial road map. Once you've dealt with your deep-seated issues around money and successfully altered your behavior, we suspect you'll find that such a roadmap is now much, much easier to follow.

Anyone can call themselves a "financial planner" so it's a good idea to look for someone with specialized certification. A Certified Financial Planner (CFP), a certified public accountant–personal financial specialist (CPA-PFS), or a chartered financial consultant (ChFC) will have training in financial planning and will report to a professional organization that keeps track of complaints against its members.

If you have friends whose financial situation seems stable and healthy, ask if they work with a financial planner. You can also ask your accountant or tax professional for a referral. Or consult a financial planning association in your area. The following are some pertinent questions to ask any planner you're considering working with.

1. "What experience do you have?" Make sure your financial planner has some experience working with individuals, not just institutions. Unless you have very specific requirements, it's usually best to work with someone who can handle a range of needs: insurance, taxes, retirement, and estate planning. Find out how the planner keeps up to date on changes in the field.

2. "What's your approach to financial planning?" You want a planner whose viewpoint matches yours on the "aggressive versus conservative" scale.

3. "Who else do you work with?" Will he or she be the only person you'll have contact with? Will your planner carry out his or her recommendations or refer you to others for that? Does the planner have financial arrangements with these other professionals? You should meet or at least get the names of anyone you may be discussing your finances with.

4. "How will I pay for your services?" Most often, planners are paid either through commissions on the products or services recommended to you, or via an hourly or flat fee. Either method is legitimate and what works best for you depends on your circumstances. The important thing is to be very clear about the arrangement—and get it in writing.

Break Out of Your Box

Here's one final exercise to help you take action and jump-start the transformation you're ready to make.

Your beliefs have gotten you where you are. They create your version of reality, which constrains and limits what you think is possible. It is important to know that regardless of your early experiences, your version of reality—how the world works and doesn't work, what you can and can't do, who you are and who you are not—is an invention on your part. It is a childlike understanding of how things are in the world, developed to help you navigate and survive your early environment. However, we live in a universe of limitless possibility. Our mental boxes—the things we often are the most certain about because we learned them in the school of hard knocks—can act like a prison we don't even know we are in. If you're not happy where you are, you have to break out of your box. But first, you have to recognize it and that's not always easy.

Think of one of Marcel Marceau's best-known acts. Solely through his movements, the famous mime created the walls of a nonexistent box. The audience saw that there *was* no box, yet his actions and gestures made its confines real. In the same way, our mental boxes are both real and imaginary. They are real for us because they're defined by our beliefs which are, in turn, shaped by our fears, our justifications, our actions and inactions. However, we lose sight of the imaginary aspect of our boxes; we forget that they're the result of mental constructions we've created. It's as if Marcel jumped into his invisible box and refused to leave, convinced the walls were real and he could not escape them. When we recognize the box for what it is, we can break free from its imaginary walls and recognize the vast possibilities that await us, and the opportunities all around us.

Here's an exercise to help you break out of your box to create a new reality. It's an open-ended, ongoing exercise, and you can return to any of the steps when you need to.

1. Visualize a breakthrough goal; something you believe may be beyond your ability to achieve. Perhaps it's getting out of debt, saving up for a Hawaii vacation, starting a new business, or retiring early. Write it down, and describe how you would feel once you've achieved this goal.

2. Identify the beliefs that keep you stuck where you are. If your current beliefs would get you something else, something else would have already been manifested in your life. Why don't you have what you want? What makes reaching that goal hard or impossible? What's standing in your way? What makes you unworthy of or unable to attain the goal?

3. Enter the world of "what if." What if you committed to removing those barriers—what would you have to do? What would you need to know? How would you have to define yourself? Identify people who have already reached the very goal you want to attain and analyze what they've done. What do they believe? How do they behave? What books do they read? If you start feeling hopeless about reaching your goal, imagine how they would behave at this point in your journey. Perhaps you've seen the acronym WWJD on a shirt, on a rubber bracelet, or on a sign. It stands for "What Would Jesus Do?" For many Christians, WWJD reminds them to change their frame of reference to what they believe Jesus would do, say, or be in their situation. It's a cue to step out of their box and create a new reality in their relationships and in their world. Ask yourself, "What would (insert name of person whose financial transformation you admire) do?"

4. Commit right now to creating a new reality. If you are not sure how to do that, simply fake it until you make it. This can be a very useful strategy. Pretend you know what you're doing and start living in your new reality *now*. Don't wait. Take the position and grow into it, learning along the way. Old habits die hard, so when you get discouraged, use the "your first thought is wrong" technique. Listen to that old self-limiting and sometimes downright insulting negative self-statement, belief, or thought, and say, "That's wrong." Then identify a more helpful belief based on your values.

AFTERWORD

Just about everyone on the planet is worried about money these days. But the silver lining to all this is that the financial meltdown has really forced all of us—as individuals and as cultures—to take a long, hard, honest look at our relationships with money. So we thought it would be interesting to ask some of the financial planners we've worked with if they had observed any *positive* effects the financial crisis has had on the attitudes and behaviors of their clients. And, because it's so much on everyone's mind, many of the clients we spoke to volunteered their thoughts on it as well. We've collected some of the most interesting observations for you here. First, the clients:

> LESLIE: *I think another thing that's surprising is just watching the economy, what's been happening on a social level or a global level—you know, the money beliefs, how they have played out, the beliefs that have driven the dysfunctional financial behaviors of an entire culture, country, generation, or maybe even a world.*

*For example, buying into the belief that one can get a 100 per-
cent mortgage with no down payment and that's in anybody's best
interest, other than the people who profit from the mortgages
themselves.*

Many people, like Leslie, are recognizing the need for wide-
spread change. And Sally reminds us that resilience and opti-
mism are always useful.

SALLY: *I hear that everyone is stressed and worried about the near
future. I understand where it comes from and I know that it will
have effects on me as well. When the events hit me, the uncertainty and people not believing in investment anymore, it makes
me feel tense. However, as the optimist that I am, I hold on to the
belief that change will happen, change is happening—and
change usually brings good things. I really do expect good things
to happen. I continue to revise my money behaviors. I continue to
try to do things differently. I do what I can and after that, I trust
that things will fall in place and that change will bring good
things.*

We were even more fascinated by the "worm's-eye" view our
financial planner clients provided. They're able to describe the
current economic situation from two complementary perspectives: that of a worried onlooker, just like the rest of us, as well
as an experienced participant in the financial marketplace.

VANESSA: *During these trying financial times I am, in a way,
grateful for the opportunity to talk about changing habits with
my friends, colleagues, and clients. Before this, many people in
my world were locked in a spendaholic spell; now they are much
more willing to examine whether their spending is in line with
their values. This is the opportunity in the crisis.*
    With my financial planning and coaching clients, I'm intro-

ducing them to the idea that there are many ways to look at current circumstances. I spend quite a bit of time brainstorming different perspectives. I also am pretty adamant about being a careful consumer of media. I encourage everyone to think about why they watch, read, or listen to the news, the TV shows, the blogs, and to look at the value that consumption brings them. If it heightens their anxiety and doesn't yield actionable steps, it might be time to give it up. If it's informative and actionable items result, then have at it.

In terms of how I am dealing with all this personally, I'm focusing even more on my personal development: reading books that feed my soul, enhancing my yoga practice, surrounding myself with like-minded friends. I gave up TV two years ago, I don't read newspapers, and I consume radio news in small, healthy doses.

Looking ahead, I'm hoping it will be better than now. I can't imagine it getting much worse. I don't really think in those terms, though. I think much more along the time lines of personal goals—where will I be five, ten, fifteen years from now. Same with my clients. Of course I plan based on historical rates of return that match my client's asset allocation, and I put them in a well-diversified portfolio. Then I hope that we won't have any more three-standard-deviation events in the next five to twenty years—but I can't predict with any certainty whether we will or won't.

ISABEL: These are hard times. I'm letting my clients who are retired know that no one understands their concerns as much as another retired person, but I'll do my best. I've encouraged a number of people to call, just to check in and let me know how they're feeling. If they prefer to write, I encourage them to send me their feelings and thoughts via e-mail. I'm trying to empathize with them and acknowledge their feelings and then also share some of the positives and how they can ride this out, show them some financial solutions and acknowledge their feelings. I am try-ing to avoid "canceling out" their concerns.

I am managing my own feelings about all of this by talking with people whom I deem to be much more knowledgeable and experienced in the financial world and getting their point of view. I talk to my therapist and also to my CPA and I take care of myself with meditation and rest.

Within five years, I would anticipate that things will be going better and on an upswing.

In ten years, I am guessing that we will still be cycling be-tween the ups and downs of the markets.

Twenty years from now, I believe we may be in another down-turn, and other crises that we have yet to imagine will probably surface. Based on what I read and what I believe and what I've seen in statistics, we will go through this again but the crisis will be different. I think the market is not a lot different from human beings' lives . . . They go through good times and bad times, healthy times and sick times, learning times and fun times.

RUSSELL: Everybody says they want change right up until the time they have to change their behaviors, actions, and attitudes. That's the heavy-lifting part of it. What the credit, financial, and economic crises are telling us is that what's been going on is not sustainable. It's not sustainable from a personal finance point of view, from an economic point of view, from a global perspective, from an environmental perspective, from an energy perspective, and also from a human capital perspective. All of these things were completely out of balance, and we were operating using nonrenewable resources to live.

I tend to run everything through a filter called sustainability. If the concept or the product is sustainable, there's hope. If it is not sustainable, there isn't much. That's the message I'm giving. Now, I think that message has a tremendous amount of hope and potential because if people, on an individual basis, get to the *point of living within their means in a sustainable manner, we are going to be better for it.*

Now how do we get people through the crisis? Many times, people already have the answer inside them. They've already had to deal with times of uncertainty and fear and anxiety, and they might be able to look back on and use those same coping tools. And in the workshops we have done we have heard of the creative things others have done during times of financial adversity, personal financial adversity. And it wasn't that bad.

GWEN: *I'm supporting my clients primarily by listening to what their fears and anxieties are. On a client interaction basis, my main job is to listen. On a technical basis, my job is to review and monitor the plans we've made in light of these different circumstances. So I kind of see it as two sides of one job.*

One of the opportunities here is that perhaps we'll learn more about the psychological side of all this money stuff. If we decided to make fiscal therapy or fiscal education a part of elementary education curriculum, then I think we could have a huge shift on the way that our society views money.

I think that in order for us to learn the lessons that life is teaching us now, there has to be an internal societal shift. We have to be able to say, "It's totally cool that my neighbor, who has the same type of job as I do, drives a better car than I do, because a better car is not my priority. My priority is, I'm sending my kids to private school. I know who I am, I'm really clear on my goals, I'm comfortable in myself. I don't need somebody outside to tell me what makes me a good person, or successful. I know that already."

The exterior work of our financial lives really is an inside job. Getting our heads right, getting our hearts right, is the real work. If we do that, then the exterior stuff takes care of itself. Understanding what my true goals are, figuring out the behaviors that will move me toward them—that's the key.

The current economic crisis, with all of its fear, uncertainty, loss, and pain, is a wake-up call for the world. In our insatiable hunger for more money, larger cars, and homes we could not afford, we abandoned reason and mortgaged our futures in an attempt to get something that money and possessions can never provide—a sense of connection, a sense of wholeness, a sense of belonging. But in the midst of our global and personal financial crises lies an opportunity. If we have the courage to get honest about our financial behaviors, examine our pasts, and challenge and change our money scripts, we have the power to transform our financial lives. It is our hope that this book has helped you make the most of this opportunity in your own life, and we applaud your willingness and courage to examine your relationship with money.

DO YOU HAVE A MONEY DISORDER?

As part of our ongoing research, we have developed the Money Disorders Scales (MDS). This test was developed after many hours of research and draws on our work with thousands of clients over the past decade. In developing the test, we administered it to more than 400 subjects, refined it, and developed a factor-analyzed set of scales that can identify symptoms associated with eight different money disorders. The test consists of fifty-three items scored on a 6-point scale ranging from "Strongly Disagree" to "Strongly Agree."

As a purchaser of this book, you can access this test at no charge at our website www.YourMentalWealth.com. Just enter the following code to take the test: YMWTEST21471. When you have completed the test, a dynamically generated individualized report will be made available to you. This report will review your results and make specific recommendations. It's important to note that a formal diagnosis can only be made by a licensed mental health professional with an expertise in financial psychology, and a test alone can never be used to diagnose any condition. However, the MDS can be a very useful screening instrument and can help you identify areas of concern.

At www.YourMentalWealth.com, you can also find the twenty-item Financial Health Scale (FHS) that we used in our research on the treatment of disordered money behaviors. It can be used as a quick measure of your financial health, and as an ongoing tool to monitor your progress toward a more balanced financial life. We also invite you to visit www.Your MentalWealth.com to access our latest news, exclusive videos, and written content related to improving your financial health. We also welcome your comments and invite you to share your stories of struggle and triumph with us.

BIBLIOGRAPHY

Adams, Kenneth M. *Silently Seduced: When Parents Make Their Children Partners—Understanding Covert Incest.* Deerfield Beach (FL): Health Communications Inc., 1991.

Alberts, Mike, SPC. "Medics getting job done in Kirkuk," *Hindustan Times,* U.S. Fed News, 7 November 2006. http://iworks.factiva.com/archive/default.aspx?an=INDFED0020061108e2b7002v4&fid=0.

All Things Considered, National Public Radio, "Client learns Madoff returns worthless," 13 December 2009. http://www.npr.org/templates/story/story.php?storyId=98229849o.

American Psychological Association. *Stress in America,* 07 October 2008. Executive summary available at http://www.apa.org/releases/women-stress1008.html.

Aquilino, W., and A. Supple. "Long-term effects of parenting practices during adolescence on well-being outcomes in young adulthood," *Journal of Family Issues,* vol. 22, 289–308 (2001).

Aubrey, Alison. "Happiness: It really is contagious," National Public Radio *Morning Edition,* 5 December 2008.

Aversa, Jeannine. "Debt-related stress leads to increasing number of health problems," Associated Press, *USA Today.* 09 June 2008. http://www.usatoday.com/news/health/2008-06-09-debt-stress_N.htm.

Aziz, S., and M. J. Zicklar. "A cluster analysis investigation of workaholism as a syndrome," *Journal of Occupational Health Psychology,* vol. 11, no. 1, 52–62 (2006).

Barber, Brad M., and Terrance Odean. "Boys will be boys: gender, overconfidence, and common stock investment," *The Quarterly Journal of Economics,* February 2001, pp. 261–292.

Baruch, Bernard M. *Baruch: The Public Years.* New York: Holt, Rinehart and Winston, 1960.

Bautista, Justo. "Woman saves boy from drowning—revives 4-year-old at crowded lake," *The Record* (Bergen County, NJ). 29 July 1998. Retrieved January 04, 2009 from HighBeam Research: http://www.high beam.com/doc/1G1-158312576.html.

Begley, Sharon. "Economists and psychologists—and the rest of us—have long wondered if more money would make us happier. Here's the answer," Newsweek.com. 15 October 2007. http://www.newsweek .com/id/43884.

———. "Scans of monks' brains show meditation alters structure, functioning," *Wall Street Journal,* 5 November 2004.

Benson, M. L., and G. L. Fox. "Concentrated disadvantage, economic distress, and violence against women in intimate relationships," in *Violence Against Women and Family Violence: Developments in Research, Practice, and Policy,* Bonnie Fisher (ed.) NCJ 193433.

Berton, Justin. "PTSD leaves physical footprints on the brain," *San Francisco Chronicle,* 27 July 2008. http://sfgate.com/cgi-bin/article .cgi?f=/c/a/2008/07/27/MNH611UUP5.DTL.

Bird, Caroline. *The Invisible Scar.* New York: D. McKay Co., 1966.

Blodget, Henry. "Why Wall Street always blows it," *Atlantic Monthly.* December 2008. http://www.theatlantic.com/doc/print/200812/ blodget-wall-street.

Bonebright, C. A., D. L. Clay, and R. D. Ankenmann. "The relationship of workaholism with work-life conflict, life satisfaction, and purpose in life," *Journal of Counseling Psychology,* vol. 47, no. 44, 469–477 (2000).

Bost, James. "Recession triggers memory of Great Depression," National Public Radio *Morning Edition.* 30 January 2009. http://www.npr.org/ templates/story/story.php?storyId=100011598.

Brenner, Marie. "Madoff in Manhattan," *Vanity Fair,* 27 January 2009. http://www.vanityfair.com/politics/features/2009/01/madoff200901 ?printable=true&currentPage=all.

Buffett, Warren. "What Worries Warren: Avoiding a 'mega-catastrophe,'" *Fortune Magazine.* 3 March 2003. http://www.fortune.com/fortune/ investing/articles/0,15114,427751,00.html.

Caginalp, Gunduz, David Porter, and Vernon Smith. "Financial Bubbles: excess cash, momentum, and incomplete information," *The Journal of Psychology and Financial Markets,* vol. 2, no. 2, 80–99 (2001).

Carey, Benedict. "Brain researchers open door to editing memory," *New York Times,* 5 April 2009. http://www.nytimes.com/2009/04/06/ health/research/06brain.html.

Caudron, Shari. "The healing power of hobbies," Reader's Digest Online. http://www.rd.com/living-healthy/the-healing-power-of-hobbies-and-pastimes/article29248.htm.

Center for Alternative Medicine at the National Institutes of Health. "Of meditation, monks, and music: Dr. Davidson speaks on systematic mind-body training," *Focus on Complementary and Alternative Medicine,* vol. XV, no. 3, October 2008. http://nccam.nih.gov/news/newsletter/2008_october/mindbodytrain.htm.

Conrad, Cecelia, and James Stewart. *African Americans in the U.S. Economy.* Rowman & Littlefield: Lanham (MD), 2005.

Csikszentmihalyi, Mihaly. "If we are so rich, why aren't we happy?" *American Psychologist,* vol. 54, no. 10, 821–827 (October 1999).

Davis, M. and P. J. Whalen. "The amygdala: vigilance and emotion," *Molecular Psychiatry,* 6, 13–34 (2001).

Deutschman, Alan. "Change or die," *Fast Company,* May 2005. http://www.fastcompany.com/magazine/94/open_change-or-die.html.

Diener, Ed, and Martin E. P. Seligman. "Beyond money: toward an economy of well-being," *Psychological Science in the Public Interest,* vol. 5, issue 1, pp. 1–31.

Dingfelder, Sadie F. "An insidious enemy: New research pinpoints the ways stress undermines our immune systems at the cellular level," *Monitor on Psychology,* vol. 39, no. 9, October 2008. http://www.apa.org/monitor/2008/10/stress-immune.html.

Dittmar, H. "Compulsive buying—A growing concern? An examination of gender, age, and endorsement of materialistic values as predictors," *British Journal of Psychology,* 96, 467–491 (2005).

Dobbs, David. "Eric Kandel: from mind to brain and back again," *Scientific American Mind,* October/November 2007, pp. 32–37.

Dunn, Donald H. *Ponzi: The incredible true story of the king of financial cons.* New York: Random House, 2004.

Fishman, Steve. "The Monster Mensch," *New York Magazine,* 22 February 2009. http://nymag.com/news/businessfinance/54703/.

Gazzaniga, Michael S. "The split brain revisited," *Scientific American: The Hidden Mind,* vol. 12, no. 1, 26–31 (2002).

Grable, John E., and So-Hyun Joo. "Student racial differences in credit card debt and financial behaviors and stress," *College Student Journal,* vol. 40, no. 2, 400–408 (2006).

Halber, Deborah. "Picower researcher finds neuron growth in adult brain," Massachusetts Institute of Technology News Office, 27 December 2005. http://web.mit.edu/newsoffice/2005/neurons.html.

Hanley, A., and M. S. Wilhelm. "Compulsive buying: An exploration into self-esteem and money attitudes," *Journal of Economic Psychology,* vol. 13, 5–18 (1992).

Hartocollis, Anemona. "Peaceful clinic flooded with patients with their own fiscal crises," *New York Times,* 31 January 2009.

Haughney, Christine. "In tough times, even the billionaires worry," *New York Times,* 10 December 2008.

Hull, Alastair. "Neuroimaging findings in post-traumatic stress disorder: systematic review," *British Journal of Psychiatry,* vol. 181, 192–110 (2002).

Joo, So-Hyun, and John Grable. "An exploratory framework of the determinants of financial satisfaction," *Journal of Family and Economic Issues,* vol. 25, no. 1, 25–50 (2004).

Juarez, Leticia. "Heroic Ponderosa firefighter recalls saving three people from burning SUV," Channel 11 News, Houston. 29 December 2008. http://www.txcn.com/sharedcontent/dws/txcn/houston/stories/khou 081229_tnt_ponderosa-firefighter-hero.1a6ebb20.html.

Kahler, R., T. Klontz, and B. Klontz. "Helping clients change: 21st century tools from a 19th century fable," *Journal of Financial Planning,* vol. 20, no. 4, 62–67 (2007).

Kausch, Otto; Rugle, Loreen; Rowland, Douglas. "Lifetime histories of trauma among pathological gamblers," *The American Journal on Addictions,* vol. 15, 35–43 (2006).

Keynes, John Maynard. *General Theory of Employment, Interest, and Money.* New York: Atlantic Publishers and Distributors, 2007.

Kindt, Merel, Marieke Soeter, and Bram Vevliet. "Beyond extinction: erasing human fear responses and preventing the return of fear," *Nature Neuroscience,* vol. 12, 256–258 (2009). Published online 15 February 2009.

Klontz, B., R. Kahler, and T. Klontz. *Facilitating Financial Health: Tools for Financial Planners, Coaches, and Therapists.* Cincinnati, OH: The National Underwriter Company, 2008.

Klontz, B., T. Klontz, and R. Kahler. *Wired for Wealth: Change the money mindsets and unleash your wealth potential.* Deerfield Beach, FL: Health Communications, Inc., 2008.

Klontz, B. T., E. M. Wolf, and A. Bivens. "The effectiveness of a multi-modal brief group experiential therapy approach," *The International Journal of Action Methods: Psychodrama, Skill Training, and Role Playing,* vol. 53, no. 3–4, 199–135 (2001).

Klontz, B. T. "The ethical practice of group experiential psychotherapy," *Psychotherapy: Theory, Research, Practice, Training,* vol. 41, no. 2, 172–179 (2004).

Klontz, B. T., A. Bivens, D. Leinart, and P. T. Klontz. "The effectiveness of equine-assisted experiential therapy: Results of an open clinical trial," *Society & Animals: Journal of Human-Animal Studies,* vol. 15, 257–267 (2007).

Klontz, B. T., S. Garos, and P. T. Klontz. "The effectiveness of brief multimodal experiential therapy in the treatment of sexual addiction," *Sexual Addiction & Compulsivity: The Journal of Treatment and Prevention,* vol.12, no. 4, 275–294 (2005).

Klontz, B. T., A. Bivens, P. T. Klontz, J. Wada, and R. Kahler. "The treatment of disordered money behaviors: results of an open clinical trial," *Psychological Services* 5(3), 295–308 (2008).

Klontz, B. T., T. Dayton, and L. S. Anderson. "The use of psychodramatic techniques within solution-focused brief therapy: A theoretical and technical integration." *The International Journal of Action Methods,* vol. 52, 113–116 (Fall 1999).

Klontz, T., R. Kahler, and B. Klontz. *The Financial Wisdom of Ebenezer Scrooge: 5 Principles to transforming your relationship with money.* Deerfield Beach, FL: Health Communications, Inc., 2006–2008.

Klontz, B. T., and P. T. Klontz. "Providing financial therapy for clients with money disorders," *Counselor: The Magazine for Addiction Professionals,* vol. 20, no. 1 (2009).

Klontz, B. T., and P. T. Klontz. "Are you a credit junkie: Plain talk about money disorders," *Recovery Living Magazine,* 72–74, February 2009.

Koehler, Brian. "Psychological trauma and the brain," ISPS-US, the United States Chapter of the International Society for the Psychological Treatments of Schizophrenia and Other Psychoses, 20 December 2006. http://www.isps-us.org/koehler/trauma_brain.html.

Koran, L. M., R. J. Faber, E. Aboujaoude, M. D. Large, and R. T. Serpe. "Estimated prevalence of compulsive buying behavior in the United States," *The American Journal of Psychiatry,* 163, 1806–1812 (2006).

Landsbergis, Paul, Susan J. Schurman, Barba A. Israel, Peter L. Schnall, Margrit K. Hugentobler, Janet Cahill, and Dean Baker. "Job stress and heart disease: evidence and strategies for prevention," *New Solutions: A Journal of Environmental and Occupational Health Policy,* vol. 3, no. 3, 42–58 (1993).

Ledgerwood, David, and Nancy Petry. "Posttraumatic stress disorder symptoms in treatment-seeking pathological gamblers," *Journal of Traumatic Stress,* vol. 19, no. 3, 411–416 (2006).

LeDoux, Joseph. *The Emotional Brain: The Mysterious Underpinnings of Emotional Life.* New York: Simon and Schuster, 1996.

Lee, Wei-Chung Allen, Jerry Chen, Hayden Huang, Jennifer Leslie, Yael Amitai, Peter So, and Elly Nedivi. "A dynamic zone defines interneuron remodeling in the adult neocortex," *Proceedings of the National Academy of Sciences,* vol. 105, no. 50, 19968–19973 (2008).

Leonhardt, David. "Economics behaving badly," *New York Times.* 3 December 2008. http://www.nytimes.com/2008/12/03/business/economy/03leonhardt.html.

Levine, Rebekah, and P. Lindsay Chase-Lansdale. "Welfare recipient, financial strain, and African-American adolescent functioning," *Social Service Review* (September 2000).

Lidz, Franz. *Ghosty Men: The Strange but True Story of the Collyer Brothers, New York's Greatest Hoarders: An Urban Historical.* New York: Holtzbrinck Publishers, 2003.

Lipton, Joshua. "Credit cards: choking on credit card debt," *Forbes,*
    12 September 2008. http://www.forbes.com/personalfinance/2008/
    09/12/credit-card-debt-pf-ii-in_jl_0911creditcards_inl.html.
Lite, Jordan. "Could a blood pressure drug dim bad memories?" *60-Second
    Science,* Scientific American website. 16 February 2009. http://www
    .sciam.com/blog/60-second-science/post.cfm?id=could-a-blood
    -pressure-drug-dim-bad-2009-02-16.
Loewenstein, George. "Preferences, behavior and welfare: emotions in
    economic theory and economic behavior," *AEA Papers and Proceedings,*
    vol. 90, no. 2, 426–432 (2000).
Loftus, Elizabeth. "Creating false memories," *Scientific American,* vol. 277,
    no. 3, 70–75 (1997).
Lohrenz, Terry, Kevin McCabe, Colin F. Camerer, and P. Read Montague.
    "Neural signal of fictive learning signals in a sequential investment
    task," *Proceedings of the National Academy of Sciences,* vol. 104, no. 22,
    9493–9498 (2007).
Mackay, Charles. *Extraordinary Popular Delusions and the Madness of
    Crowds.* Boston: L.C. Page & Company, 1932.
Mallia, Joseph, and Matthew Chayes. "Wal-Mart worker dies in Black
    Friday stampede," *Newsday,* 29 November 2008. newsday.com/news/
    local/nassau/ny-limart1129,0,167903.story.
McDaniel, Deangelo. "Risking life to save another: Hartselle officer says
    he's no hero after ending a hostage situation," *Decatur Daily,* 25 January
    2007. Accessed via HighBeam Research: http://www.highbeam.com/
    doc/1G1-158312576.html.
Medintz, Scott. "Secrets, lies and money," *Money,* 1 April 2005.
    http://money.cnn.com/magazines/moneymag/moneymag_archive/2005/
    04/01/8254979/index.htm.
Miller, William R., and Stephen Rollnick. *Motivational Interviewing:
    Preparing people for change.* New York: Guilford Press, 2002.
Moyers, Bill, Betty Flowers, and David Grubin. *Healing and the Mind.*
    New York: Random House, 1995.
Neuner, M., R. Raab, and L. A. Reisch. "Compulsive buying in maturing
    consumer societies: An empirical re-inquiry," *Journal of Economic
    Psychology,* vol. 26, 509–522 (2005).
Noah, Timothy. "Fun with Bailout Numbers: The financial pages discover
    the word quadrillion," *Slate Magazine,* 09 Oct. 2008. http://www.slate
    .com/id/2201961/.
Norvilitis, Jill M., Bernard Szablicki, and Sandy D. Wilson. "Factors
    influencing levels of credit-card debt in college students," *Journal of
    Applied Social Psychology,* vol. 22, issue 5, 935–947.
O'Hanlon, Larry. "Study: A lack of control causes people to see patterns
    that don't exist," *Discovery Channel,* MSNBC.com. 2 October 2008.
    http://www.msnbc.msn.com/id/26996326/.
Petry, Nancy M. *Pathological Gambling: Etiology, Comorbidity, and*

Treatment. Washington, D.C.: American Psychological Association, 2005.

Picower Institute for Learning and Memory at MIT. "Researchers identify cell type that remodels brain circuitry," *Neuroscience News,* vol. 3, no. 3 (2009).

Pollak, Daniela, Francisco Monje, Lee Zuckerman, Christine Denny, Michael Drew, and Eric Kandel. "An animal model of a behavioral intervention for depression," *Neuron,* vol. 60, no. 1, 149–161 (2008).

Postrel, Virginia. "Why asset bubbles are part of the human condition regulation can't cure," *Atlantic Monthly.* December 2008. http://www.theatlantic.com/doc/200812/financial-bubbles.

Price, Russ Alan, and Lewis Schiff. *The Middle-Class Millionaire: The rise of the new rich and how they are changing America.* New York: Random House, 2008.

Raghubir, Priya, and Joydeep Shrivastava. "Monopoly money: the effect of payment coupling and form on spending behavior," *Journal of Experimental Psychology: Applied,* vol. 14, no. 3. http://www.apa.org/journals/releases/xap143213.pdf.

Riger, S., and S. Staggs. The Impact of Intimate Partner Violence on Women's Labor Force Participation, submitted to the National Institutes of Justice, 2004. NCJ 207143. http://new.vawnet.org/category/Documents.php?docid=315&category_id=188.

Robinson, B. E. "The workaholic family: A clinical perspective," *The American Journal of Family Therapy,* vol. 26, 65–75 (1998).

Robinson, B. E., and L. Kelley. "Adult children of workaholics: Self-concept, anxiety, depression, and locus of control," *The American Journal of Family Therapy,* vol. 26, 223–238 (1998).

Robinson, B. E., J. J. Carroll, and C. Flowers. "Marital estrangement, positive affect, and locus of control among spouses of workaholics and spouses of nonworkaholics: A national study," *The American Journal of Family Therapy,* vol. 29, 397–410 (2001).

Robinson, John P., and Steve Martin. "What do happy people do?" *Social Indicators Research,* vol. 89, no. 2, 115–139 (2008).

Rodriguez-Villarino, R., M. Gonzalez-Lorenzo, A. Fernandez-Gonzalez, M. Lameiras-Fernandez, and M.L. Foltz. "Individual factors associated with buying addiction: An empirical study," *Addiction Research and Theory,* vol. 14, no. 5, 511–525 (2006).

Roosevelt, Franklin Delano. "More important than gold: FDR's first fireside chat," History Matters. Created by the American Social History Project / Center for Media and Learning (Graduate Center, CUNY) and the Center for History and New Media (George Mason University). http://historymatters.gmu.edu/d/5199.

Salkin, Allen. "You try to live on 500K in this town," *New York Times.* 8 February 2009. http://www.nytimes.com/2009/02/08/fashion/08half mill.html?ref=nyregion&pagewanted=print.

Salomon, A, E. Bassuk, A. Browne, S. S. Bassuk, R. Dawson, and
    N. Huntington. *Secondary Data Analysis on the Etiology, Course and
    Consequences of Intimate Partner Violence Against Extremely Poor
    Women.* Submitted to the National Institute of Justice, 2004. NCJ
    199714.

Sapolsky, Robert M. "Depression, antidepressants, and the shrinking
    hippocampus," *Proceedings of the National Academy of Sciences,*
    October 23, 2001, vol. 98, no. 22, 12320-12322.

Schneider, J. "The increasing financial dependency of young people on
    their parents," *Journal of Youth Studies,* vol. 3, no. 1, 5–20
    (2000).

Seal, Mark. "Madoff's World," *Vanity Fair,* April 2009. http://www.vanityfair
    .com/politics/features/2009/04/madoff200904?printable=true&current
    Page=all.

Shapiro, Thomas. *The Hidden Cost of Being African American: How Wealth
    Perpetuates Inequality.* Oxford University Press US, 2005.

Shefrin, H., and M. Statman. "The disposition to sell winners too early and
    ride losers too long: Theory and evidenc," *The Journal of Finance,*
    vol. 40, no. 3, 777–790 (1985).

Shiv, Baba, and Alexander Fedorikhin. "Heart and mind in conflict: The
    interplay of affect and cognition in consumer decision making," *The
    Journal of Consumer Research,* vol. 26, no. 3, 278–292 (1999).

Smeesters, Dirk, and Naomi Mandel. "The sweet escape: Effects of
    mortality salience on consumption quantities for high- and low-
    self-esteem consumers," *Journal of Consumer Research,* vol. 35,
    no. 2, 309–323 (2008).

Spence, J. T., and A. S. Robbins. "Workaholism: Definition, measurement,
    and preliminary results," *Journal of Personality Assessment,* vol. 58, no. 1,
    160–178 (1992).

St. George, Donna. "Unhappy people watch more TV than happy people,
    U-Md. researcher finds," *Washington Post,* 23 November 2008. http://
    www.washingtonpost.com/wp-dyn/content/article/2008/11/22/AR
    2008112201985.html.

Steketee, G., R. O. Frost, and M. Kyrios. "Cognitive aspects of compulsive
    hoarding," *Cognitive Therapy and Research,* vol. 27, no. 4, 463–479
    (2003).

Sullivan, Cris, and Maureen Rumptz. "Adjustment and needs of African-
    American women who utilized a domestic violence shelter," *Violence
    and Victims,* vol. 9, no. 3, 275–286 (1994).

Tatzel, M. "Money worlds and well-being: An integration of money
    dispositions, materialism and price-related behavior," *Journal of
    Economic Psychology,* vol. 23, no. 1, 103–126 (2002).

Tedeschi, Richard, and Lawrence Calhoun. "Posttraumatic growth: A new
    perspective on psychotraumatology," *Psychiatric Times,* vol. 21, no. 4
    (2004).

Thaler, Richard H. "From Homo economicus to Homo sapiens," *Journal of Economic Perspectives*, vol. 14, no. 1, 133–141 (2000).

Tolin, D., R. Frost, and G. Steketee. *Buried in Treasures: Help for Compulsive Acquiring, Saving, and Hoarding*. Oxford, England: Oxford University Press (2007).

Torre, Pablo S. "How (and why) athletes go broke," *Sports Illustrated*, 23 March 2009. http://vault.sportsillustrated.cnn.com/vault/article/magazine/MAG1153364/index.htm.

Trachtman, R. "The money taboo: Its effects in everyday life and in the practice of psychotherapy," *Clinical Social Work Journal*, vol. 27, no. 3, 275–288 (1999).

Usborne, David. "$5m payout wrecked my life, says 9/11 widow," *The Independent*, 15 June 2005. http://www.independent.co.uk/news/world/americas/5m-payout-wrecked-my-life-says-911-widow-494169.html.

van der Kolk, B. A., and A. C. McFarlane. "The black hole of trauma," *Traumatic Stress: The Effects of Overwhelming Experience on Mind, Body, and Society*. Bessel A. van der Kolk, Alexander C. McFarlane, and Lars Weisaeth (Eds.). New York: Guilford Press, 1996.

Verghese, Joe, Richard B. Lipton, Mindy J. Katz, Charles B. Hall, Carol A. Derby, Gail Kuslansky, Anne F. Ambrose, Martin Sliwinski, and Martin Buschke. "Leisure activities and the risk of dementia in the elderly," *New England Journal of Medicine*, vol. 348, 2508–16 (2003).

Weber, Deborah, and Cecil Reynolds. "Clinical perspectives on neurobiological effects of psychological trauma," *Neuropsychology Review*, vol. 14, no. 2, 114–129 (2004).

Whitson, Jennifer, and Adam D. Galinsky. "Lacking control increases illusory pattern perception," *Science*, vol. 322, no. 5898, 115–117, (2008).

Wilson, Michael. "Old habits bedevil plane crash survivors who vow to change," *New York Times*. 8 February 2009. http://www.nytimes.com/2009/02/08/nyregion/08crashes.html?ref=nyregion.

Zeller, Tom Jr. "The Lede: Savings Rate at Depression-Era Lows . . . Does it Matter?," *New York Times*, 1 February 2001. http://thelede.blogs.nytimes.com/2007/02/01/savings-rate-at-depression-era-lows-does-it-matter/?scp=1&sq=%22negative%20savings%20rate%22&st=cse.

Zimbardo, Philip, and John Boyd. *The Time Paradox: The New Psychology of Time that Will Change Your Life*. Free Press: New York, 2008.

ACKNOWLEDGMENTS

Jointly, we are grateful for a truly extraordinary team who has helped make this book possible. We could not have done it alone. Special thanks to those clients of ours who shared their experience, strength, and hope for this book. You are our greatest teachers. Thanks to Brad's sister and Ted's daughter, Brenda Klontz Anderson, who provided incredible support by taking care of the details so we could focus on the big picture. Thanks to our managers, Kerry Hansen and Lori Cloud of Big Enterprises, who came into our lives at just the right moment. Their expertise has added tremendous velocity to our work. Thanks to our agent, Laurie Liss, of Sterling Lord Literistic for her professionalism, encouragement, and support. You really know your stuff. Thanks to our personal editor, Jan Werner, who kept us headed in the right direction and whose expertise and hard work kept us on track to meet a tight deadline. You are a joy to work with. Thanks also to Brad's stepmother and Ted's wife, Margie Zugich, who spent many hours reading and proofing this book. Thanks also to Gary Seidler, Rick Kahler, and our friends and mentors Sharon Wegscheider-Cruse and Dr. Joe Cruse.

Thanks to our wonderful and supportive team at Broadway Books. Special thanks to Talia Krohn, our editor, whose vision inspired us. Your dedication, red pen, creativity, and insights made this book a much better one. Thanks also to Roger Scholl, editorial director of Broadway Business; Meredith McGinnis, associate director of marketing; Tara Delaney Gilbride, director of publicity; Dennelle Catlett, senior publicist; and Michael Palgon, deputy publisher. All of you have been big supporters of the book, and we really appreciate it.

We have some individual acknowledgements to offer, too.

BRAD: I want to thank my business partner, coauthor, and father, Ted. It is a unique blessing to have the relationship we have, that allows us to create together and do the work we do. I love every minute of it. I want to thank my wife, Dr. Joni Klontz Wada, whose support, encouragement, and love make me a better person. The book benefited immeasurably from your in-depth knowledge and insights into the psychological issues around women and money. Thanks to my family, friends, and mentors who believe in me, root for me, and help me think outside the box. Special thanks to Wanda Turner, Dr. Jim Turner, Philip Morgan, Dr. Alex Bivens, Dr. Martin Johnson, Tim Cusack, Dr. Larry Kutner, Lee White, Dr. Rick Delaney, Dr. Kevin Pyle, Gary Seidler, Joey Villanueva, Rick Kagawa, Saundra Davis, Rick Long, Robert "Fixer" Smith, Steve Bucci, John Wada, Diane Wada, and Sonya Britt.

TED: I am grateful for my son, Brad, who helped us put what we do into a form that could be tested and demonstrated to be effective. He then took the results and without pause wrote and rewrote and refined the study until he got it published in the APA journal. That's what started us on this path, and his vision and determination made it all possible. In addition, this project would not have been possible without the loving support of my best friend and wife of thirty years, Margie. Thanks also to my "angels"—Elaine Walker, MaryAnn McCready, Dr. Bill Mayhall, the thousands of clients who taught me so much throughout all the years, and my many friends and family who continue to cheer me on. I am also eternally grateful for my money disorders. While they did a lot of damage, they also gave me a seemingly unquenchable desire to learn from my experiences and own up to my part in those situations. I am committed to never experiencing them again, and perhaps most importantly, I'm determined not to pass them down to future generations.

INDEX

Abusive relationships, 112, 195
Acceptance, as stage of grief,
    213–214
Addictive behavior (*see* Money
    disorders)
Adoptive children, 159
Adrenaline, 35, 38
African Americans, 113–114
After-the-fact realizations, 47
Age of Turbulence, The
    (Greenspan), 58, 80
Alienation from others, 112
Amen, Daniel G., 264
American Association for Marriage
    and Family Therapy,
    272–273
American Counseling Association,
    272
American Psychological
    Association, 20, 220, 272
Amygdala, 35, 44, 94–95
Anger, as stage of grief, 213
Animal brain, 37–39, 42, 43, 45,
    48, 51, 60–62, 67, 71,
    94–95, 123, 124, 130, 156,
    234
Anxiety, 27, 37, 46, 61, 67, 95,
    149, 166, 167, 207, 270
Apple Tree exercise, 239–241
Appreciation, 264–265
Archetypes, 123
Arizona State University, 28
Associated Press/AOL poll, 20
Average household income, 81
Avoidance of money (*see* Money
    avoidance disorders)

Bankruptcy, 99, 144, 173, 177
Banks, mistrust of, 107
Bargaining, as stage of grief,
    213
Baruch, Bernard, 85
Beck, Aaron, 267
Beck, Judith, 267
Behavioral therapy, 217
Belly breathing, 234–235
Berkshire Hathaway, 152
Beta-blockers, 271

Betrayal, dealing with past, 243–244

Bettelheim, Bruno, 123

Biofeedback, 270–271

Bird, Caroline, 107

Black Swan, The (Taleb), 54

Bluebeard fairy tale, 175–176

Bost, James, 107

Boyd, John, 207–208

Brain
    animal, 37–39, 42, 43, 45, 48, 51, 60–62, 67, 71, 94–95, 123, 124, 130, 156, 234
    emotional, 35, 37, 43, 45, 47, 48, 96
    frontal lobes of, 98
    gamma waves of, 237
    hemispheres of, 48–50
    limbic, 35
    physical changes in response to trauma, 96–97
    prehistoric, 32
    rational, 37–39, 42, 43, 45–48, 54–56, 228, 234
    regeneration of, 228–229
    reptilian, 34, 37
    split-brain experiments, 49, 96, 212
    structure of, 33–38, 48–49

Brainstem, 34

Break Out of Your Box exercise, 275–277

Breathing, 42, 44, 47, 234–235

Brothers Grimm, 122

Bubbles, market, 81–86

Buddhism, 36

Buffett, Warren, 52, 83, 152

Buyer's remorse, 173

Calhoun, Lawrence, 216

Capital Resources and Insurance, 116

Cardiac patients, 31–32

Cerebellum, 34

Certified Financial Planner (CFP), 274

Certified public accountant-personal financial specialist (CPA-PFS), 274

Change, resistance to, 25–26, 253–254

Chartered financial consultant (ChFC), 274

Chest breathing, 235

Christmas Carol, A (Dickens), 150–151

Clutterers Anonymous, 272

Cognitive-behavioral therapy (CBT), 266–268

Cognitive therapy, 217

Collapse (Diamond), 57

Collective unconscious, 122–123

Collyer family, 157

Comfort zone, financial, 65–76, 78–79, 112–113, 143

Compassion meditation, 237

Compulsive buying disorder, 133, 158, 173–174

Compulsive hoarding (*see* Hoarding behaviors)

Concentration meditation, 237

Corpus callosum, 49

Cortisol, 38

Crab-barrel effect, 72

Credit counseling, 229

Credit default swaps, 84, 152

Crisp, Quentin, 80

Culture, financial trauma and, 113–118

Damasio, Antonio, 57–59

Davidson, Richard, 237

Debt, 75, 113 (*see also* Money disorders)

Debtors Anonymous, 174, 229, 272

Decision-making process, 42
    emotions and, 57–62

Defense mechanisms, 102, 132, 136–140
Delayed gratification, 209
Denial, 40–41, 136
    financial, 102, 132, 134, 136–140, 230–231
    as stage of grief, 213
Dependency, financial, 102, 119–120, 133, 175, 176, 193–200, 209
Depression, 97, 166, 207, 270
    as stage of grief, 213
Derivatives, 152
Descartes' Error (Damasio), 57
Diamond, Jared, 57
Dickens, Charles, 150–151
Diener, Ed, 24
Dissociation, 139–140
Divorce, 99, 139, 174, 184, 186, 200
Domestic violence, 195
Dopamine, 173, 270
Dot-com bubble, 83, 85–86
Durst Organization, 20

Electroencephalography (EEG) research, 97–98
Embezzlement, 99
Emergency response plan, 183–184
Emotional brain, 35, 37, 43, 45, 47, 48, 96
Emotional needs, 21, 22
Emotional release, 211–218, 268–269
Emotions, decision-making process and, 57–62
Enabling, financial, 133, 175, 176, 187–193
Endocrine system, 35
Epilepsy, 49
Erasmus University, 28
Excessive risk aversion, 132, 134, 151–153, 208
Excitement, 39, 41
Exercise, physical, 263–264

Exercises
    Apple Tree, 239–241
    Break Out of Your Box, 275–277
    Creating Money Mantra, 250–252
    Knees-to-Knees, 254–258
    Money Atom, 221–225
    Money Egg, 225–227
    Rewriting Money Scripts, 245–247
    Understanding Your Money Story, 241–243
Experiential therapy, 217, 268
Explanatory mechanism, 48–51, 212
Extraordinary Popular Delusions and the Madness of Crowds (Mackay), 81–83
Exuberance, 58

Facebook, 64
Facilitating Financial Health: Tools for Financial Planners, Coaches, and Therapists (Klontz, Kahler, and Klontz), 273
Fairy-tale metaphor, 122–123, 134, 154, 175
False positives, 54, 96
Family experience, financial trauma and, 99–106
Fear, 27, 39, 41, 46, 58, 64, 95, 149
    facing, 230–232
Fedorikhin, Alexander, 55
Fight-or-flight response, 35, 38–40, 42, 94, 211, 267
Financial comfort zone, 65–76, 78–79, 112–113, 143
Financial crisis, 19–20, 30–31, 79, 99, 122, 152, 191, 279–284
Financial denial, 102, 132, 134, 136–140, 230–231
Financial dependency, 102, 119–120, 133, 175, 176, 193–200, 209

Financial enabling, 133, 175, 176, 187–193
Financial flashpoints, 39, 51, 61, 90–91, 94, 123, 151, 164, 170
Financial Health Scale (FHS), 286
Financial ignorance, 139
Financial incest, 133, 175, 185–187
Financial infidelity, 133, 175, 180–184, 191
Financial planners, 274–275
Financial rejection, 132, 134, 140–149
Financial status, differences in, 77–78
Financial trauma, 99–125
    culture and, 113–118
    family experience and, 99–106
    gender and, 118–122
    societal, 106–108
    socioeconomic issues and, 108–113
Financial Wisdom of Ebenezer Scrooge, The: 5 Principles to Transform Your Relationship with Money (Klontz, Klontz and Kahler), 151
Flashbulb memories, 95
Flexibility, importance of, 56–57
Fooled by Randomness (Taleb), 54
Foreclosure, 99
Foster children, 159
401(k)s, 67
Freeze response, 40, 42, 94, 139, 152, 267
Freud, Sigmund, 229
Frontal lobes of brain, 98
Fugita, Stephen, 116
Functional magnetic resonance imaging (fMRI), 96
Future-oriented (F-O) person, 208, 209

Galinsky, Adam, 53
Gamblers Anonymous, 166, 272

Gambling, 152, 153, 161–162
    pathological, 133, 164–166, 208, 266
Gamma waves of brain, 237
Gandhi, Mahatma, 217
Gazzaniga, Michael, 49, 50
Gender issues
    financial dependency and, 193–195
    financial infidelity and, 181–182
    financial trauma and, 118–122
Gerdes, Lee, 97–98
Gilbert, Daniel, 23–24
Grable, John, 131
Graham, Benjamin, 52, 83
Great Depression, 40, 107–108, 117, 161, 169
Greenspan, Alan, 58, 80
Grief, stages of, 213–214
Griffin, Joe, 20–21
Guilt, 28, 112, 140–141, 143, 149, 189, 230
Gut feelings, 59–60

HALT acronym, 232
Happiness, income levels and, 23–24, 110–111, 167
Healing and the Mind (Moyers and Lerner), 36
"Heart and Mind in Conflict" (Shiv and Fedorikhin), 55
Hemispheres of brain, 48–50
Herd instinct, 63–65, 80–86, 88–89
Hidden Cost of Being African American, The (Shapiro), 114
Hippocampus, 35, 97
Hoarding behaviors, 107–108, 109, 133, 156–161
Holland, tulipomania in, 81–83
Hormones, 35, 38
How We Decide (Lehrer), 60
Human givens approach, 20–21, 24
Hypothalamus, 35, 38

Imagination, 61
Income levels, happiness and,
    23–24, 110–111, 167
Infringement, 97
Insight-oriented therapy, 217
Intelligent Investor, The (Graham),
    52, 83
International reply coupons (IRCs),
    87
Interpreter mechanism, 50, 52
Invisible Scar, The (Bird), 107
Isaza, Pamela, 43

Japanese Americans, 114–117
Joo, So-Hyun, 131
Journaling, 217
Jung, Carl, 122–123

Kabat-Zinn, Jon, 238
Kagawa, Kiyoshi, 115–118
Kagawa, Rick, 116–117
Kandel, Eric, 259
Kennedy, Joseph, 85
Keynes, John Maynard, 56
Klein, Gary, 60
Knees-to-Knees exercise,
    254–258
Kornfield, Jack, 238
Kübler-Ross, Elisabeth, 213

Late fees, 136
Learned helplessness, 200,
    271
Learned safety, 271
LeDoux, Joseph, 49
Left brain hemisphere, 49–50
Lehrer, Jonah, 60
Lerner, Michael, 36
Limbic brain, 35
*Limitless You: The Infinite
    Possibilities of a Balanced
    Brain* (Gerdes), 97
LinkedIn, 64
Loftus, Elizabeth, 214
Lottery winners, 144

Mackay, Charles, 81–83
MacLean, Paul, 34, 35
Madoff, Bernie, 88
Magnetic resonance imaging
    (MRI), 96
Mandela, Nelson, 217
Mantras, 250–252
Marceau, Marcel, 276
Market bubbles, 81–86
Maslow, Abraham, 20–21
McFarlane, Alexander, 93
Medications, 270
Meditation, 36, 45, 216, 236–238,
    268
Memory, 35, 140, 214–218, 259,
    271
Mental health professionals,
    265–266, 272–273
Miller, Edward, 32
Mindfulness meditation, 236–238
Momonoi, Fumiko, 115–117
Momonoi, Yoshio, 115, 116
Money Atom exercise, 221–225
Money avoidance disorders, 101,
    102, 109, 110, 134–153
    common scripts, 135–136
    excessive risk aversion, 132,
        134, 151–153, 208
    financial denial, 102, 136–140,
        230–231
    financial rejection, 132, 134,
        140–149
    underspending, 132, 134,
        149–151, 209
Money disorders, 124–125
    avoidance (*see* Money avoidance
        disorders)
    definition of, 129
    money-worshiping (*see*
        Money-worshiping disorders)
    relational (*see* Relational money
        disorders)
    screening test for, 132, 201,
        285–286
    symptoms of, 131

Money Disorders Scale (MDS),
    285–286
Money Egg exercises, 225–227
Money magazine, 181
Money mantras exercise, 250–252
Money scripts, 51, 90, 113–114,
    119–124, 130–132,
    134–136, 145, 156,
    179–180, 193–194, 201,
    224–225, 227, 238–239,
    242–243, 245–250, 259–261
Money-worshiping disorders,
    154–174
  common scripts, 156
  compulsive buying disorder,
      133, 158, 173–174
  hoarding behaviors, 107–108,
      109, 156–161
  overspending, 28–30, 91, 133,
      158, 169–173, 208
  pathological gambling, 133,
      164–166
  unreasonable risk taking, 133,
      161–164
  workaholism, 133, 156,
      166–169, 209
Monkey mind, 36
Montague, Read, 83
Moyers, Bill, 36
Murder-suicide, 122, 195
Music, 235–236
Musicophilia (Sacks), 235
MySpace, 64

National Association of Social
    Workers, 272
National Debt Clock, 20
Needs, hierarchy of, 21
Neocortex, 36, 37, 95
Nervous system, 35
Neurofeedback therapies, 270–271
New York Times, 31, 220
NFL players, 144
Norepinephrine, 38
Northwestern University, 53

O'Brien, David, 116
Obsessive-compulsive personality
    disorder, 159, 270
On Death and Dying (Kübler-Ross),
    213
Online spending, 172–173
Overdraft charges, 136
Overspending, 28–30, 91, 133,
    158, 169–173, 208

Pandora's box, 176
Pascal, Blaise, 54
Past-negative (P-N) person, 208,
    210
Pastoral counseling, 217
Past-positive (P-P) person, 208,
    209–210
Pathological gambling, 133,
    164–166, 208, 268
Picower Institute for Learning and
    Memory, 228
Plane crash survivors, 31
Plott, Charles, 84–85
Ponzi, Charles, 87
Ponzi schemes, 87–88, 99
Positive attitude, 265, 267
Positive self-talk, 44
Postrel, Virginia, 84, 85
Posttraumatic growth, 216–217
Posttraumatic stress response, 97,
    164, 211
Poverty, vow of, 142, 144–145,
    147
Prayer, 238
Prefrontal cortex, 55, 97
Prehistoric brain, 32
Present-fatalistic (Pr-F) person,
    208–209
Present-hedonistic (Pr-H) person,
    208
Price, Stephen, 43
Prince Charming fairy tale, 119,
    120, 176, 193, 195, 200,
    209
Procrastination, 98

Professional athletes, 144
Psychodrama, 221
Psychological Services, 220, 266
Psychotherapy, 216, 217

Racial discrimination, 113–115
Randomness, 54
Rational brain, 37–39, 42, 43,
    45–48, 54–56, 228, 234
Real estate bubble, 83, 86
Rejection of money (*see* Money
    avoidance disorders)
Relapse prevention, 233
Relational money disorders,
    175–201
  common scripts, 179–180
  financial dependency, 119–120,
    133, 175, 176, 193–200, 209
  financial enabling, 133, 175,
    176, 187–193
  financial incest, 133, 175,
    185–187
  financial infidelity, 133, 175,
    180–184, 191
Relative deprivation, 79–81, 83
Reptilian brain, 34, 37
Resilience, sense of, 109
Reynolds, Chip, 43
Right brain hemisphere, 49–50
Riley, Michael, 60–61
Risk taking
  excessive risk aversion, 132,
    134, 151–153, 208
  unreasonable, 133, 161–164
Role reversal, 215
Roosevelt, Franklin D., 115

Sacks, Oliver, 235
SAFE process, 182–184
Savings rates, 170
Scrooge, Ebenezer (Dickens
    character), 150–151
Secret money behaviors (*see*
    Financial infidelity)
Security Exchange Company, 87

Self-hypnosis, 238
Seligman, Martin, 24
Serotonin, 270
Shame, 25, 27, 28, 46, 112, 129,
    160, 169, 189, 230, 231
Shapiro, Thomas, 114
Shiv, Baba, 55
Slavery, 113, 114
Smiling, 269
Smith, Adam, 62
Social isolation, 72
Societal financial trauma, 106–108
Socioeconomic issues, financial
    trauma and, 108–113
Somatic markers, 59–60
Spenders Anonymous, 272
Spending plan, 183
Split-brain experiments, 49, 96,
    212
Sports, 44–45
Stanford University, 55
Stress, 20, 27, 45 (*see also* Money
    disorders)
  deciding under, 53–56
  neurobiology of, 94–99
  physical reactions to, 206
Stumbling into Happiness (Gilbert),
    23–24
Subprime mortgage collapse, 152
Suicide, 122, 195
Superstitions and rituals, 54
Support groups, 217, 229, 272

Tai-chi, 238
Taleb, Nassim, 54
Technology stocks, 83, 85–86
Tedeschi, Richard, 216
Television viewing, 264, 281
Therapists, finding, 272–273
Thich Nhat Hanh, 217, 238
Time paradox, 207–210
*Time Paradox, The: The New
    Psychology of Time That Will
    Change Your Life* (Zimbardo
    and Boyd), 207

Training, principle of, 43–46
Trant, Dan, 142
Trant, Kathy, 142
Trauma
    financial (*see* Financial
        trauma)
    neurobiology of, 94–99
Triggers, identifying, 232–234
Triune brain, 34–38, 48
Tulipomania, 81–83
Twitter, 64
Tyrrell, Ivan, 20–21

Underspending, 132, 134,
    149–151, 209
Understanding Your Money Story
    exercise, 241–243
Unfinished emotional business,
    205–227
    changing memories,
        214–217
    dealing with past betrayal,
        243–244
    exercises in resolving (*see*
        Exercises)
    origin of, 211–214
    time paradox and, 207–210
    writing down, 249
University of Texas—Austin, 53

Unreasonable risk taking, 133,
    161–164
Uses of Enchantment, The
    (Bettelheim), 123
USS *Missouri*, 60

Vallejos, T. J., 43
Values, 247–249
Van Der Kolk, Bessel, 93
Visualization, 44, 61
Volunteering, 264
Vow of poverty, 142, 144–145, 147

Wagner, Dick, 23
Whitson, Jennifer, 53
Workaholism, 133, 156, 166–169,
    209
Work ethic, 109
World War II, 114–115, 161

X-rays, 96

Yoga, 238
YourMentalWealth.com, 132, 201,
    266, 285, 286

Zimbardo, Philip, 207–208, 210
Zimbardo Time Perspective
    Inventory (ZTPI), 208